What Readers Say about *Recovery by Choice*

(Continued from back cover)

I'm going to use it as a 'sober souvenir,' to help during those tough times to remin[...] better I feel now that I'm a sober person. The workbook really has made me re-e[...] helped me through some tough times already. – N.D.

I have absolutely loved the workbook.... I can tell this book is going to make a lot of difference. – R.B.

I am very pleased. I was especially impressed with Chapter 8 - My History. – W.G.

I've got to say I love this book, I wish I had done this when I first got sober, the questions make me think, think, think! – J. H.

I still adore my Recovery by Choice book and have become voracious about letting people know that designing your own recovery program, the one that works for you, is possible and extremely satisfying. – M.G.

I just worked through the Recovery by Choice book offered at lifering.org and it was phenomenal for me. I think everyone of us should have it, and work it at your own pace. It's intense but so hugely helpful. The workbook is like a hand to hold. I needed it so much. – L.M.G.

I have done some introspection over the years, but this workbook is really specific. It's helping me put my finger on what my real issues have been. How I "solved" problems before, and what my options are now. – M.G.

I think you'll really like the workbook. It is easily the most useful exercise book I've ever seen. Simply full of wisdom for building a recovery program. – J.X.

I got the workbook quite recently and have started completing parts. It is a very useful book and I personally found the chapter on feelings extremely enlightening. – M.O.

I think it's excellent, it helped me a lot. – G.L.

I have the workbook and love it, it really makes you think about your addiction, hope you get one! You'll love it too. – Liz FL

I was amazed at the depth of the workbook, and go to it when I need some extra support or things to ponder late at night. – L.F.

It is helping clients of all ages (16-60). I am a licensed addictions counselor. – V.S.

It is an excellent book – helped me immensely. Besides being a workbook in which you can fill out answers to checklists and other questions, it has hints, tips, and suggestions that have worked for other people. These suggestions were very valuable to me. – G.M.

You will be amazed by what it will show you about yourself. I was shocked! It is also kind of fun to go through. – RP.

The workbook is a cool thing, its main purpose seems to be to make you think about yourself, your life. As you sit there reading it, by yourself, you can't really lie to yourself. – B.M.

The workbook helped me to create a staying-sober plan that has worked well. Now I'm off to review it and make some updates. One whole year with NO hangovers and NO regrets! – L.L.

My LifeRing workbook arrived yesterday and it is brilliant. At least now I can read in bed of an evening and see the words, and remember in the morning what I read! – T.D.

The workbook is a godsend (Can I use that word on a secular message board?) – F.J.

Received my workbook 3 days ago and have spent about 5 hours working with it. Really stirred up a lot of thinking and self-realization. Still sober, day 13. It feels like I'm really "getting it." – R.M.

This book has been helpful for my clients. I intend to use it more. – V.S., LCPC, CCDC

This is the most comprehensive, clear, practical, and effective tool I've seen in 30 years of reading recovery literature. Hands down. The section on relapse is far and away the best I've ever seen. I'd call it a must read. – G. M.

I have found the workbook very helpful and go back to it often. It's straightforward, makes a lot of sense and is very practical. Great job! – Angela N.

It will help you notice those "curve balls" before you can pretend you didn't see them coming. – Jeanne M.

Anyone recovering from addiction to alcohol or drugs would benefit immensely from a thorough study of this valuable tool. – John D.

We don't have a Big Book, we don't have a small book, but we do have a workbook! – Margherita M.

I am greatly impressed.… It has a depth that is wonderful to find, addressing those many questions that WE all know but which are so hard to get TO much less to grow past. I know already that this will be the mainstay of my work. – Anthony W.

Your workbook is a dream! – Charles B.

I knew you/we (all in recovery) had something special the first time I opened my beta copy. … There's nothing else like it out there that I have found. – Ben G.

It's GREAT! – Amy L.

We've had excellent feedback from using this workbook. MUCH MORE positive feedback than I've heard about other 'methods,' so I'll continue to use it. One [patient] said it's the first time (in several attempts at treatment) that they've had to 'work' and it was helpful. Thanks again. – Sue H.

A VERY helpful and well written workbook. – Roger L.

I highly recommend it … It is really changing how I look at sober life, relapses, and my life in general. – Cynthia M.

The workbook is a tremendous tool, and an outstanding body of work. – Mike C.

I think it will be quite useful for people at many different stages of recovery. – Bill W.

A marvelous piece of work. It's been helpful to me. – Richard B.

The workbook is awesome. I have given two of them to friends in recovery and had nothing but good reviews. – Patrick B.

I was knocked out by the range and quality of information in the book. – Aongus C.

"Recovery by Choice" is absolutely excellent. It has a wealth of information, checklists, etc. that helped me make a plan of "how" I would do this. It costs about $20, but it is well worth every penny, in my opinion. By the way, a person doesn't need to order the book online, if you'd rather not – it is possible to print out an order form and send a check, if you prefer. That is what I did, and it only took a couple days for me to get the book. I am so glad I got this book; it was very helpful for me. – Gal M.

I like the workbook because it helps me take a look at myself and my environment that can trip me up. – L.J.

It is useful much like scaffolding is to a building: It is used, and then when the work is completed, it comes down. – T.S.

It is a valuable resource for me as the exercises are a way for me to be honest with myself and discover/apply new techniques and ways to successfully stay sober. – C.L.

I was a little skeptical that filling out checklists was going to help but I am already thinking otherwise. – S.M.

I found the T-charts really useful when I was first trying to stop. They gave me the chance to work out how I might react in certain situations. Since then I have sailed through two weddings … just shows it can be done! I found the workbook really helpful. -- H.H.

The Daily Do's section helped me immensely! – L.S.

Recovery By Choice

Living and Enjoying Life
Free of Alcohol and Other Drugs

A Workbook

Fourth Edition

By Martin Nicolaus

LifeRing Press

Recovery by Choice: Living and Enjoying Life Free of Alcohol and Other Drugs
By Martin Nicolaus

LifeRing Press
Toll free: 1-800-811-4142
Questions: publisher@lifering.org
Online orders: https://lifering.org

ISBN: 9780965942935

Disclaimer: Nothing in this book is intended as medical diagnosis or medical advice. All names of individuals given for illustration are fictitious and the incidents and events described are composites.

Fourth Edition
Reprinted 2016 by Kindle Direct Publishing
Note: The page layout of this printing varies from the original printing of the Fourth Edition released in 2011. Format changes have shifted some sections to different pages, and the spacing of some subsections has been adjusted. The content is otherwise identical to the 2011 printing of the Fourth Edition.

Content Overview

Introduction: Exercising the power of choice is essential to addiction recovery. Why treatment needs to match the individual. The key to success is effective self-treatment. How to work this book. Introduction to the nine domains. Page 15

A Tool for a Sober Lifetime: Life is a series of small decisions having big consequences. The Sobriety T-Chart is a tool to guide each decision in the direction of reinforcing the recovering person's sober self. Page 29

First Domain: My Body. Give yourself a medical checkup. Look at the wide range of areas where alcohol and other drugs may have had an impact, and flag those where you see issues. Make a plan to get more information and professional help if indicated. Page 35

Second Domain: My Exposure. Survey your immediate environment and flag the points where you are exposed to triggers. Safely dispose of your supplies. Chart a route to avoid slippery places. Create safe spaces. Learn a tool for building your recovery reflexes (the Daily Do). Page 57

Third Domain: My Activities. How are you spending your time? Which of your activities are dangerous to your sobriety, and which are safe? Decide which activities to avoid for now. Look for new activities that will help your recovery. Learn to do a problem activity clean and sober. Page 73

Fourth Domain: My People. Some people support your sobriety, some people oppose it, and some don't know about it. Figure out which is which, and develop strategies for dealing with each kind of person. Page 91

Fifth Domain: My Feelings. Recapture your ability to feel good, clean and sober. Become aware of common emotional issues in recovery. Master three big methods for handling powerful trigger feelings. Identify issues where you want professional help. Page 115

Sixth Domain: My Life Style. Identify issues and make plans for change in your work, housing, social life, finances, and other real-life areas. Page 149

Seventh Domain: My History. Recall who you were before you became addicted, try to figure out how your life became sidetracked, trace the pluses and minuses of your history, and say good-bye to your addicted self. Page 165

Eight Domain: My Culture. Learn to identify and respond to the messages about alcohol and other drugs in your culture. Find your place in your culture and decide on your role in it. Page 209

Ninth Domain: My Treatment and Support Groups. Learn about chemical dependency treatment and support groups and make a plan to get what you need from them. Page 231

Preventing Relapse: Learn about warning signs of relapse, develop ways to stay on track, and spot the areas in your personal recovery program that need more work. Page 259

My Recovery Plans: Day Plan, Page 289. Week Plan, 293. Life Plan, 297.

Table of Contents

My Recovery Plan for My Life......................297

Table of Main Worksheets

Introduction

"Recovery by choice" seems at first a contradiction in terms. Isn't it the essence of addiction to alcohol and other drugs that we lose the power to choose?

Yes and no. Yes, once a person has crossed the line into addiction, if they[1] then put alcohol or other drugs into their body, they will not have the power to choose to stop. Once they get rolling they are like a truck without brakes. I know, I lived it.

But an addicted person can decide not to climb back into that truck. Not ever.

The power to make that decision, and to stick with it, doesn't come all at once, at least not for most people. But that doesn't mean they're too paralyzed ever to make it. The power to choose recovery may begin with small decisions having a horizon of seconds, minutes or hours. Shall I glance again at the beer billboard? Shall I pass by 3rd and Pine where I might run into my dealer? Do I spend the evening with people who drink and drug or with people who don't? Getting as far as choosing to live clean and sober in 24-hour blocks already marks great progress. Each successful decision strengthens and informs the power to make further decisions with wider horizons. Shall I attend a weeklong conference? Shall I spend the summer doing A or B? Shall I go back to school in Minnesota and get a degree, or move to San Diego and live with X? All the fractional decisions empower the person to make and persist in the global choice: shall I live my life as a clean and sober person, or shall I die a drunk and an addict?

Like a muscle or a mental skill, the power to choose recovery vitally requires material on which to exercise. Given no choices to make, or only pseudo-choices, it withers. The notion that addicted persons are too paralyzed to make choices is a self-fulfilling prophecy. If they are given no choices, they will be paralyzed. Paralysis, however, is not the optimum condition in which to start a long and difficult journey.

Successful recovery from addiction requires making choices. Addiction is systemic and dynamic. It shifts shapes, evolves, and insinuates itself into the infinitely varied details of our many different lives. Sure-fire recipes and miracle cures that

---

[1] This book uses the plural pronoun "they" in place of the awkward "he or she" to refer to a singular person of either gender. Although this construction may offend grammatical purists, it is commonplace now in the spoken language and serves important goals of equity and economy.

require no thinking or choosing may work for localized, static disorders such as heartburn or hemorrhoids, but not for the bio-psycho-social monster that is addiction. Because it assumes all the diverse and changing forms of the individuals whose lives it destroys, addiction requires a response that is itself flexible, individualized, and capable of adapting and evolving. Recovery from addiction requires the ability to respond intelligently and in a resilient manner to an infinite variety of different situations – it requires the power to think and make choices.

Effective treatment of addiction is individualized. The National Institute of Drug Abuse (NIDA) of the National Institute of Mental Health (NIMH) conducted a comprehensive study of treatment methods in 1999 and found, as the first fundamental principle: "No single treatment is appropriate for all individuals. Matching treatment settings, interventions, and services to each individual's particular problems and needs is critical to his or her ultimate success in returning to productive functioning in the family, workplace, and society."[2]

Where can a person find addiction treatment that meets this first and most basic criterion? Clinical treatment in most programs is too short, and the average facility has too little resilience or resources to engage with the client's individual needs. Support groups can be wonderful, or not, and you can go there as long as required; but you are there only a few hours, and at their best they can only resonate with and support the work you do yourself. The only person in a position to give the individual in recovery the kind of extended personalized therapeutic attention that is required for success is you, the individual whose recovery it is to be. That's where this workbook comes in.

This is a how-to book for building a lifetime personal recovery program based on abstinence from alcohol and drugs. Using this book, you can become "the author and the arbiter of your own recovery."[3] You can create "a program that keeps you in charge."[4] You can learn to act with confidence as your own therapist.[5] You can empower your sober self.[6]

The basic method of this book is to offer you choices. You will hear many different voices addressing various recovery issues in a few words from a variety of angles. It is up to you to position yourself in this array of choices in a way that works for you to keep you clean and sober. The commentaries that lead from section to section will ask you to exercise your intellect, search your feelings, apply your experience, and use your judgment about a broad range of issues. The book offers

---

[2] Principles of Drug Addiction Treatment: A Research-Based Guide. National Institute on Drug Abuse, NIH, Oct. 14, 1999.

[3] "The first principle of recovery [from trauma] is the empowerment of the survivor. She must be the author and arbiter of her own recovery. Others may offer advice, support, assistance, affection, and care, but not cure. Many benevolent and well-intentioned attempts to assist the survivor founder because this fundamental principle of empowerment is not observed." Judith Herman, MD, in *Trauma and Recovery*, 2nd Ed. 1997 Basic Books (New York), p. 133. .

[4] The expression is that of Doug Althauser, You Can Free Yourself from Alcohol and Drugs: Work a Program That Keeps You in Charge, 1998, New Harbinger (Oakland).

[5] Relapse prevention "is most successful when the client confidently acts as his or her own therapist following treatment." Linda A. Dimeff, G. Alan Marlatt, "Relapse Prevention," in Reid K. Hester and Miller, Handbook of Alcoholism of Treatment Approaches: Effective Alternatives, 2nd ed., 1995, Allyn and Bacon (Boston), p. 177.

[6] See my *Empowering Your Sober Self: The LifeRing Approach to Addiction Recovery*, LifeRing Press 2014.

some answers, but its main contribution is to raise questions for you to think about. The therapeutic concept is that the consideration of choices will awaken and energize your healthy, recovery-seeking mental and emotional powers, engage and strengthen your motivation, stimulate you to take intelligent action on your own behalf, and teach you how to be in charge of your own recovery. The ultimate aim of the method is to facilitate your autonomy as a clean and sober person.

Constructing your individualized custom-made recovery program presents certain challenges. The emphasis on making choices, figuring things out for yourself and making your own plans for action places greater demands on a person's emotional and intellectual capacities than memorizing answers, taking things on faith, and "doing what you are told." This is not for everyone. If you are more inclined to coast than to pedal, you may find this approach too strenuous.

However, the build-it-yourself method has advantages.

A strong and consistent finding in studies of recovery motivation is that people are more likely to persist in a course of action, and to succeed at it, when they have chosen it themselves. The same therapeutic method works better when the person has elected it than when it is imposed.[7] People are more committed to a plan that addresses their personal concerns and to a program that is of their own making.[8]

When people become active and figure things out for themselves, they learn better. MIT learning theorist Peter Senge writes in his best-seller *The Fifth Discipline: The Art and Practice of the Learning Organization*, "Self-concluding decisions result in deeper convictions and more effective implementation. ... People are more effective when they develop their own models – even if mental models from more experienced people can avoid mistakes."[9] By going through the process of developing your own model – as distinct from merely copying a recipe – you experience what Senge calls a "deep learning cycle," which entails "the development not just of new capacities, but of fundamental shifts of mind, individually and collectively." The evidence of "deep learning" is that we can do things we couldn't do before – in this case, to lead and enjoy our lives without alcohol or drugs.

Despite the widespread currency of blame-deflecting medical metaphors, many well-meaning people still approach the recovering client as a Bad Person, a reject from the character assembly line. We who are in recovery all too often internalize these self-flagellating definitions that facilitate relapse. Recovery approaches based on such moral judgments tend to operate on the policy, "The Beatings Will Continue Until Morale Improves."

Science can help here, if we use it. Decades of brain research into addiction have shown that long-term use of addictive substances impairs a person's power to take

---

[7] William R. Miller, "Increasing Motivation for Change" in Reid K. Hester and Miller, Handbook of Alcoholism of Treatment Approaches: Effective Alternatives, 2nd ed., 1995, Allyn and Bacon (Boston), p. 95
[8] Miller, p. 95.
[9] Peter Senge, The Fifth Discipline: The Art and Practice of the Learning Organization, (1990).

pleasure from reality.[10] Recovery means, in important part, learning or relearning to "get off on reality."[11] That is why this workbook presents numerous opportunities to develop the positive side of your reality. Get into new activities, hang out with new people, experience new feelings, get to know and to appreciate the positive qualities you've had all along, increase your self-esteem, build up a healthy ego, work toward a positive self-image, do something every day that makes you feel good – these are essential building blocks of recovery from addiction.

This book is intended basically for self-study (bibliotherapy). You could work it in isolation if necessary. But the book grew out of, and is adapted for, self-help recovery in a group setting.[12] Some people can and do recover alone, but many people find that it's more effective and a lot more fun to do it with a congenial support group. For this reason, many of the topic areas contain the suggestion to take the topic to a group for discussion and feedback.[13]

Although it is not designed as a clinical protocol, this book may improve your treatment experience.[14] If you are having friction with staff because the legacy approach is not working for you, you may be able to persuade your counselor to permit you to use this workbook as a demonstration of your commitment to your recovery. The book also contains a series of suggestions to help you obtain what you need from your treatment program in a positive, sobriety-directed manner. You may also be able to use this book to identify particular areas of your concern where professional service providers may be helpful with referrals, suggestions, or pointers to other readings.

The veteran addiction treatment counselor and historian of recovery, William L. White, writes that the basic aim of professional addiction treatment is "to create a setting and an opening in which the addicted can transform their identity and redefine every relationship in their lives, including their relationship with alcohol and other drugs."[15]

In keeping with this concept, this workbook is organized around key relationships in people's lives: the person's relationship to his or her body, to the places and things of addiction, to life activities and situations, to other people, to one's feelings, and to various aspects of life style, culture, and personal history. Blanks are provided for those who wish to add other personal concerns. What you will be doing as you proceed, bit by bit, is to reinvent yourself as a person who does not use drugs or alcohol.

---

[10] Eliot Gardner, "Brain Reward Mechanisms," in *Substance Abuse, a Comprehensive Textbook, 3rd Ed.*, Lowinson et al., editors. Williams and Wilkins, Baltimore, 1997, p. 52.

[11] The phrase is Dr. Gardner's.

[12] When the book is used in a group setting, the group leader will want to select, condense, or abbreviate the material. Groups move through a text much more slowly than individuals. Without abbreviation, a group might take years to complete this book.

[13] All meetings of LifeRing Secular Recovery allow cross-talk (supportive free conversation) during all or part of the meeting's time so that participants can, if they wish, get direct feedback from other group members. See *How Was Your Week, Bringing People Together in Recovery the LifeRing Way,* LifeRing Press 2003.

[14] My *Empowering Your Sober Self: The LifeRing Approach to Addiction Recovery* (LifeRing Press 2014) is a comprehensive introduction with numerous references to the practice of treatment professionals.

[15] *Slaying the Dragon: The History of Addiction Treatment and Recovery in America*, p. 342.

How to Work This Book

The book opens with a simple tool, the Sobriety T-chart. The basic idea behind the T-chart is to make recovery one's priority in analyzing life choices. This is the core design that replicates itself in a thousand different ways at many different scales and in many settings throughout the book. Except for the first chapter and the last, which serve as the frame, this book is organized like a fractal pattern, [16] not like an assembly line. Once you get the basic design, the order in which you work is an individual matter. Feel free to move through the book in any sequence you see fit. Work it backward if you prefer. Let your life be your guide. If you feel you are in a high-risk zone for relapse, jump ahead to the Relapse chapter and then go wherever you see the need. If your feelings concern you most, start with the Feelings domain. If you have people trouble, jump to the People domain. The labeled tabs in the outside margin and numerous cross-references in the text may facilitate your explorations. Skip material that doesn't speak to you. If you encounter topics that stress you to the point where you are at risk for relapse, back off. Let sleeping dogs lie until they and you are ready to face each other in a non-threatening way.

This book contains numerous checklists, many of them prefaced with the tag "People Say." Put a checkmark before an item that resonates with you. Leave the others blank. These are not test questions and there is no answer book and no score or grade. Working most of these checklists is like entering a virtual meeting or chat room. Imagine that a person in the room with you is speaking the item. How do you feel about it? Does it strike a chord with you?

Just like in a real meeting, there is no consistent pattern to the checklist items. Some of the choices are complementary; check all that ring with you. Some are mutually exclusive. Some will seem obviously right to you, no-brainers. Some may seem annoyingly stupid. Some may be wobblers for you and unsettle you and get you thinking and feeling. Those may be your best ones.

Try to let the checklist material sink in a little; don't rush through it too fast. But try not to agonize forever, either; if you are spinning your wheels, just make a note or leave it blank and move on to the next. Items that leave you stuck may be particularly good ones to bring to a support group meeting.

The final section of the last chapter, titled "My Personal Recovery Program," is blank. The point is for you to write it yourself. This will be the place to pull together all the detailed plans you may have made in the previous chapters into the beginnings of an over-all life plan for your recovery.

Feel free to revise your work as you go. Few great plans go from first draft to completion without extensive alterations. Changing a plan is the rule, not the exception. If you relapse, it means there's a bug in your program, so it's time to

---

[16] Fractal patterns are complex branching geometrical constructions, infinitely scalable, generated by simple formulas. They are distinct from linear progressions. Snowflakes, trees, ferns, river networks, galaxies, and blood vessel branches are examples of fractals in nature. Here, the simple basic formula of A v. S (explained in the first chapter) replicates recursively to generate the complex branching structures that make up the different work areas of the book.

deepen the analysis and make some revisions. It will be helpful for you to learn to recognize your near-relapse situations – moments when your path takes you to the edge of a cliff – so that you can change your course and revise your plan before you actually tumble over. Learning sobriety has much in common with learning to ride a bicycle.

One of the most useful things you can do with this book after you have worked with it is to share your personal program with others. People new to recovery may benefit tremendously from seeing your finished book, or at least the summary that you wrote at the conclusion. If you are part of a LifeRing recovery group, your group may after a while want to collect its members' personal recovery plans (last section of Chapter 14), with the authors' permission, and put them into a binder for newcomers to look at.

Some chapters of this workbook have places for you to revisit, for example after three months or after a year of sobriety. In this way the book can help you chart your own progress over time. Even after you have basically finished your work with the book, it can serve as a useful refresher for you later on, when your memories of your early recovery may have faded.

This workbook will probably do you the most good if you express yourself freely and fully in its pages. But please keep in mind the obvious fact that books may get lost or fall into the wrong hands. Do not write information that would put you at risk of harm. If you absolutely must commit such things to paper "to get them out of your system," write them on a separate sheet and handle them separately. When you refer to other people, use their first names or pseudonyms.

Many points in this workbook suggest that you may want to get more information about a specific topic. The fastest way to get a large quantity of information these days is on the Internet. The LifeRing web site, *www.lifering.org,* is a good starting point. It will lead you to numerous other resources. It may be quicker, however, to ask a knowledgeable person, such as a counselor or a librarian. Don't hesitate to broadcast a general request for information to your meeting or your online community.

Do not be surprised if you find that there is fundamental and vehement disagreement among experts about practically every issue involved in addiction and recovery. Perhaps even more than in other fields, this is an area where your survival may sometimes require that you ignore the babble of warring authorities, including this book, rely on your own wits, and do whatever works to keep you clean and sober.

Acknowledgements

I was first exposed to many of the issues raised in this workbook as an outpatient in 1992-1994 in the Kaiser Permanente Chemical Dependency Recovery Program in Oakland California. It was my good fortune to have its then Medical Director, Laurence Bryer MD as my case manager, its Program Coordinator, Robert Boyd

PhD, as one of my group leaders, and its then Medical Director, Dr. Nicola Longmuir MD, as my physician. I also owe debts to my other Kaiser counselors, Leslie Chatham PhD, Jennifer Palangio PhD, and Janet Robinson LCSW, among others. Jeffrey Blair MFCC and Joann Cook LCSW have been sources of valuable counsel during follow-up. They will probably find in these pages the evidence of many seeds they sowed years ago.

In the gestational stages of this workbook I had the unique opportunity to lead a weekly LifeRing meeting with patients at the Dual Diagnosis Crisis Intervention Unit at the Herrick Campus of Alta Bates Hospital in Berkeley, California. Attempted suicide with alcohol/drug involvement is the most common reason why people are brought to this locked ward. Many of the patients are veterans of chemical dependency treatment and traditional recovery groups. There I came face to face each week with the failures of every recovery approach, including my own. These patients helped me like no others to be clearer, more positive, more modest, and more aware of the gravity of the choices we make. I am grateful to Jane Haggstrom RN, PhD, the Patient Care Manager, and to the other Herrick 4N staff members for their many kindnesses and support in connection with this meeting.

I began writing this book in earnest when the Merritt-Peralta Institute (MPI) at Summit Hospital in Oakland California decided in the Spring of 2000 to host a LifeRing meeting as a supplement to its 12-step offerings. This is a 28-day inpatient program based on the Minnesota Model. A significant portion of patients in the program, over time, had been asking for an alternative approach. Almost the first question from the MPI patients in our first LifeRing meeting was, "Do you guys have a workbook?" This book is a response to the MPI patients' eager, insistent, and legitimate demand for some tool that spelled out the LifeRing approach in some detail. I am grateful to David Cohn MD, then the MPI Medical Director, and to Terry Arnold LVN, Clinical Coordinator, for their permission to hold the LifeRing meeting and to test out portions of the workbook with the MPI clients; and to the whole MPI staff, but especially Chuck Marisco CDC, Kathy Koshgarian RN, MSN, Sue Hinde RN, and Carolyn Robinson CNA for their professional cooperation and friendship.

I need to acknowledge here a general philosophical indebtedness to the following authors of recovery books: the late Jean Kirkpatrick, founder of Women for Sobriety; James Christopher, founder of Secular Sobriety Groups (SSG, later SOS); Jack Trimpey, founder of Rational Recovery; Charlotte Kasl, author of *Many Roads, One Journey* (1990) and founder of the Sixteen Steps groups; and to the late Dr. James R. Milam, principal author of the classic *Under the Influence: A Guide to the Myths and Realities of Alcoholism* (1981). Over the course of three decades these therapeutic pioneers cleared and cultivated the mind-space without which the abstinent choice-based recovery approach exemplified in this workbook could not have been built.

I also owe special intellectual debts to six contemporary American treatment professionals.

Doug Althauser, MEd, CSAC, MAC, Program Coordinator of the Kaiser Permanente Chemical Dependency Recovery Program in Honolulu Hawaii, is the author of *You Can Free Yourself from Alcohol and Drugs – Work a Program That Keeps You in Charge* (New Harbinger, Oakland, 1998). This remarkable book first demonstrated to my mind that it is possible to "square the circle" – to combine structure and order with freedom and choice in chemical dependency treatment. The purpose, plan, and particulars of the present self-help workbook differ in many respects from Althauser's more sequential and institutional approach. Althauser's is mainly a clinical protocol; this workbook is mainly bibliotherapy. But the core concept here is the same, and I am deeply grateful to his work for showing the way.

Professors Reid K. Hester and William R. Miller, authors of *Handbook of Alcoholism Treatment Approaches: Effective Alternatives,* first opened my eyes to the evidentiary basis underlying or not, as the case may be, the legacy substance abuse treatment and support enterprise. This workbook has drawn substantial inspiration and ideas from the Hester-Miller *Handbook's* survey of modern evidence-based treatment approaches.

I owe a special debt to William L. White for his book *Slaying The Dragon, The History of Addiction Treatment and Recovery in America.* His work is a fascinating read from any standpoint – history written as well as one ever sees it. I found it particularly mind-stretching to read about the great variety of recovery efforts in American history. White's panorama allowed me to see more clearly than before that the contemporary landscape is, after all, a transitional one, and that the inexorable processes of change will have, and are having, their way. As a veteran treatment professional and educator of treatment professionals, White has written some of the most empathetic and eloquent passages about the treatment process that I believe I shall ever read. His description of treatment as the presentation of choices[17] is the methodological keel of this workbook.

Eliot L. Gardner MD of the Albert Einstein College of Medicine in New York is the author, among other works, of a review article, *Brain Reward Mechanisms*, summarizing fifty years of addiction research with laboratory mammals.[18] Gardner's article cemented in my mind the conviction that addiction has a neuro-physiological foundation; or, to put it another way, that addiction happens not so much in the "mind" as in the brain. Experimenters routinely take normal little rodents, lacking (as far as we know) any inkling of civilization or its discontents, and turn them into alcoholics/addicts by infusing their bloodstreams, via needle or vapor chamber, with sustained high doses of the substance for a period of time. Off they go then, transformed, pressing a lever thousands of times to get the next dose, ignoring food, sex, companionship, sleep, pain and everything else, until they fall dead from exhaustion.

---

[17] "What we are professionally responsible for is creating a milieu of opportunity, choice and hope. What happens with that opportunity is up to the addict and his or her god. We can own neither the addiction nor the recovery, only the clarity of the presented choice, the best clinical technology we can muster, and our faith in the potential for human rebirth." *Slaying the Dragon*, p. 342.

[18] "Brain Reward Mechanisms," in *Substance Abuse, a Comprehensive Textbook, 3rd Ed.*, Lowinson et al., editors. Williams and Wilkins, Baltimore, 1997, p. 52.

This simple method for manufacturing addicted mammals, replicated in thousands of studies, suggests, to my mind at least, that searching for the causes of human addiction in lofty fields such as personality, psychology, psychiatry, sociology, history, morality, "spirituality," theology, philosophy, or aesthetics is misdirected. These higher, uniquely human functions may assist an individual's recovery, or not, but they are superfluous to produce addiction. NIDA's finding that the cause of addiction in humans is excessive intake of addictive substances, reported by its director Alan Leshner PhD in another context,[19] is consistent with Gardner's survey of the laboratory studies and possesses strong therapeutic and prophylactic value. This finding underlies the *My History* chapter here, and informs the workbook's general approach.

Finally, I am grateful to the National Institute on Drug Abuse (NIDA) for the Oct. 1999 publication of its science-based survey of addiction treatment, quoted at the outset. This workbook is in major part an effort to translate the principal NIDA findings about the qualities of effective treatment into a format useful to individuals who are treating themselves.

The main purpose of this book is therapeutic. But the book also has a secondary, organizational purpose. I hope that the book will help to make more people acquainted with the LifeRing approach that has helped me and so many others make our recoveries. Building a personal recovery plan is a fundamental part of the LifeRing recovery approach; it flows from the third "S" in the LifeRing "Three S" philosophy: Sobriety, Secularity, and Self-Help.[20] The choice-based method of this workbook, leading to a diversity of individual abstinence plans, is an implementation of the LifeRing concept of "small-p" programs.[21] The workbook's technical approach goes back to a suggestion in an early work that one way to start building one's personal recovery program is to make a T-chart.[22] I hope that people will make use of this workbook to form more LifeRing recovery meetings – "life rings," as someone aptly called them.

These living loops of positive feedback form the main source of the many voices you will hear in the checklists that make up the core of this workbook.[23] Since I stopped drinking and using on Oct. 2, 1992, I estimate I've attended close to a thousand LifeRing meetings,[24] but I still hear new matter all the time. The *LSRmail* email list created by Tom Shelley of St. Petersburg Florida, with its hundreds of

---

[19] Leshner, "Addiction is a Brain Disease, and It Matters," *Science*, Oct. 3, 1997.

[20] For more on the "Three-S" philosophy, read *Empowering Your Sober Self* (LifeRing Press 2014), or *How Was Your Week?* (LifeRing Press 2003), Chapters 9-11. Although building one's own recovery plan is basic to the LifeRing approach, nothing requires the LifeRing participant to do it in writing or to use any particular book or device. This workbook is merely one item in an open-ended secular toolbox available to the LifeRing participant.

[21] On building "small-p" v. "Big-P" programs, see Ch. 11 of *How Was Your Week?*

[22] This reference is to *Handbook of Secular Recovery: A Brief Introduction to the Philosophy and Practice of LifeRing Secular Recovery* (originally published as *Sobriety Handbook: The SOS Way*, 1997), LifeRing Press, 1999, p. 27. These works are now out of print, replaced by *How Was Your Week, Bringing People Together in Recovery the LifeRing Way,* LifeRing Press 2003.

[23] Few of the checklist items constitute verbatim quotations. I have called up from memory the gist of what I heard and rephrased it to fit the concise checklist format. In a few cases I have set down words that I believed people were thinking but not saying, or that were implied in conduct.

[24] Prior to the formation of LifeRing, the meetings I attended were known as SOS.

participants and tens of thousands of posts, has been another inexhaustible mine for this book.[25] Additional material came from the patients in the Dual Diagnosis Crisis Intervention meeting and from participants in the MPI inpatient program, described above, and from the Focus Group, described below. To all of these I am grateful.

The progress of this workbook has benefited greatly from the feedback generously provided by a number of participants in LifeRing Secular Recovery. Scott Newsom, Ph.D. of Houston TX reviewed the earliest versions of the manuscript and made a number of valuable general and particular suggestions, for which I am particularly grateful. Patrick Brown of Ryan TX provided valuable feedback both as to the general concept and to particulars. Marjorie Jones of Oakland CA and Robbin Lou, Berkeley CA, each took the trouble to review early drafts and give me the benefit of their feedback as to form and content. Jones also moderated the LifeRing convenor's email list, *lsrcon*, on which discussions of the various drafts posted online from 0.70 forward were conducted.

I owe special thanks to the members of the first Workbook Focus Group that met on Thursday evenings and then Mondays at the Kaiser Permanente CDRP facility in Oakland beginning in August, 2000. Veteran Oakland LifeRing convenor Bill Somers was a mainstay of this working group, but it consisted mostly of newcomers then in the first 90 days of their recoveries and participating, as I had years earlier, in the Kaiser early education program. Together we went through many of the chapters line by line. These were the perfect critics and collaborators, because it is for them and others beginning their recoveries that this book is primarily written. They were at the same time ruthless and infinitely forgiving, critical of the smallest detail yet supportive of the effort, unmerciful in their exposure yet gracious in their praise. They were a joy to work with, and they profoundly reshaped this book for the better. They were Larry S., Craig S., Sam L., Steve H., Amy L., Kenny C., Lynda T., Bert Y., John L, Ronnie Z., Martin Z., David Lee B., Sharon B., and Sonya R., and others. I am especially grateful to Chet G., Amy L., Gillian E. and Sylvia S. for detailed feedback in writing. Thanks also to Gary E. and Dennis T. for suggestions and feedback.

If the people with whom I had the good fortune to work in writing this book are typical, there is no thoughtfulness deficit in early recovery. I have at various times taught college undergraduates, graduate students, freedom schools, adult classes, and study groups, and I don't believe I've ever seen a sharper, brighter and more motivated group of minds. It is to them that this work is gratefully dedicated.

– Marty N.,12/28/00

Preface to the Third Printing

Additional thanks are due to the many readers who told me about how they used this book and how it has helped them with their recoveries. The positive response to this work from individuals in recovery, and also from treatment professionals, has

---

[25] For a selection of posts from this remarkable online community, see *Keepers: Voices of Secular Recovery* (LifeRing Press, 1999).

necessitated a third printing. This printing corrects typographical errors, changes some fonts, refreshes the cover, and incorporates a few small additions and deletions in content. It is otherwise identical to the first and second printings. – M.N. 8/15/06

Preface to the Fourth Printing

Thousands of people have now used *Recovery by Choice*, and a growing number of treatment professionals have been adopting it for their clients. The book is entering into more and more clinics and other institutions. From the institutional side – as well as from many clients – there has been a growing demand to enhance the structural features of the work, and to move in the direction of a treatment protocol or manual.

Recovery by Choice is a guidebook for self-treatment. This is a recovering person's own book. If a conventional treatment manual – a guidebook for treating others, a professional's book – based on the concepts underlying *Recovery by Choice* ever comes into being, it will be a separate work.

Nevertheless, certain adaptations to the demand for more structure can be made without undermining the workbook's self-help foundations. In my recent book, *Empowering Your Sober Self*, I introduced the new framework, suggesting that the global territory of recovery work is divisible into "a series of nine specific work areas or domains."[26] This edition of the workbook embodies that change. The terms "domain" or "work area" refer simply to the major issue clusters that most people in recovery find they need to grapple with. They are:

(1) My Body: issues of physical and mental well-being
(2) My Exposure: environmental triggers to use alcohol or other drugs
(3) My Activities: issues concerning what we do and how we spend our time
(4) My People: relationship issues, and their many connections with recovery
(5) My Feelings: emotional awareness and the achievement of sober good feelings
(6) My Life Style: practical issues of survival and management in recovery
(7) My History: issues about one's family of origin and forming a new identity
(8) My Culture: recognizing the addiction-related messages in our cultures
(9) My Treatment and Support Groups: learning to get help and take care of oneself

---

[26] *Empowering Your Sober Self: The LifeRing Approach to Addiction Recovery* (LifeRing Press 2014), p. 103.

Throughout this printing from here forward, the terminology of "domain" or "work area" has mostly taken the place of the previous language, which referred merely to conventional literary divisions called, of course, chapters.

The change is in one sense "merely semantic," a repackaging of the existing content under new labels. But it is more. The new language highlights the three-dimensional framework of the recovery project, much like an anatomical model identifies and highlights discrete but connected structures and systems that make up the body.

The new semantics facilitates a more visual orientation. Instead of, "I'm working on Chapter 4," workbook activists can now say, "I'm in the Third Domain – where are you?"

People can benefit from the enhanced sense of security that comes from the feeling of being inside a defined space or structure.
Study groups can form devoted to a specific domain or to a subset of the domains, with an enhanced sense of focus and mission.

People can ask themselves and others how many of the domains they have worked through, thereby giving themselves a clearer sense of progress and accomplishment.

Treatment professionals can more easily track a client's progress by determining which domain, or how many domains, they have worked through.

People can form different personal profiles based on which domains they found most challenging, rewarding, upsetting, or transformative.

People can form relationships based on shared experiences with a particular domain or with the whole series of domains.

All this, and more, arises from the transition upward from the flat literary convention of chapters to the three-dimensional paradigm of domains. Language is powerful; language is not just labels, it conveys content, meaning, and structure.

None of these changes diminishes the choice-based structure of the work. We are not moving backward toward the soul-sucking linear assembly-line model that was so admired in the age of the Model T Ford. People in this book remain individuals, not widgets. People can still start anywhere they choose, and they can enter and leave the domains in any order that works for them. They can determine which domains apply to them deeply, or only somewhat, or not at all. They can skip domains or repeat domains, entirely based on their particular needs and priorities. The object of the whole effort remains for each person to build a Personal Recovery Program. The transition to the domain (work area) framework enhances the individually tailored self-treatment project that is the core of this book, and gives it more depth, color, and definition.

In addition to this transformative change, the fourth printing contains a number of other edits. I have rewritten parts of Chapter 1, formerly titled "My Decision." I have added several sections to the first Domain, My Body (chapter 2), updated some of its other sections, and added a note there about psychoactive medications. I have rewritten most of the Third Domain, My Activities (chapter 4), streamlining and filling in gaps. I have reorganized the ending of the Seventh Domain, My History (chapter 8). There are numerous minor additions, deletions and changes elsewhere. As a result of the accumulation of these edits, the page numbers, worksheet numbers, and in some cases the sub-section numbers are different from the previous printings. The typography has been updated and the cover has a new design. Because of the extent of these updates, this is not merely a new printing but a new edition.

I am grateful to Jim R. and Lloyd E., both convenors of Oakland LifeRing groups dedicated to workbook study, and to numerous participants in my own workbook study groups and to a workbook email list for suggestions and comments leading up to this edition. I owe a special debt to Jim R. and to Lynn C. for extensive, thorough and very helpful editorial contributions to this edition.

– MN 1/21/2011

A Tool for a Sober Lifetime

Yogi Berra[1] said, when you come to a fork in the road, take it. We say, when you come to a fork in the road, make a Sobriety T-chart.

Every real-life decision has two basic branches. One leads you to a stronger recovery, the other leads you toward relapse.

Sometimes that's true in an obvious way. You come to a corner. Turn one way, you'll pass a familiar bar or a drug house and you'll be triggered and you may relapse. Turn the other way, and you have better survival chances.

Many times it's not so obvious, and it helps to stop, think, and work it out. This chapter introduces a tool for making the right decision at every fork in the road.

The basic idea is this.

Choices that strengthen your recovery and reduce your relapse risk are choices that empower your sober self. We abbreviate those choices as "S."

If you choose, instead, the path that raises your risk of relapse, you are reinforcing your addict self ("A").

So, basically, whenever you come to a fork in the road, one branch leads to A and the other leads to S.

The tool in this chapter is a standard decision-making tool, a T-chart. This particular T-chart is adapted for the special purpose of helping you make sobriety the priority in your life. This simply means choosing "S" over "A" whenever you come to a point of decision. So, the name of this decision-making tool is the Sobriety T-Chart.

The Sobriety T-Chart is a simple but effective device for applying the Sobriety Priority when life hands you a less than obvious decision to make. It's a tool

_____

[1] New York Yankees' All-Star catcher and Major League baseball manager (1925-), also famous for his sayings, such as, "You can observe a lot by watching," "We make too many wrong mistakes," and "Ninety per cent of this game is half mental." The Yogi Bear cartoon character was modeled on him.

for looking around the corner, and for thinking several moves ahead, like a chess player.

You work the Sobriety T-Chart this way.

First, draw a big T.

On the left side of the T-chart, draw a big A and on the right side, an S. Like this:

A | S

Now, define the issue that you need to decide. Keep it sharp and practical. Frame it so that it can be answered yes or no.

Examples: Do I go to a party where people will be drinking? Do I move in with a new roommate? Do I switch from five eight-hour days to a four tens work schedule?

Write the issue above the top of the T.

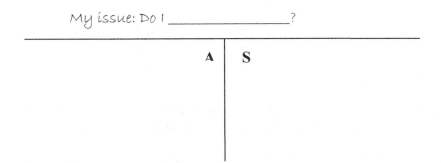

My issue: Do I _____?

A | S

Now, brainstorm the issue. How will your life change if you say "yes" to the question? As a thought comes to you, write it down underneath. If you think of something that will strengthen your sobriety, write it on the right side (under the S). If it's something that will undermine your sobriety, write it on the left side, under the A.

When you've listed all the likely consequences of the issue for your recovery, stop and think. Weigh the sides, maybe discuss it with people, sleep on it if necessary, and then make your move. The next page has an example.

Weighing the A and the S in every issue is a way to make sense out of the messy confusion that life sometimes hands us. Identifying and choosing the S in everything you do is the practical meaning of making sobriety your priority in life. Even when you don't have paper and pencil handy, the mental habit of weighing every decision in terms of sobriety v. relapse – S against A – is a powerful recovery tool.

In the following chapters of this book, you'll enter nine domains (work areas) where you may need to invest some effort to rebuild your life. As you work in these domains, you will be applying the core idea behind the T-chart to a great variety of different issues. Successful recovery involves choosing the sobriety-empowering option, the S, whenever you come to a fork in the road.

Here is an example.

Suppose a friend, D., has told you there is a room available in D.'s apartment and asked you whether you are interested. Write the issue on the top of the chart. Below, on the left side, write all the specific ways in which moving in with D. would probably count against your recovery and increase your risk factors for relapse. On the right side, write all the specific ways in which moving in with D. would probably help your recovery and empower your sober self (your S).

Worksheet 1: Sobriety T-chart (Example)

Issue:	Should I move in with D.?
How it would endanger my recovery (A)	**(S) How it would empower my recovery**
D's main squeeze is probably a drunk	D does not drink or use or smoke
D's other roommate keeps wine in fridge	I will be in a neighborhood with less drugs
There is a liquor store right on the corner	I'll have a nicer room, less stress
I'll have to work longer hours to afford it	It's quieter, not so much loud partying
I hate the purple paint trim in the	I'll be able to bicycle to work, save
hallway, makes me want to drink	commute money
I'll have to listen to D's dog barking at	I'll live closer to F and L (sober friends)
night sometimes, drive me nuts	and spend more time with them
	I'll get away from my druggy roommates
	I'll get to play with D's dog
	There's a washer-dryer there, don't have to
	go to the stinky laundromat
	Good light, I can have house plants
	Eventually I can find my own place in
	that neighborhood

Start by brainstorming – write down whatever happens to come up first. Don't agonize over the proper order, or worry about being very organized. Skipping around is fine.

You may find that you can't decide right away whether some factor is a plus or a minus for your recovery. In this example, the fact that D. has a dog has its pluses and its minuses, and at first the person who made this chart couldn't decide where to put the dog. By breaking "dog" down into more detail (companion to play with, v. pest that robs you of sleep) the over-all choice may become clearer.

You may also find yourself moving things from one side to the other as you think about them … that's par for the course. One of the most useful things about the Sobriety T-Chart is to get your brain asking everything whether it empowers your A or your S.

If the decision doesn't become clear in short order after you list the pro-sobriety and the pro-relapse factors, you may want to set up a more elaborate chart that uses weights, as in Example 2 below.

Worksheet 2: Sobriety T-Chart Using Weights (Example 2)

Issue: Move in with D?			
How it would endanger my recovery (A)			**(S) How it would empower my recovery**
D's main squeeze is probably a drunk	-2	5	D does not drink or use or smoke
There is a liquor store right on the corner	-2	3	I will be in a neighborhood with less drugs
I'll have to work longer hours to afford it	-2	3	I'll have a nicer room, I'll feel better about myself, less stress
		1	It's quieter, not so much loud partying
		1	I'll be able to bicycle to work, good exercise
		2	I'll live closer to F and L (sober friends) and spend more time with them getting support
D's other roommate keeps wine in fridge	-3	5	I'll get away from my druggy roommates
I'll have to listen to D's dog barking at night sometimes	-1	2	I'll get to play with D's dog, good company
I hate the purple paint trim in the hallway, makes me want to drink	-1	2	Good light, I can have house plants, cheer me up
		1	Eventually I can find my own place in that neighborhood

The maker of this Sobriety T-Chart has used a rating system of 1-5 to assign a personal weight to each factor in the decision. The weights you use are up to you.

For example, how should you weigh the fact that D's other roommate keeps wine in the fridge? If wine was your thing, and drinking somebody else's was never a real problem for you (in fact, you kind of preferred that!), then you might want to give this factor your heaviest minus score. But if refrigerator wine held no charm for you and you never sneaked other people's drinks (at least when there was a chance to get caught!) then this fact would get negligible weight in your scheme of things.

After you've assigned each factor its weight, you can almost make your decision by arithmetic. Almost, because a long list of small plus factors probably shouldn't be allowed to outweigh a single deadly negative. For example, what if the maker of this T-chart has a history of relapsing or near-relapsing when walking by a liquor store?

Some decisions are too complex to be solved in a single T-chart. At first approach, the problem has more than two branches. To make the right decision, you will need to move in stages. First, simplify the problem down to two basic choices. Then make a second T-chart, or even a third. Ultimately, you'll probably make your decision by intuition. But your gut feeling will be more educated and trustworthy if you've first worked through the details of the various options by analyzing each option in terms of the Sobriety Priority: how it tips the scales from A to S, or the reverse.

Note also that your chart can be the start for action plans that help your sobriety. For example, if the purple trim in the hallway bothers you, talk to D. about letting you paint it over. Also, if you move there, because the room has good lighting, you'll want to be shopping for houseplants. Reshaping your environment to support your sobriety is a strong thing you can do for your sober self, and your Sobriety T-Chart led you there.

You can work the Sobriety T-Chart by yourself. You can also work it in a group setting. If you have a board or butcher paper to work with, you can draw the big T there, and you (or another group member) can put up the ideas as they come. We've done this many times in workbook study groups, and it's been illuminating and fun. Putting out the pro-recovery and anti-recovery consequences of life decisions for friends to look at can give you an extra measure of insight and assurance that you're doing the right thing.

On the next page is a blank Sobriety T-Chart to photocopy. You can also make your own any time on a napkin or the back of an envelope. You could get fancy and set up a computer spreadsheet. And of course you can use this tool in your mind, without any pencil, paper, or computer whatsoever. This tool is simple but deep. Its basic idea – to make sobriety your priority in every life decision for as long as you live – is the guiding thread of this workbook.

Worksheet 3:   Sobriety T-Chart (blank)

SOBRIETY DECISION TOOL

The issue: _____

How it would reinforce my addict self [A]		[S] How it would empower my sober self

My decision:_____

[Chapter Two]

First Domain: My Body

The most important decision you can make in recovery is not to put alcohol or other drugs into your body. As part of your decision to treat your body better from now on, you may want to give yourself an informal health checkup. This will include not only the direct effects of drinking/using on your body but also neighboring issues such as nutrition and exercise, diseases such as hepatitis and HIV, and common mental health concerns that often go alongside excessive drinking/using, such as depression and anxiety.

This work area looks into "body" and related health issues and lets you flag items that you may want to address as part of your recovery. It makes sense to discuss these issues with a professional. Only a physician or other licensed health-care provider is qualified to make a diagnosis of your individual case and to prescribe medications.

In these checklists, check all items that apply to you. This is not an exam and there is no grade, score, or answer book. Read *How to Work This Book* in the Introduction at Page 19 if you are unclear about what is expected. At the exit of the domain is a checklist where you can flag topics about which you want more information.

1.   Detox

__ I am not sure whether I need medical supervision to detox
__ I plan to detox under medical supervision and I have an appointment
__ I have detoxed off this drug before and feel confident I can detox without
    medical supervision

1 Body

2 Exposure

3 Activities

4 People

5 Feelings

6 Life Style

7 History

8 Culture

9 Treatment

1 Body   2 Exposure   3 Activities   4 People   5 Feelings   6 Life Style   7 History   8 Culture   9 Treatment

2.   Telltale Signs

__ I have some telltale visible signs of my drinking/using on my body, namely:
    __ red eye
    __ burst veins in nose or rest of face
    __ pot belly, overweight
    __ flabby, fluid-filled abdomen
    __ anemic, emaciated
    __ needle track scars
    __ nose perforation
    __ bulbous nose
    __ stained fingers
    __ skin abscesses
    __ yellow skin
    __ dry, red, itchy skin
    __ premature wrinkles, signs of aging
    __ burst veins in legs
    __ swollen glands in neck
    __ shaky hands
    __ swollen finger tips
    __ shrunken testicles
    __ scar, fracture or other injury I got while under the influence
    __ bad teeth, missing teeth, bad gums, sores in mouth
    __ other, _____
    __ Nobody could tell I drank/used, I look completely normal.

3.   Hidden Body Damage

__ I already know that I have the following internal body damage directly from my drinking/using:
    __ liver damage (hard, swollen liver)
    __ heart damage
    __ irregular heart beat
    __ recurrent pneumonia
    __ reduced immunity
    __ shortness of breath
    __ kidney damage
    __ loss of bladder control
    __ pancreas problems
    __ recurrent diarrhea
    __ Hepatitis C
    __ diabetes
    __ problems with digestive tract
    __ blood sugar too low or too high
    __ low libido (sex drive)
    __ brain damage
    __ amnesia, memory loss

__ muscle weakness, atrophy
__ seizures
__ tingling in hands, feet
__ numbness in hands, feet
__ loss of balance
__ low energy
__ skipped menstrual periods
__ impotence
__ vitamin deficiency, anemia
__ insomnia, sleep disturbances, nightmares
__ nerve damage
__ damaged esophagus
__ other, namely _____
__ I'm not aware of any internal body damage that stems directly or indirectly from my drinking/using

4.   Doctor Visits

__ I have had an all-around medical checkup within the past year and I'm OK
__ I haven't had a checkup because I'm a little afraid what the doctor will find
__ I haven't been to a doctor because I procrastinate
__ I plan to see a doctor because I want to know if I'm OK
__ I haven't been to the doctor because I can't afford to go
__ I've been to the doctor recently and I have been diagnosed with the following medical problem(s) I didn't already know about:

_____

__ When I see a doctor I tell them honestly about my drinking/using if they ask
__ When I see a doctor I tell them honestly about my drinking/using even if they don't ask
__ When I see a doctor, I tell them about some of my drinking or using but not the full story
__ When I see a doctor, I keep quiet about my drinking/using
__ When I see a doctor, I tell the truth about my drinking/using but ask the doctor not to write it in the chart
__ A doctor has advised me to stop drinking/using
__ A doctor has advised me to cut down on drinking/using
__ A doctor has never talked to me about my drinking/using even though I told them the whole story of what I did
__ A doctor probably would have told me to stop if I had told them the real story of my drinking/using
__ No doctor has ever asked me about my drinking/using
__ I'm going to defer going for a checkup
__ I plan to go for a checkup on _____(date) with Dr.
    _____

Body

1 Body   2 Exposure   3 Activities   4 People   5 Feelings   6 Life Style   7 History   8 Culture   9 Treatment

1 Body   2 Exposure   3 Activities   4 People   5 Feelings   6 Life Style   7 History   8 Culture   9 Treatment

5.   Teeth and Gums

__ I have had my teeth and gums checked within the past year and they're OK
__ I haven't had my teeth and gums checked because I know there's no problems
__ I haven't had my teeth and gums checked because I know they're bad
__ I haven't had my teeth and gums checked because I can't afford to
__ I've been to the dentist and I have the following problems

_____

__ The condition of my teeth and gums has not been affected by my drinking/using
__ My drinking/using has affected my teeth or gums this way

_____

__ I'm going to defer going to a dentist

__ I'm going to see Dr. _____ on _____ (date)

6.   Nutrition

__ I'm not happy with the way I eat – I feel I eat too much
__ I'm not happy with the way I eat – I feel I don't eat enough
__ I'm not happy with the way I eat – I feel I eat the wrong kind of stuff
__ I suspect I might have a food allergy that might contribute to cravings
__ When I drank and used I still ate a healthy diet
__ My drinking/using meant that I got too many calories and got overweight
__ My drinking/using meant that I didn't eat enough and lost weight
__ My drinking/using wrecked my eating and I may have malnutrition
__ I'm too heavy. I think I would feel better if I weighed _____ lbs
__ I'm too skinny. I think I would feel better if I weighed _____ lbs
__ I have no idea how much I should weigh; I'd like more information
__ Since I got clean and sober I lost / gained _____ lbs
__ I feel OK about my weight change since I got clean and sober
__ I feel bad about my weight change since I got clean and sober
__ I need to pay special attention to my nutrition because I have diabetes
__ I have talked to a nutritionist and we worked out a personalized diet plan for me
__ I have never talked to a nutritionist
__ I have read about nutrition and recovery and I recommend the following source
       of information about it:

_____

__ It might help my recovery to make certain changes in the way I eat, namely:

_____

__ I don't need to make changes in my diet for my recovery

7. Vitamins, Minerals, Herbs, Supplements

___ I've never thought about taking vitamins, minerals, herbs, or supplements

___ I am taking _____ because it _____

_____

___ I have read something about the role of vitamins, minerals, herbs and
     supplements in recovery and I recommend the following source of
     information:

_____
___ I don't plan to start taking vitamins, minerals, herbs, or supplements
___ I plan to start taking

_____

8. Caffeine

___ I don't drink coffee, tea, or caffeinated soft drinks
___ I drink coffee, tea, or caffcinated soft drinks occasionally or lightly
___ I drink _____ cups of coffee (tea) on a normal day
___ I drink _____ cans or bottles of caffeinated soft drinks on a normal day
___ If I don't drink coffee, tea, or caffeinated soft drinks, I get headaches for a while
___ Since I stopped drinking/using, I find that I am drinking more coffee, tea, and/or
     caffeinated soft drinks
___ Since I stopped drinking/using, I find that I am not drinking as much coffee, tea,
     and/or caffeinated soft drinks
___ Coffee, tea, or caffcinatcd soft drinks have nothing to do with my drinking/using
___ I feel I ought to stop caffeine because it's another mind-altering drug
___ I feel OK with continuing caffeine because its effects are trivial compared to
     alcohol and/or "drugs"
___ Coffee, tea, or caffeinated soft drinks help me overcome my cravings to
     drink/use
___ Coffee, tea, or caffeinated soft drinks help me overcome cravings for a short
     time but make my cravings come back worse when the caffeine wears off
___ Drinking beverages containing caffeine, for me, is a trigger to drink alcohol
___ Drinking beverages containing caffeine, for me, is a way to counteract the urge
to drink alcohol
___ I'm finding that caffeine only lends me energy, and then takes it away again
___ I plan to reduce my caffeine consumption
___ I'm going to switch to decaffeinated coffee, tea, and caffeine-free drinks
___ I don't plan to change my caffeine intake pattern

1 Body   2 Exposure   3 Activities   4 People   5 Feelings   6 Life Style   7 History   8 Culture   9 Treatment

1 Body   2 Exposure   3 Activities   4 People   5 Feelings   6 Life Style   7 History   8 Culture   9 Treatment

9.   Sugar

__ I rarely eat sweets
__ I eat a small amount of sweets every day
__ I eat a lot of sweets and I am somewhat concerned about it
__ Eating sweets has nothing to do with my former drinking/using
__ When I stopped drinking/using, my sweets consumption didn't change
__ When I stopped drinking/using, I got cravings to eat more sweets
__ When I stopped drinking/using, I lost interest in sweets
__ When I get a craving to drink/use, I eat some sweets instead and that makes the
     cravings go away
__ Eating sweets after a while triggers my cravings to drink/use and makes them
     worse
__ I have been checked by a doctor and I don't have hypoglycemia [low blood
     sugar]
__ As much sweets as I eat, maybe I have hypoglycemia; I should get checked
__ I am eating so many sweets I am concerned that I may be developing diabetes
__ I have been diagnosed as diabetic
__ I'm going to reduce or cut out refined-sugar sweets
__ I'm not going to make changes in my sugar consumption

10.   Salt

__ Whenever I drank alcohol, I found myself gobbling salty snacks
__ Whenever I ate a salty snack, I got an urge to drink alcohol
__ I'm concerned about my salt intake because of my blood pressure
__ I'm concerned about my salt intake because of other health effects
__ I'm eating so much salt I wonder if I'm addicted to it
__ I've been eating a low salt or salt-free diet
__ I plan to cut back on salt as part of my recovery
__ I'm not concerned about salt and don't plan to make any changes in my salt
     intake

11.   Nicotine

__ I don't smoke cigarettes, never did

__ I used to smoke, but I quit. It's been _____ (*time*) since my last cigarette

__ Whenever I drank/used, I also smoked cigarettes

__ I never or rarely smoked cigarettes while I drank or used

__ The more I drank, the more I smoked, and vice versa

__ I smoke more than two packs a day

__ I smoke menthols

__ I smoke non-filters

__ I get nicotine from cigars

__ I smoke a pipe

__ I get nicotine from chewing tobacco or snuff

__ I get nicotine from smokeless products

__ I would like to quit smoking now

__ I have tried to quit smoking but failed _____ times

__ I would like to quit smoking but don't know how

__ I have no intention to quit smoking, ever

__ I will quit smoking someday but not now

__ I'm going to quit smoking on _____(date)

__ My smoking has no effect on my staying sober and clean

__ If I couldn't smoke, I couldn't stand to remain clean and sober

__ Even though I'm clean and sober I still feel like a drug addict with my smoking

__ When I get a craving to drink or use, I smoke a cigarette instead to make it go
     away

__ When I smoke a cigarette, it brings on a craving to drink or use

__ Smoking makes me feel relaxed

__ Smoking first makes me feel relaxed and then it makes me feel tense and
     stressed until I have another one

__ Smoking makes me feel depressed

__ I smoke and I've been checked for lung cancer and other smoking related
     diseases and I'm OK

__ I smoke and I haven't had a cancer checkup for some time and maybe I ought to

__ I smoke and I notice I'm coughing a lot and am short of breath and I don't like
     the way I feel

__ I have a smoking-related disease, namely

     _____

__ I feel it's impossible to quit drinking, drugging and smoking at the same time

__ I feel I can quit drinking, drugging and smoking all at the same time

__ I feel that I'm making progress by switching from cigarettes to products that
     give me nicotine without smoking

__ I don't see the point of substituting one form of nicotine addiction for another;
     the point is to get free of the addiction, period

__ I'm not going to make changes in my nicotine intake at this time

1 Body   2 Exposure   3 Activities   4 People   5 Feelings   6 Life Style   7 History   8 Culture   9 Treatment

1 Body   2 Exposure   3 Activities   4 People   5 Feelings   6 Life Style   7 History   8 Culture   9 Treatment

12.   Pain

__ I am in chronic pain due to an injury/illness and I use(d) alcohol/drugs to self-
      medicate
__ Due to my drinking/drugging I suffered an injury which is a source of constant
      pain
__ Before surgery I advised my doctor that I was addicted to opiate-based pain
      medications
__ My doctor prescribed opiate-based pain medications for me after surgery and
      when I was better I discontinued the medications without trouble
__ I keep a supply of prescription pain medications on hand "just in case"
__ When I'm done with pain I throw away my unused pain meds
__ My doctor prescribed opiate-based pain medications for me and I felt I got
      hooked on them and could not stop taking them
__ I have a prescription for opiate-based pain medications and I find myself taking
      them just to get high
__ I am afraid to take any pain medications, even plain aspirin, because I have been
      told they would endanger my sobriety
__ I have been told that alcoholics should accept pain as a punishment
__ I drank while taking pain medications and almost killed myself
__ I take prescribed opiate-based pain pills when I have pain and then I throw the
      rest away
__ I want to explore methods of pain management that don't involve opiates
__ I am not sure whether I am handling my pain in the best way and I would like to
      see a physician specializing in pain management about it
__ I don't have an issue with pain

13.   Exercise

__ I am physically active and get plenty of exercise each week
__ I get some exercise each week but a little more wouldn't hurt
__ While I drank/used I was an active athlete and in good physical condition
__ While I drank/used I got very little exercise other than bending the elbow
__ I am seriously out of shape now
__ I've noticed that I feel better when I take some exercise
__ I would like to exercise more but can't figure out how or what or when
__ I know perfectly well how to exercise more but I just don't do it
__ I have noticed that when I exercise it is easier to resist my cravings to drink/use
__ I am disabled and cannot exercise except in very limited ways
__ I am going to exercise more, starting _____ (date)
__ I am not going to change my exercise patterns

14. Sleep, Rest

___ Bedtime is a time when I crave a drink to help me get to sleep
___ I always slept fine and still do
___ When I drank/used, I didn't "go to sleep," I passed out
___ When I drank/used, I had this sleep problem:

_____

___ Since I stopped drinking/using, I am sleeping fine
___ Since I stopped drinking/using, I am having trouble getting to sleep
___ Since I stopped drinking/using, I am having trouble staying asleep
___ When I have trouble getting to sleep, I take _____ to help me
___ I am afraid that inability to get to sleep sober will cause me some harm
___ I would like more information about the effects of alcohol and drugs on sleep
___ I have talked over my sleep problem with a doctor
___ My sleep problem might have something to do with my caffeine consumption
___ I have sleep apnea, or think I might have it
___ I am often tired during the day
___ I take naps during the day
___ I feel that I am sleeping too much now. I sleep ___ hours a day.
___ I just can't get up in the morning because:

_____

___ I feel fine in the mornings now
___ It feels great not to wake up with a hangover any more
___ I am not concerned about my sleeping patterns

15. Dreams

___ There hasn't been any change in my dreaming since I got sober
___ My dreaming has changed this way

_____

___ I have had dreams in which I drank/used
___ When I woke up from my drinking/using dream I was relieved that it was just a
        dream
___ I have had dreams in which I almost drank/used but stopped myself in time
___ I have had dreams in which I saw myself as a person who does not drink/use
___ I have talked about my dreams with my support group
___ I have talked about my dreams with a counselor
___ I am not concerned about my dreams
___ I want more information about dreams in recovery

1 Body   2 Exposure   3 Activities   4 People   5 Feelings   6 Life Style   7 History   8 Culture   9 Treatment

1 Body   2 Exposure   3 Activities   4 People   5 Feelings   6 Life Style   7 History   8 Culture   9 Treatment

16.   My Brain

__ I'm pretty sure my brain is basically fine

__ I'm worried that I may have suffered memory loss or other possible brain damage due to drinking/using

__ I'm concerned that I may be suffering from clinical depression, or that I may have something else wrong with my brain

__ Sometimes I hear realistic voices telling me things and I worry I'm losing my mind

__ Sometimes I feel as if other people can see I have a problem and they treat me funny

__ I am aware that I am a person just like everyone else

__ I am thinking about getting a mental checkup because of my concerns about my brain

__ I have seen a mental health professional and I have been told I am OK

__ I have seen a mental health professional and I have been diagnosed with

_____

__ I would like more information about the effects of drinking/drugging on my brain

17.   Medications

__ A doctor has prescribed the following medication(s)

_____

__ The medication I am taking has a potential for abuse

__ I know exactly how much of this medication I am supposed to take

__ I sometimes take this medication just to get high or to escape or feel better

__ Staying clean and sober is especially important for someone taking this medication because

_____

__ I want more information about the medication I am taking

__ I am taking Antabuse (disulfiram) because I know that if I drink while on Antabuse I will get very sick

__ I plan to take Antabuse before certain situations that hold high risk of relapse for me

__ I cannot take Antabuse because of my liver or other health issues

__ I have one of the exceptional metabolisms that is not affected by Antabuse

__ I have taken Antabuse and drank and gotten very ill but kept drinking anyway

__ I feel that taking Antabuse has strengthened my sobriety and kept me from relapse

__ I feel uncomfortable relying on Antabuse and feel I should be able to do without it

__ I plan to take Antabuse until I feel steadier in my sobriety and then discontinue it

__ I want more information about Antabuse

__ I am taking naltrexone (ReVia®, Vivitrol®) to reduce my cravings

__ I want more information about naltrexone and other medications designed to reduce cravings

__ I detoxed with buprenorphine (Suboxone®, Subutex®)

__ I want more information about buprenorphine as an alternative to methadone

__ My physician has prescribed bupropion (Welbutrin®, Zyban®) to help me quit smoking

__ My doctor has prescribed varenicline (Chantix®) to help me quit smoking and/or to reduce my alcohol cravings

__ I am taking methadone

__ I plan to take methadone indefinitely

__ I plan to take methadone for _____ (*time*) and then get free of it

__ My doctor has prescribed acamprosate (Campral®) to reduce my alcohol cravings

__ My doctor has prescribed baclofen (Lioresal®) to help me through withdrawal or to cut down my cocaine use

__ My doctor has put me on gapabentin (Neurontin®), ibogaine, D-cycloserine (Seromycin®), kudzu, modafinil, NAC, nalmefene, propranolol, ondansetron (Zolfran®), topiramate (Topamax®), nepicastat, fluoxetine, tiagabine, vigabatrin (Sabril®), or zonisamide to help me overcome my addiction

__ I am aware of and on guard against the possible side effects – including some very serious ones – of the particular anti-addiction medications that I am taking

__ I want more information about the range of modern medications that are available now to help with recovery from addiction

18. Medical Marijuana

__ I have a serious chronic disease such as cancer or AIDS that depresses my appetite or makes me nauseous, and I have a prescription for marijuana that helps me eat without vomiting, so that I don't lose too much weight

__ I'm undergoing temporary treatment such as chemotherapy that makes me feel sick, and I have a prescription for marijuana that enables me to feel more normal

__ I have been diagnosed with glaucoma and my doctor tells me that using marijuana has improved the fluid pressure in my eyes

__ I understand that inhaling the smoke of anything is bad for the lungs, so I take my medically prescribed marijuana in a non-smoking form

__ I have gone to a doctor who gives marijuana prescriptions for a fee to anyone who claims to suffer from "stress," and who doesn't?

__ I have a prescription for marijuana but there's really nothing medically wrong with me (yet)

__ I am aware that today's marijuana is many times more potent than it was during the 1960s when it was widely considered a harmless recreational drug

__ I don't use marijuana, medically or otherwise

1 Body   2 Exposure   3 Activities   4 People   5 Feelings   6 Life Style   7 History   8 Culture   9 Treatment

1 Body   2 Exposure   3 Activities   4 People   5 Feelings   6 Life Style   7 History   8 Culture   9 Treatment

19. Depression

__ I have been diagnosed with clinical depression

__ I sometimes feel really down but there's been some hard things happening in my life

__ I feel really down most of the time and I can't put my finger on any obvious reason

__ I can't get out of bed for days on end and just lie there with the blinds shut

__ I am a chain-smoker because I feel it helps me with my depression

__ I'm scared to go to a health care professional about the way I feel

__ Maybe if I tell a doctor I'm depressed all the time I will get a prescription for a pill that will make me high legally

__ I am taking anti-depressant medications currently, namely

    __ Prozac®

    __ Zoloft®

    __ Welbutrin®

    __ Other, namely: _____

__ I have taken anti-depressant medication and never felt a high, that's not what it does

__ I know people who have been helped by anti-depression medications

__ I know people who have had problems with anti-depression medications

__ I used to take prescription anti-depressant medications but I quit because

    __ I felt better

    __ I forgot to take them

    __ I gained weight

    __ I couldn't sleep

    __ I had no libido (sex drive)

    __ I couldn't perform sexually

    _____

__ I want more information about new medications (beyond Prozac etc.) to treat depression

__ I am aware of the possible interactions between my depression medication and alcohol/drugs/nicotine

__ I used to use alcohol and/or illegal drugs to medicate my depression

__ A doctor told me to use alcohol/drugs to medicate my depression

__ Medicating my depression with alcohol/drugs/nicotine had the following effect:

_____

__ I feel my basic problem is depression, and I used alcohol/tobacco/drugs to medicate that

__ I feel my basic problem is alcoholism/nicotine/other drug addiction, and my use of alcohol/nicotine/drugs got me depressed or made my depression worse

__ I can't tell whether my basic problem is depression or addiction

__ I am getting professional help for my depression

__ I have a support system specifically for my depression, separate from my addiction recovery support system

__ The doctor who is helping me with my depression knows the full story about my drinking/using/smoking

___ I haven't told the doctor who is treating me for depression about my
    drinking/using/smoking

___ My chemical dependency counselor knows the full story about my depression

___ I haven't told the counselor who is treating me for addiction about my
    depression

___ Staying clean and sober and quitting smoking is especially difficult for a person
    with depression because

_____

___ Staying clean and sober and quitting smoking is especially important for a
    person with depression because

_____

___ I plan to address my depression issue as part of my recovery from alcohol/drugs

___ I want more information about depression and depression medications

___ I don't see a depression issue in my life at this time

About Psychoactive Medications

Modern medicine offers a large and growing variety of pharmaceuticals that go to the brain and affect your thoughts, feelings, moods, and attitudes. These psychoactive medications may be useful sobriety tools, but many of them may also become drugs of abuse.

How can you make sure that your medications are sobriety tools and not fuel for addiction? There are no absolute guarantees, but these two basic guidelines will give you a margin of safety:

1. Be totally honest with your physician about your use of alcohol and other drugs, including nicotine. You can ask the physician not to write this information into your chart if you are concerned about your privacy, but you must practice full disclosure, without cutting corners.

2. Select a physician who is experienced in treating addictions. Ask whether your physician is a member of the American Society of Addiction Medicine (ASAM) or its equivalent in other countries. If not, ask what other training or experience they have in addiction treatment. Many physicians have no training in addictions and have no clue about the impact of their prescriptions on persons with pre-existing addiction issues.

If both of these conditions are met, and if you take the medicine as prescribed, and are aware of the possible side effects, you may enjoy the benefits of decades of research into the neuropharmacology of the brain. The right medication can be a powerful aid to your recovery. But no pill yet invented or on the horizon is a magic bullet. All of them are meant to be taken as part of a holistic recovery effort that requires your own work to reshape your attitudes and behaviors, including participation in appropriate recovery support groups, if available.

1 Body   2 Exposure   3 Activities   4 People   5 Feelings   6 Life Style   7 History   8 Culture   9 Treatment

1 Body   2 Exposure   3 Activities   4 People   5 Feelings   6 Life Style   7 History   8 Culture   9 Treatment

20.   Chronic Anxiety

__ I have been diagnosed with Generalized Anxiety Disorder
__ I used to drink/drug to medicate my chronic anxiety
__ The effect of my drinking/using on my chronic anxiety was

_____
__ Staying clean and sober is especially difficult for a person with chronic anxiety
     because

_____
__ Staying clean and sober is especially important for a person with chronic anxiety
     because

_____
__ I want more information about chronic anxiety
__ I plan to address my chronic anxiety as part of my recovery
__ I don't have a chronic anxiety issue

21.   Bipolar Disorder

__ I want more information about bipolar disorder
__ I have been diagnosed with bipolar disorder
__ I used to drink/do drugs to medicate my bipolar disorder
__ The effect of my drinking/drugging on my bipolar disorder was

_____
__ The doctor who is treating me for bipolar disorder knows the full story about my
     drinking/using
__ I have a support system specifically for my bipolar disorder
__ Staying clean and sober is especially difficult for a person with bipolar disorder
     because

_____
__ Staying clean and sober is especially important for a person with bipolar disorder
     because

_____
__ I plan to address my bipolar disorder as part of my recovery
__ I don't have an issue with bipolar disorder

22. Panic Attacks

__ I want more information about anxiety attacks or panic attacks
__ I suffer(ed) from anxiety attacks or panic attacks
__ The effect of my drinking/drugging on my panic attacks was

_____

__ I have seen a health care provider about my panic attacks
__ Staying clean and sober is especially difficult for a person with panic attacks
      because

_____

__ Staying clean and sober is especially important for persons prone to panic
      attacks because

_____

__ I plan to address my issue with anxiety/panic attacks as part of my recovery
__ I don't have an issue with anxiety/panic attacks

23. Post-Traumatic Stress Disorder

__ I have been diagnosed with Post-Traumatic Stress Disorder (PTSD)
__ I feel constantly on my toes ready to spar with attackers
__ Sometimes I feel completely cut off from my feelings, and have no sense of
      what is going on inside me
__ Sometimes I feel as if I were outside my body watching from a distance what is
      happening to me
__ Sometimes my normal thought process is interrupted by frightening images that
      come without warning
__ I am aware of some very painful things that happened to me in the past when I
      was defenseless and had no one to help me
__ The relationship between my drinking/using and my PTSD is:

_____

_____

__ I want more information about PTSD
__ I don't have an issue with PTSD in my life

1 Body   2 Exposure   3 Activities   4 People   5 Feelings   6 Life Style   7 History   8 Culture   9 Treatment

24. Schizophrenia

__ I sometimes have strange thoughts or feelings that make me suspect I may have schizophrenia, such as: [28]
    __ Odd or unusual things happening that I can't explain
    __ I feel I can predict the future
    __ I am being controlled by something or someone else
    __ I go out of my way because of superstitions that I have
    __ Sometimes I can't tell if what's happening is real or imaginary
    __ I can read other people's minds, or they can read mine
    __ I suspect that people are plotting to harm me
    __ I have superpowers
    __ My mind is playing tricks on me
    __ People are talking to me who don't really exist
    __ Someone is speaking my own thoughts out loud
    __ I worry that maybe I'm going crazy
__ I have several of these possible signs of schizophrenia, but only while I'm high on cocaine or other drugs, or during withdrawal, never while I'm straight
__ I have several of these possible signs of schizophrenia while I'm high or during withdrawal, and I wonder if the drug is just unmasking an underlying schizophrenia that I wasn't aware of before
__ I have several of these possible signs of schizophrenia while I'm high or during withdrawal, and I'm concerned that the drug may be reinforcing these schizophrenic tendencies and that I'll go seriously crazy if I continue using
__ I suspect I might have schizophrenia but I'm avoiding going to a doctor about it
__ I've been diagnosed as having schizophrenia and am being treated for it
__ I was using alcohol and/or other drugs before I developed schizophrenia
__ I started using alcohol and/or other drugs after my schizophrenia developed
__ I can't remember which came first, the drugs or the schizophrenia, or they came on together
__ Drugs like alcohol and nicotine (etc.) help me control my schizophrenia symptoms and make me feel better
__ Drugs like alcohol and nicotine (etc.) trigger my schizophrenia symptoms and make me feel worse
__ I have schizophrenia medications, but I prefer alcohol and nicotine (etc.)
__ I'm on schizophrenia medications and I'm aware that taking alcohol and especially nicotine can mess with the effective dosage of my medications
__ I'm trying to get treatment for both addiction and schizophrenia, but the addiction people don't want me because of my schizophrenia and the mental health people don't want me because of my addiction
__ Having both schizophrenia and addiction together is very depressing and I sometimes give up hope
__ I have times when I'm mentally clear and my schizophrenia is quiet, and it's super-important that I'm also clean and sober during those times
__ I have times when I'm mentally clear and my schizophrenia is quiet, and during those times I can take positive steps to help myself
__ I don't have a schizophrenia issue at this time

---

[28] Adapted from the Yale University PRIME Screening Test

25. Hepatitis C

__ I have been diagnosed with hepatitis C
__ The relationship between my drinking/using and my getting hepatitis-C is

_____

__ Staying clean and sober is especially difficult for a person with hepatitis because

_____

__ Staying clean and sober is especially important for a person with hepatitis-C
    because

_____

__ I plan to address my hepatitis issue as part of my recovery from alcohol/drugs
__ I don't have a hepatitis issue

26. HIV

__ I am HIV positive
__ I might be HIV positive but I'm avoiding getting tested
__ The relationship between my drinking/using and my becoming HIV+ is

_____

__ Staying clean and sober is especially difficult for a HIV+ person because

_____

__ Staying clean and sober is especially important for a person who is HIV+
    because

_____

__ I want more information about the relationship between HIV status and
drinking/using
__ I am a support person for someone who is HIV+ and it is important for me to
    keep my act together
__ I plan to address my HIV situation as part of my recovery from alcohol/drugs
__ I don't have an HIV issue

1 Body   2 Exposure   3 Activities   4 People   5 Feelings   6 Life Style   7 History   8 Culture   9 Treatment

1 Body   2 Exposure   3 Activities   4 People   5 Feelings   6 Life Style   7 History   8 Culture   9 Treatment

27.   Tuberculosis

__ I have tested positive for tuberculosis
__ The relationship between my drinking/using and my getting tuberculosis is

_____
__ Staying clean and sober is especially difficult for a person with TB because

_____
__ Staying clean and sober is especially important for a person with tuberculosis
    because

_____
__ I want more information about my tuberculosis risk
__ I plan to address my tuberculosis as part of my recovery from drugs/alcohol
__ I don't have an issue with tuberculosis

28.   Genes

__ My biological parents, or one of them, had serious alcohol/drug problems
__ I have a lot of alcoholics in my family tree going back several generations
__ I'm not aware of any alcoholics in my family tree
__ I want more information about the role of genetics in alcoholism/drug addiction

29.   Getting Older

__ I am getting older
__ I could handle the drinking/drugging when I was younger but it's time to stop
    now
__ It's about time I took responsibility for my life
__ I feel I have aged or worn out my body prematurely due to drinking/using
__ I didn't start drinking heavily or using until I got older
__ I feel it is harder to stay clean and sober as I get older because

_____
__ One of my motivations for drinking/using was to feel less old
__ I feel that staying clean and sober is especially important as I get older because

_____
__ I have children and I want them to have a sober role model
__ My parents were drunks/addicts and I don't want my kids to grow up the same
    way
__ I have grandchildren and I want them to have a sober grandparent
__ I want more information about addiction and getting older

30.   Dying

___ I know people who have died from alcoholism / drug addiction
___ I have almost died because of my drinking/drugging
___ I don't care if I die drunk or stoned
___ I want to die sober
___ If I don't get sober I will probably die of a drug overdose or of liver disease
___ My basic reason for drinking/using is/was to kill myself
___ I tried to overdose on alcohol/drugs so that I would die
___ I don't care if people remember me as a drunk or addict
___ I want people to remember me as a sober person
___ I have made a will
___ I don't plan to make a will, let the government do with my stuff what it sees fit
___ I don't really want to live, but I don't want to die drunk or addicted either
___ I want to live, that's why I want to stay sober
___ I want to donate my liver to a transplant candidate, if it's any good
___ I've made written plans for my funeral/cremation
___ I've left instructions whether to resuscitate me or not
___ I have been diagnosed with a terminal disease and want to go out sober
___ I have been diagnosed with a terminal disease and might as well go out
        drinking/using
___ I expect there will be _____ persons at my funeral
___ I am never going to die

31.   Pregnancy

___ I am pregnant or plan to become pregnant
___ I was drinking/using when I got pregnant
___ I would not have become pregnant if I had been clean and sober at the time
___ I would like to terminate the pregnancy
___ I would like to have the baby and have it be healthy
___ I am informed about the risks of drinking/using during pregnancy
___ I am aware that alcohol could damage my baby even before I may know for sure
        that I am pregnant
___ Staying clean and sober is especially important for a person who is or might
        become pregnant because

_____
___ I acted like I didn't care if my baby was born brain-damaged because of my
        drinking
___ I acted like I didn't care if my child turned out to be a drunk/addict like I am
___ I don't want to be the addicted mother that mine was
___ I would like my child to have a clean and sober mother
___ I am going to make sure my baby and I get medical attention
___ I will stop drinking, using and smoking at least until the baby is born
___ I can always abstain from drinking/using/smoking while I am pregnant but I
        have trouble afterward the baby is born
___ Pregnancy is not an issue for me

1 Body   2 Exposure   3 Activities   4 People   5 Feelings   6 Life Style   7 History   8 Culture   9 Treatment

1 Body   2 Exposure   3 Activities   4 People   5 Feelings   6 Life Style   7 History   8 Culture   9 Treatment

32.   Checklist of Concerns

The checklist on the next page pulls together the work you have been doing in this domain.

After reviewing your work, make a checkmark in the "Yes" column for any topic that concerns you.

Make a checkmark in the "Info" column if you want more information about that topic, then ask a counselor or other health-care provider, or get the information in other ways.

If you have Internet access, you can get a great deal of information about any of these areas, but only a qualified professional can give you a diagnosis or prescribe medications.

One relatively efficient way to start getting online information about a health concern is to go to wikipedia.org, read the material there, and follow the links at the bottom of the article.

The scientific literature on a health issue is searchable through the PubMed website at http://www.ncbi.nlm.nih.gov/pubmed, or just google "PubMed."

In the "Summary of my Concern" column of the worksheet on the next page, write a short description of your concerns about that topic – just a word or two that sums it up.

At the end of the book, you can use this worksheet – and similar worksheets at the exit of other domains – to put the pieces of your recovery issues together into a lifetime recovery plan.

Worksheet 4:   My Body Checklist

MY CONCERNS ABOUT MY BODY			
Yes ✔	Issue	Info ✔	Summary of my Concern
	Detox		
	Telltale Signs		
	Hidden Body Damage		
	Doctor Visits		
	Teeth and Gums		
	Nutrition		
	Vitamins		
	Caffeine		
	Sugar		
	Salt		
	Nicotine		
	Pain		
	Exercise		
	Sleep, rest		
	Dreams		
	My Brain		
	Medications		
	Medical Marijuana		
	Depression		
	Chronic Anxiety		
	Bipolar Disorder		
	Panic Attacks		
	Schizophrenia		
	Hepatitis C		
	HIV		
	Tuberculosis		
	Genes		
	Getting Older		
	Dying		
	Pregnancy		

1 Body

2 Exposure

3 Activities

4 People

5 Feelings

6 Life Style

7 History

8 Culture

9 Treatment

1 Body   2 Exposure   3 Activities   4 People   5 Feelings   6 Life Style   7 History   8 Culture   9 Treatment

33. My Plan for My Body

Having reviewed and prioritized the material in this domain, the main issue I intend to focus on concerning the condition of my body is:

_____

_____

The main thing I intend to do about this issue is:

_____

_____

Today's date: _____

34. Three-Month Review

Three months after finishing your work in this domain, what changes if any do you notice in your body, your health, and the way you feel?

_____

_____

_____

35. One-Year Review

One year after finishing your work in this domain, what changes if any do you notice in your body, your health, and the way you feel?

_____

_____

_____

_____

[Chapter Three]

Second Domain: My Exposure

One of the most common challenges in recovery is dealing with the sight, smell, feel or sound of "our" drug or of people, places and things that remind us of it.

Typically, years of repetitive using/drinking have etched our minds with learned associations such as "see Bud label ⇨ want drink" or "see corner of Pine and 23rd ⇨ want drug." Becoming consciously aware of these patterns, and of the things that trigger them, is half the battle. Once you know what to watch out for, you can take action.

In this domain you can map out areas in your life where you are exposed to drugs/alcohol and make decisions on how to deal with that issue. You can learn tools that will let you not only survive but prevail as a clean and sober person in a sometimes tough and dirty world.

36. People Say: About Exposure

___ I can't escape seeing and being exposed to alcohol or drugs

___ Although I can't escape exposure to alcohol/drugs completely, I could reduce my exposure to them

___ I still have my alcoholic beverage (and/or my drug) in the house

___ I threw out all my stuff

___ When I see an advertisement for alcohol, especially for my main brand, it sets off thoughts about drinking in my brain

___ Sometimes when I see an advertisement for alcohol, I let my eyes linger on it and I take in all the details

___ When I see an advertisement for alcohol, I turn my eyes away and look at something else

___ Sometimes when I see actors on TV or in the movies pretending to drink or use drugs, it makes me want to do some myself for real

___ When I see drinking or drug use on the screen, it makes me glad I'm not doing that any more

___ When I see actors drinking or smoking, it makes me mad because I know that the liquor and tobacco companies paid to have them do it

___ When I see actors on TV drinking and/or smoking, I change the channel

___ When I see actors drinking/smoking/using, I don't notice it

1 Body   2 Exposure   3 Activities   4 People   5 Feelings   6 Life Style   7 History   8 Culture   9 Treatment

1 Body   2 Exposure   3 Activities   4 People   5 Feelings   6 Life Style   7 History   8 Culture   9 Treatment

__ If a movie has a lot of positive images of drinking/drugging in it I'll walk out

__ When I pass a liquor store, I have to pull myself together so as not to go in and buy

__ When I pass a liquor store I don't feel anything, I just ignore it, it's not for me

__ When I go through the alcohol aisle in a supermarket, it means nothing to me

__ When I go through the alcohol aisle in a supermarket I get thoughts about drinking

__ When I go through the alcohol aisle in a supermarket I get memories of my hangovers

__ When I see my former dealer I get a craving to use

__ When I see my former dealer I keep moving; this person has nothing for me

__ When I see my former dealer my thoughts turn to homicide

__ When I see people doing my drug I get a craving

__ When I see people doing my drug I am so glad it's not me

__ If I handle a bottle or can of my main brand of alcohol, I get a craving to drink some

__ There's no way I would handle a container of alcohol; why would I?

__ It doesn't affect me one way or the other to handle my brand of drink or my drug

__ When I pass a bar or tavern and see people drinking inside, I get a desire to go in and drink with them

__ When I smell a bar I get sickened by the stench

__ When I pass a bar or tavern, I'm glad I'm not in there any more

__ I go in to bars and taverns to hang out with people I know, but I drink non-alcoholic beverages and it doesn't bother me more than I can handle

__ I go in to bars and taverns to socialize, and I drink non-alcoholic beverages, but it's somewhat of a struggle to stay clean and sober what with everybody else drinking

__ When I'm in bars or taverns with drinking friends I tell them how much better I feel now that I don't drink any more

__ I look for opportunities to go to bars and/or druggy environments when I don't have to, so as to prove to myself how strong my resistance is

__ I'm an entertainer (or bartender, server, cook) and have to be around the stuff every working minute

__ When I see performers drink/use I worry that kids will take them for role models

__ If I see drug tools like pipes, razor blades, straws, roach clips, needles, etc., I get a craving

__ If I smell wine or beer or other drinks, especially my main brand, I start thinking about how good it would be to have some

__ If I smell alcohol I inhale deeply and savor the flavor

__ If I smell marijuana smoke, I get an urge to smoke some

__ If I smell marijuana smoke I inhale deeply and see if I can get high

__ If I smell cigarette smoke, I get an urge to smoke some

__ If I smell alcohol or weed, I start thinking about my hangovers and paranoid trips

__ If I smell alcoholic beverages, I get a feeling of nausea like I want to throw up

__ If I smell marijuana smoke, I start to gag and go for some fresh air

__ If I smell cigarette smoke, I blow out and get away from it

__ If I had my way, I would live in an environment that was free of drugs and alcohol and tobacco

37.   Thinking About What People Say

In the "People Say" section above, some people kept supplies in the house. Do you think this is a good idea for you? _____

Some people lingered over alcohol advertisements. Do you think this is a smart thing for you to do? _____

Some people deliberately went into drinking/using environments when they had no need to, supposedly to test themselves. Do you think this is a wise policy for you? _____

Some people inhaled and savored the smell of their substance, instead of "huffing" the odor out. Which do you think is the better decision for your sobriety? _____

38.   My Current Exposure

In the *My Current Exposure* Worksheet on Page 60, put a check mark in the first column for any current source of exposure to alcohol/drugs that applies to you.

In the third column, assign yourself Risk Points for each item you have checked.

The Risk Points are based on how big a pull this item has on your mind.

- Does the sight or sound or feel or smell of this item make you want to drink/use? A little bit? Quite a bit? A lot?

- How much mental work does it cost you to clear that urge out of your mind?

Use any Risk Points ranking system that you feel comfortable with, for example 0 –10, 1-3, "low – medium - high," or something else. High points = high risk.

People differ considerably in what is risky for them and in how much of a given risk they can comfortably put up with. What may be harmless to one person can be a landmine for another. The point is for you to know about you.

Keep in mind that your own mood will vary. Right at this moment you may be feeling so confident that nothing could trip you up. But what about later this evening if you feel lonely and depressed? Try to base your Risk Point scores on your most vulnerable state of mind.

After you finish this worksheet, you'll use your Risk Points scores to make a plan for dealing with the most urgent trouble spots in your current environment.

In later chapters you'll explore the triggers to drink or use that operate in your mind independently of your immediate surroundings.

1 Body   2 Exposure   3 Activities   4 People   5 Feelings   6 Life Style   7 History   8 Culture   9 Treatment

Worksheet 5:   My Current Exposure

✔	MY CURRENT EXPOSURE CHECKLIST	Risk Points
	Source of Exposure	
	At the place I stay:	
	There is an open container of my main alcoholic beverage	
	There is a closed container of my main alcoholic beverage	
	There is an open container of a kind of alcoholic beverage I didn't much care for	
	There is a closed container of a kind of alcoholic beverage I didn't much care for	
	There is a stash of my main "drug"	
	There is a stash of another drug that I sometimes did	
	There are some roaches or pipes with residue in them	
	There are shot glasses, snifters, steins, stemware, martini shakers, stirrers, openers, or other containers or utensils specifically designed for alcoholic beverages	
	There are empty alcoholic beverage containers that are waiting to be put out for recycling or as garbage	
	There are roach clips, pipes, stash boxes, rigs, or other containers or utensils specifically designed for "drugging"	
	There are alcoholic beverage posters or advertisements	
	There are posters that celebrate "druggy" people	
	There are empty alcoholic beverage bottles that are used for decoration or as candle holders or vases	
	There is non-alcoholic beer and/or wine	
	There is Dijon mustard (made with wine) in the refrigerator	
	There is cooking sherry in the kitchen cabinet	
	There is vanilla extract in the spice shelf	
	There are addictive prescription medications in the medicine cabinet	
	There is Sterno in the camping closet	
	There are CDs or albums of music that strongly remind me of drinking and/or drugging	
	There are books and/or magazines for alcoholic beverage enthusiasts, for example, wine connoisseur magazines, homebrew beer books, etc.	
	There is a person who lives with me who drinks and/or uses	
	There are people who visit me who bring alcohol/drugs into the house when they come	
	There are people who come visit me who ask me for alcohol/drugs and get annoyed if I don't have any	
	There are neighbors who drink in a public way	
	There are neighbors who do drugs in a public way or who knock on my door wanting to sell me some or give me a free sample	
	There is a bar nearby and I'm exposed to the noise	
	I keep alcohol to serve to friends who visit me	
	My favorite TV programs contain beer or wine commercials	
	My favorite radio station carries beer or wine commercials	
	My favorite books have heroes/heroines who drink/do drugs	

1 Body   2 Exposure   3 Activities   4 People   5 Feelings   6 Life Style   7 History   8 Culture   9 Treatment

✓	MY CURRENT EXPOSURE CHECKLIST Source of Exposure	Risk Points
	I have artwork on the walls that celebrates drinking	
At Work or School:		
	I have a supply of my drink/drug at work	
	I work around open containers of alcohol professionally for example, as bartender, flight attendant, food server, chef, entertainer	
	I work around closed containers of alcohol professionally, for example, as supermarket checker, truck driver	
	I handle or dispense prescription drugs that are addictive, for example,. as physician, nurse, paramedic, pharmacist	
	I see a drug dealer at work from whom I used to score	
	I am a drug dealer	
	A lot of the people I work with are using drugs and/or drinking	
	My supervisor shows up bombed half the time	
	My supervisor expects me to drink and/or use drugs during lunch or after hours	
	The people I work with expect me to drink/use at lunch or during breaks or after work	
	My work requires me to travel and this means a lot of exposure to alcohol/drugs	
In Transit:		
	I can't leave my house without passing a liquor store or bar or dealer	
	On my everyday commute I would have to make a detour to avoid passing a liquor store/bar/drug dealer	
	On my usual trips I cannot avoid passing liquor billboards	
	I have a supply of drugs/alcohol hidden in my car	
	I feel I need to have a drink before I get behind the wheel of my car	
	I'm a frequent flyer and the airlines always serve drinks	
	When I get on an airplane I feel I need to drink to control anxiety	
Where My Family or Friends Stay:		

1 Body   2 Exposure   3 Activities   4 People   5 Feelings   6 Life Style   7 History   8 Culture   9 Treatment

Left margin: 1 Body   2 Exposure   3 Activities   4 People   5 Feelings   6 Life Style   7 History   8 Culture   9 Treatment

✓	MY CURRENT EXPOSURE CHECKLIST	Risk Points
	Source of Exposure	
	At my family's/friends' houses they typically drink/use drugs	
	Whenever I go there they expect me to drink/use with them	
	Whenever I go there they try to give me alcohol or drugs to take home	
	The person I'm in a relationship with drinks/uses there	
	When I Go Out	
	The only places to go for entertainment in this town are bars	
	The only place to meet my friends is in bars	
	In about every movie I see, the hero or heroine drinks/uses/smokes	
	Every place where you can go for entertainment in this town, even the library and the aquarium, I've always been drunk/stoned and they all remind me of drinking/using	
	The only entertainment I've ever known is to stay home and drink/use	
	At parties I go to there is heavy drinking/drugging	
	At parties I go to, the only people I know are drinkers/users	
	All the family occasions feature heavy drinking	
	My favorite restaurant serves dishes cooked in wine or with liquor	
	The restaurant has a wine bottle on every table	
	The server always asks whether I want a cocktail	
	The server always suggest I should have wine with dinner	
	The restaurant has wine bottles on the walls and ceiling	
	I have to pass through the bar to get to the dining room	
	The sign for the restaurant has a neon cocktail glass	
	Other Places Where I Get Exposed to Alcohol/Drugs	

39.   What Can I Do About My Exposure?

What can you do about the sights, sounds and smells of alcohol/drugs in your environment?

Can you eradicate them from the world? Probably not. But maybe you can create a clean space in your immediate environment.

Can you flee from them altogether for the rest of your life? Unlikely. But maybe you can take a vacation from them, or change your scene, or alter your daily routine to avoid the worst of them or to spend less time around them.

If you can't fight or flee the sights, sounds and smells of alcohol/drugs, there are still things you can do to filter them out. You can change the channel or hit "mute" when beer ads come on. You can flick your eyes back on the road when you see a liquor billboard or a drug deal. You can "huff out" the smoke of drugs or the smell of alcohol.

What if you are a bartender, food server, chef, entertainer, flight attendant, or other professional who is surrounded by alcohol during your working hours? What if you live in a household where everyone else drinks/uses? Many people in heavily saturated environments nevertheless achieve complete abstinence. Most successful drug dealers don't use.

People who abstain successfully in wet or druggy environments maintain a firm boundary in their minds between "me" and "them." Drinking/using is something "they" do. It's not something "I" do, no matter what. If you find that keeping up this kind of boundary doesn't work for you, survival as a sober person – and survival, period – may require changing professions.

Environmental triggers cannot cause you to drink or use unless you allow them to. By becoming aware of the danger points and slippery places you can put up your shields in time and go on alert. The real question is how much effort it costs you to maintain your shields, and how long you can keep them up before fatigue sets in. That's where a safe place and a safe time become vital, so that you can recharge your sobriety batteries.

Many people say that the danger of exposure declines for them as they get more sober time. An exposure that might cost them major effort in the early months of sobriety, such as going to a rock concert, becomes easy later on, as they become stronger and more self-aware in their sobriety.

Conditioned reflexes like "see bottle – want drink" can also be turned in favor of your sobriety. You can substitute: "see bottle – remember hangover." You can also create protective, empowering triggers like "see recovery book – want sobriety." Many people credit their successful recoveries in part to adoption of an everyday exercise (a "Daily Do") that affirms their sobriety and etches the commitment to living clean and sober deeply into their minds. (More about that on Page 70.)

You'll find additional work on how to handle cravings in the Third Domain (Activities), Fourth Domain (People) and Fifth Domain (Feelings).

40. Exposure Risk Worksheet

In the *Most Hazardous Exposure Risk Worksheet* on Page 65, copy your three highest risk point items from the *My Current Exposure* Worksheet starting on Page 60. For each high-risk item, write why this item is a particular risk for you, and outline a plan for dealing with it. Could you avoid this exposure altogether? If you cannot avoid it, what can you do to minimize it or to make yourself less vulnerable to it? These might be good issues to bring to a group for feedback.

Here is an example of a filled-in *Most Hazardous Exposure Risk Worksheet*:

Worksheet 6:   Most Hazardous Exposure Risk Worksheet (Example)

MOST HAZARDOUS EXPOSURE RISK WORKSHEET
My No. 1 Exposure Risk: *Going to the corner of 23rd and Main*
Why this is especially risky for me: *This is where I used to score crack. If I even drive within three blocks of there I start getting a craving and if I actually go to that corner I'll relapse, I know I will.*
Specifically, what I plan to do about this risk is: *Don't go there. If I have to make a detour, no problem. Better to spend a few pennies more for gas and spend a couple of extra minutes making the detour than to get sucked back into using!*
My No. 2 Exposure Risk: *My friend Ronnie's house*
Why this is especially risky for me: *We always smoke and drink and do any drugs available when we go there. That's about all we ever do when we go there. I can't imagine being there and not doing drugs.*
Specifically, what I plan to do about this risk is: *That's easy. Don't go there. If Ronnie invites me over I'll say I'm busy with something else.*
My Third Highest Exposure Risk: *Watching football on TV at home*
Why this is especially risky for me: *I always start out with a few beers and my friends come over and then we go on to the other stuff and by the time the game is over we're more wasted than the players.*
Specifically, what I plan to do about this risk is: *This will take some effort but I can do it. To begin with, I'm going to go over to my sister's house where they don't drink or use, and watch the game there. Later in the season when I have more clean and sober time I'm going to see who my true friends are and have a clean and sober football party at my house. If they can't support me getting a clean and sober life, what kind of friends are they?*

1 Body   2 Exposure   3 Activities   4 People   5 Feelings   6 Life Style   7 History   8 Culture   9 Treatment

Worksheet 7:   Most Hazardous Exposure Risk Worksheet

MOST HAZARDOUS EXPOSURE RISK WORKSHEET
My No. 1 Exposure Risk:
Why this is especially risky for me:
Specifically, what I plan to do about this risk is:
My No. 2 Exposure Risk:
Why this is especially risky for me:
Specifically, what I plan to do about this risk is:
My Third Highest Exposure Risk:
Why this is especially risky for me:
Specifically, what I plan to do about this risk is:

1 Body

2 Exposure

3 Activities

4 People

5 Feelings

6 Life Style

7 History

8 Culture

9 Treatment

1 Body   2 Exposure   3 Activities   4 People   5 Feelings   6 Life Style   7 History   8 Culture   9 Treatment

41.   Make an Exposure Hot Spot Map

On a separate sheet, sketch a map of the area where you live and/or work; or get a street map. On the map, mark the danger zones where your risk of exposure to drugs/alcohol is especially high. Then, plan a route that avoids or minimizes your travel through those toxic places.

For example, a hot spot map done by a workbook study group participant featured smoke shops, a certain coffee shop, tattoo parlors, the nearby commuter train station, a community college, and certain intersections where she used to buy or use marijuana. Your map needn't be fancy or drawn to scale. But if you are handy with computers, you could use a mapping program such as Google Earth. You can overlay slippery places and other notations on the map, plan a relatively safe route, then print your work and keep it with you as a reminder during your travels.

What do you do if your whole community is saturated with danger spots and there is no possible route that avoids all of them? Write your ideas:

_____

_____

_____

42.   Make an Exposure Floor Plan

On a separate sheet, sketch out the floor plan of the place where you live, including major pieces of furniture, doors, stairs, etc. Mark pieces of furniture, cabinets, and other spots where you habitually kept a supply or drank/used.

Then make a plan to transform or avoid those areas: move or replace furniture, paint the area a different color, add pictures, plants, or other eye-catchers, replace carpets or curtains, and change your behavior pattern so that you don't linger unnecessarily in spots where your memories of drinking/using are strongest.

43.   The Triggers in My Closet

Are there clothes in your closet or your dresser that you usually wore when you drank or used? Are there items with wine stains or burn holes, or that smell of smoke? Do you have jewelry or trinkets that have drug memories in them? Now might be a good time to clean house.

44.   My Safe Space

Do you have a place where you can be completely free of all exposure to alcohol/drugs (except the thoughts and feelings that may be in your own mind)? _____

Is your home such a place? _____

If one part of your home is not safe, is there another part where you can retreat and be away from the sight and smell of alcohol and drugs?

Can you make and enforce a rule to keep drugs/alcohol out of your space? _____

Do you have a drug and alcohol-free place to go to outside your home? _____

What could you do to create a safe space, or to enlarge the one you have, or to create additional safe places for you?

_____

_____

_____

45.   Safe Disposal Methods

If you decide to get rid of the substances in your home, you will probably have to handle them (and smell them) in the process. Some people have relapsed doing that. What to do?

This is where a friend in recovery comes in very handy. You two can "clean house" together.

Illegal drugs are best flushed down the toilet. Use a hammer on your drug tools and put them beyond repair before throwing them in the trash, otherwise you'll be tempted to retrieve them. The toilet is also perfect for cheap wine, beer and liquor.

Are there some fancy bottles that seem too good to pour down the drain? You can gift-wrap them lovingly and give them away immediately to the first comer, or leave them on the street. If you have crystal stemware wine glasses, brandy snifters and other high-priced drinking paraphernalia that are "talking to you," you might store them out of sight in a seldom-opened cupboard, or pretend that they're holiday items and box them up, put them away, and forget them.

This is a fun topic to talk about with a group.

1 Body   2 Exposure   3 Activities   4 People   5 Feelings   6 Life Style   7 History   8 Culture   9 Treatment

1 Body   2 Exposure   3 Activities   4 People   5 Feelings   6 Life Style   7 History   8 Culture   9 Treatment

46.   My Safe Time

Do you have a regular time when you are ordinarily removed from all exposure to alcohol/drugs (except the thoughts that may be in your mind)? _____

What could you do to create such a time, or to make more time of this kind in your day?

_____

_____

_____

47.   "Dry Drunk" Episodes

Sometimes the sight, sound, smell or feel of a familiar drug can make the body think that you've had some. (Ever had a "contact high"?) Some people in early recovery have experiences where they feel and act as if they were intoxicated (for example, they get very depressed, animated, manic, irritable or unsteady) and wake up the next morning with a headache and other typical hangover symptoms. Episodes of this type are sometimes known as "post-acute withdrawal symptoms" or "dry drunks." (Do not confuse the "dry drunk" symptoms with the term of insult that some people use to attack other people's sobriety.)

In experiments, people who believe they are drinking alcohol, but aren't, sometimes show typical signs of intoxication, including symptoms you cannot fake, such as rapid eye movements and changes in blood pressure. This kind of physical response to a mental cue occurs also with some other bodily systems. For example, laboratory animals trained to associate a sound with an injection of bacteria that arouse their immune systems will eventually produce the immune response to the sound alone.

Dry drunk episodes, if you experience them, are another reason to minimize your exposure to drinking/drugging triggers and to make changes in your activities and life style.

Have you had "dry drunk" episodes? If so, write about them here:

_____

_____

_____

48. My Recovery Triggers

Some people find that surrounding themselves with "recovery stuff" helps to trigger sober thoughts and gives them sober energy, just as being around alcohol/drugs may trigger relapse thoughts. Such objects may be recovery books, knick-knacks, and jewelry with an explicit recovery theme. They may also be ordinary objects that have a special recovery meaning for you. In the table below, make a list of the recovery-related objects in your life. After you finish the table, ask yourself how your inventory of recovery things compares with your stock of paraphernalia for using/drinking.

Worksheet 8:   My Recovery Triggers

MY RECOVERY TRIGGERS
Explicit recovery books and other objects I own:
1)
2)
3)
4)
5)
6)
7)
8)
Other objects that have a special recovery meaning for me:
1)
2)
3)
4)
5)
6)
7)
8)

1 Body

2 Exposure

3 Activities

4 People

5 Feelings

6 Life Style

7 History

8 Culture

9 Treatment

49.   My "Daily Do"

In the famous experiment where he was trained to salivate when a bell rang, Pavlov's dog had little choice but to follow instructions. You can do better. You can be the trainer as well as the dog. You can condition yourself to think "see white powder – remember bankruptcy" instead of your old reflex craving response. You can also groove new neural pathways that keep recovery uppermost in your mind. There is a rich arsenal of time-tested techniques for re-educating your mental reflexes. The key ingredient in all of them is repetition, daily if not more often.

Here is a sampler of such "Daily Do" exercises people use. Some of them work on the aversion principle: link drinking/using with bad things that happened to you. Some of them work on the affirmation principle: underline your strong qualities and your sober victories and build your confidence. There's no reason why you shouldn't use both flavors, alternately or together, in whatever combination suits your mood and your personality. The repetition may be more important than the content.

Put a checkmark next to the ones that appeal to you, and start doing them. Better yet, make up your own.   Vary them from time to time to keep them fresh. Many people say that their "Daily Do" is the most effective single tool in their sobriety toolkit, and regard it as the secret of their successful long-term recovery.

A. Aversion Flavor:

___ Every morning I get in front of the mirror and say out loud "When I drank/used I woke up in the morning with vomit all over me." *(Vary this from time to time with other negative things that happened to you when you drank/used.)*

___ I tape a piece of paper to my mirror that says "I am an alcoholic/addict, I do not drink or use no matter what." I read it out loud every morning.

___ I put a rubber band around my toothbrush, that reminds me when I brush how I let my teeth and gums rot when I drank/used.

___ On my digital wristwatch I turn on the hourly beeper (or set an alarm shortly before my regular drinking time, or at some arbitrary other time) to remind myself that I am an alcoholic/addict and do not drink or use.

___ Every morning I take mega-vitamins and remind myself, as I swallow the huge pill, that drinking/using was bad for my body chemistry.

___ I ask for decaf coffee in the mornings because I get cravings when I crash after the regular coffee buzz; choosing decaf reminds me how unpleasant it is to have cravings.

___ I keep a copy of my DUI sentence taped to my dresser mirror where I look at it every morning when I get up.

___ I keep a list of the ten stupidest things I did during my drinking/using on a bright yellow piece of paper folded in my wallet in front of my bills. Every time I go to my wallet I see the paper and it reminds me.

___ Other

B. Affirmation Flavor:

__ Every morning I take time out and say out loud to myself, "I am a worthwhile, intelligent human being. I will not drink or use today." *Make up your own text on this theme, for example:*

__ "I am a capable, competent, caring and compassionate person. I respect myself and I deserve respect from others."

__ "The past is behind me. Today I am a new happy sober person."

__ "I am responsible for my choices. I choose to live my life clean and sober."

__ I use a favorite recovery keyword as my computer password.

__ I keep pictures of my children where I can see them to remind me that they deserve a sober parent.

__ On a wall calendar I put a star for every day I have been free of drugs and alcohol.

__ On my mirror I tape the saying, "It's not my fault. I will not beat myself up today."

__ I do meditation every day and get to a quiet place in my mind where I do not feel cravings.

__ I have a list of three difficult crises that I went through clean and sober. I keep it in my wallet to remind myself that my sobriety has survived heavy storms.

__ I keep recovery literature laying around my tables and shelves where my eye frequently falls on it.

__ I have a special silver necklace that I bought for myself as a getting-sober present. Whenever I feel the slightest urge, I touch it. It reminds me what I'm doing.

__ Other

_____

50.   My Plan for My Exposure

Based on the preceding, summarize here the main thing that you plan to do about your current exposure to the sight, sound, smell and touch of addictive substances.

What I plan to do about my exposure is:

_____

_____

_____

_____

I am starting my Daily Do exercise ___ Today ___ Later

Today's date: _____

1 Body   2 Exposure   3 Activities   4 People   5 Feelings   6 Life Style   7 History   8 Culture   9 Treatment

1 Body   2 Exposure   3 Activities   4 People   5 Feelings   6 Life Style   7 History   8 Culture   9 Treatment

51.   Three-Month Review

Three months after finishing your work on this chapter, what changes if any are there in your environment, as far as your exposure risk goes?

_____

_____

_____

_____

Looking back on it, were your Risk Point scores realistic, or did you underestimate some of your risks?   Yes   No   If you underestimated, why do you suppose that happened?

_____

_____

I am keeping up my Daily Do exercise Yes No

52.   One-Year Review

One year after finishing your work on this chapter, what changes if any are there in your environment, as far as your exposure risk goes?

_____

_____

_____

_____

I am keeping up my Daily Do exercise __ Yes ___No

Chapter Four

Third Domain: My Activities

"I never dreamed I could do _____ clean and sober." Many people wove drugs and/or alcohol so tightly into the activities of their life that it may take some time and effort to get them untangled again. In this domain, you can start taking your life back from alcohol/drugs, thread by thread.

Sometimes drinking/using became a person's whole life and they had no other activities to speak of. Recovery in that case may mean starting from scratch.

When you get clean and sober, you can celebrate a string of victories as you learn to do things clean and sober that you never thought you could. You can use your freed-up time to follow old dreams or develop new interests and pursuits.

This work area contains two main tools for getting your life activities untangled from drinking/using.

Part One centers on the *My Activities Checklist*. This worksheet is a long, detailed list of common everyday activities that people do. Here you indicate whether this is an activity that usually found you under the influence, or whether you were usually clean and sober then.

After you finish this checklist, there are some questions aimed at helping you sift through the material, reflect on it, and make a personal plan for change. This part concludes with a worksheet of possible new activities that might fill your newly freed up time with clean and sober pleasure, or even passion.

Part Two of this domain is a worksheet for learning to do a single activity clean and sober. This checklist brings in a series of tools that people use to go safely through their personal trouble spots and come out smiling, clean and sober.

1 Body

2 Exposure

3 Activities

4 People

5 Feelings

6 Life Style

7 History

8 Culture

9 Treatment

53.   The *My Activities* Checklist

The next worksheet is a long list of common activities that people do, as well as some that are not so common. There are plenty of blanks for you to add activities of yours that are missing from the list.

For each activity, you put a checkmark in the first column, column (A), if this is an activity that you almost always did while under the influence of alcohol or other drugs. For example, if you generally watched television while drinking, or drank while watching television, you check column A next to the activity "Watch TV."

But if this is an activity that you almost always did clean and sober, you put a checkmark in the third column, column (S). For example, if you generally went off to work sober, or you were generally sober while going off to work, you check column S next to the activity "Leave for work."

And if this activity sometimes found you clean and sober, sometimes not, depending, then check the middle column, "It depended." For example, if you sometimes baby-sat clean and sober, sometimes under the influence, depending, you check the middle column next to the activity "Baby-sit."

If you never did this activity, leave the line blank.

If you're not sure or can't remember, put a question mark in column A.

Worksheet 9:   My Activities

MY ACTIVITIES In the past, did I do this activity under the influence, or clean and sober? *Activity*	Almost always drunk/high [A]	It depended	Almost always clean/sober [S]
On Work Days:			
Get out of bed			
Shower, dress			
Eat breakfast			
Look for a job			
Spend the day not working			
Leave for work			
Arrive at work			
Start working			
Take first break			
Have lunch by myself			
Have lunch with others			
Resume work after lunch			
Take second break			
Quit work			
Work overtime			
Attend an onsite meeting			
Give a presentation			
Get evaluated			
Evaluate someone else			
Attend an offsite meeting			
Business travel, by car			
Business travel, by air			

MY ACTIVITIES			
Eat meals on business trip			
Business overnight stay			
Work at home			
Go out after work			
Start trip home			
Arrive home after work			
Stop at a store			
Eat the evening meal			
Relax in the evening			
Watch TV			
Be home alone			
Get to sleep			
Sleep through the night			
Go to the gym, exercise			
Walk the dog			
Days off			
Get out of bed			
Shower, dress			
Eat breakfast			
Clean house			
Grocery shop			
Other shopping			
Home repairs			
Car repairs			
Watch TV, movies			
Read a book			
Read newspaper			
Hang out do nothing			
Take a nap			
Be at home with others			
Be at home alone			
Go to sleep			
Sleep through the night			
Gym, exercise			

1 Body   2 Exposure   3 Activities   4 People   5 Feelings   6 Life Style   7 History   8 Culture   9 Treatment

1 Body   2 Exposure   3 Activities   4 People   5 Feelings   6 Life Style   7 History   8 Culture   9 Treatment

MY ACTIVITIES			
Walk the dog			
Social Things			
Baby-sit			
Visit a friend			
Phone a friend			
Do email or chat rooms			
Entertain guests			
Go on a family vacation			
Go on a first date			
Go out with family			
Go out with a steady date			
Go to a bar			
Go to a birthday party			
Go to a club			
Go to a family meal			
Go to a funeral			
Party with strangers			
Party with people I know			
Go to a wedding			
Go to church			
Go to a game			
Try to seduce somebody			
Have sex with spouse			
Make casual chit chat			
Spend time with my kids			
Spend time with my S.O.			
Spend time with parents			
Visit friend in prison			

MY ACTIVITIES			
Hobbies/Recreation			
Bird watch			
Build things			
Build web site			
Care for animal			
Climb a mountain			
Collect things			
Compose music			
Cook, bake			
Dance, or dance lessons			
Design			
Do crafts			
Do ham radio			
Exercise			
Garden			
Get a degree			
Go bicycling			
Go boating			
Go camping			
Go dancing			
Go fishing			
Go for hike			
Go for walks			
Go on vacation			
Go sightseeing			
Go skating			
Go to a sports event			
Go to auctions			
Go to club meetings			
Go to plays or concerts			
Home decorate			
Invent			
Make ceramics			
Make movies			
Martial arts			

MY ACTIVITIES		
Paint		
Play an instrument		
Play board games		
Play card games		
Play on computer		
Play solo sports		
Play team sports		
Read a book		
Restore things		
Ride horses		
Ride motorbike		
Sculpt		
Sail		
See movies		
Sew-knit-embroider		
Sing		
Surf		
Stargaze		
Take a class		
Take pictures		

MY ACTIVITIES		
Trace genealogy		
Visit library		
Visit museum		
Volunteer		
Windsurf		
Work out in gym		
Work puzzles		
Write a book		
Write poetry		
Yoga		
Other		

Right margin tabs: 1 Body   2 Exposure   3 Activities   4 People   5 Feelings   6 Life Style   7 History   8 Culture   9 Treatment

54.   Questions after Working the *My Activities* Checklist

Now that you've finished this worksheet, you have a useful picture of some recent life patterns. Look back through the long list and think about what it all means. Here are some questions to consider and work through.

A. Patterns in my Drinking/Using

Do you notice any pattern in the activities that you generally did while you were using alcohol or other drugs? (You checked the left column, column A)

For example, are you a person who was generally clean and sober (S) at work but drinking or on drugs (A) at home? Or vice versa?

___ I was generally clean and sober at work
___ I was generally under the influence while at work
___ I was generally clean and sober at home
___ I was generally under the influence while at home

Were you generally sober in activities that you did alone, but under the influence when with other people? Or the reverse?

___ I was generally clean and sober when alone
___ I was generally under the influence when alone
___ I was generally clean and sober with other people
___ I was generally under the influence with other people

Do you notice any calendar patterns in your drinking/using? For example, were you sober Monday through Friday and used mostly on weekends? Was Friday (payday) a specially dangerous day for you? Did you have fairly regular periods of sober days or weeks followed by binges? Write your observations here:

_____

_____

_____

Worksheet 10: Time Card

Time	A	S
6 AM		
7 AM		
8 AM		
9 AM		
10 AM		
11 AM		
Noon		
1 PM		
2 PM		
3 PM		
4 PM		
5 PM		
6 PM		
7 PM		
8 PM		
9 PM		
10 PM		
11 PM		
Midnight		
1 AM		
2 AM		
3 AM		
4 AM		
5 AM		

Do you notice any **clock patterns** in your drinking/using? For example, were you a person who was usually sober until 5 o'clock and then started drinking? Based on your entries in the *My Activities* checklist, fill out this time card (left). Put a check mark in column A if you were usually under the influence during that hour; put a checkmark in column S if you were usually sober. If you had different patterns on different days, make a copy of the time card and fill it out for each type of day separately. Based on this time card, how many hours were you clean and sober (S), and how many hours were you under the influence (A)? (Include hours passed out and hung over or in withdrawal as hours under the influence).

Hours clean and sober:

_____

Hours under the influence:

_____

Percentage of time clean and sober:

_____%.

Do you notice any other on/off patterns in your drinking/using? Or were you under the influence in almost everything you did, all the time? Write your observations on a separate sheet.

B. Strategic Decision: Learn or Avoid?

Look again in the *My Activities* checklist (starting on Page 75) at the activities where you checked column A – activities where you were generally under the influence.

For each of your column A activities, you have an important decision to make: whether to learn how to do this activity clean and sober, or whether to avoid this activity altogether, at least for now.

You may not have much of a choice. For example, if "go to sleep" was an activity that you never did clean and sober in the past, and even though getting to sleep clean and sober at this time seems practically impossible, you'll still have to learn it.

If you do have a choice, consider the options: Avoid or Learn.

From the *My Activities* checklist, copy the activities for which you checked Column A into this next worksheet:

Worksheet 11: Avoid or Learn

Activity that I usually did while drinking/using (First column in My Activities Checklist)	Avoid	Learn

Then, for each activity, consider and decide whether to check "Avoid" or "Learn."

- Consider choosing "Avoid" here if you can live at all without doing this activity. If you almost never did this activity clean and sober in the past, and the activity isn't absolutely necessary for your survival, why go

1 Body   2 Exposure   3 Activities   4 People   5 Feelings   6 Life Style   7 History   8 Culture   9 Treatment

there? You run a high risk of setting yourself up for relapse. A common example: going to a bar. Unless you're the bartender and this is the only way you can make a living, is it a brilliant thing to go to such places in your early recovery?

- If you select "Learn" here, be sure to work Part Two of this domain, the *Learning to do One Activity Clean and Sober Worksheet* starting on Page 88. You'll want to give some thought to how you are going to learn to do this activity, how to handle problems that may come up, who is available to support you, etc. Do the *Learning to do One Activity Clean and Sober Worksheet* for each activity that you've decided to learn.

- If you are in doubt whether you can learn how to do an activity clean and sober, try asking people in your support group (if you have one) to share their experiences. Sometimes all you need is a little encouragement and the living example of someone else who has confronted this issue.

Your decision about "Avoid" or "Learn" is not forever; it's just for right now and the near future. As you get stronger and more experienced in your recovery, you will eventually be able to shift activities from your "avoid" column to your "learn" column.

Let's take a closer look at the decision whether to avoid or learn.

C. The Courage to Choose "Avoid"

In a real war, the winning general is the one who chooses when and where to do battle. Offering to fight at all times and in all circumstances is a fool's game. Many a war has been won by armies that mastered the art of evasion and retreat. They avoided battles in which they were outmatched. In this way they gradually built up their forces and slowly migrated toward a terrain where they had superiority.

▶ *"Retreat until your enemy is exhausted, then attack."* – *Sun Tsu, Art of War.*

You, too, are gradually constructing and strengthening the forces of your sober self, and your life path is migrating toward stronger ground for your recovery.

There is a saying in aviation: "There are bold pilots, and there are old pilots, but there are no old bold pilots."

If you are deliberately flying into high-risk situations when you don't have to, why?

_____

_____

Do you feel somehow less of a person if you decide to avoid an activity that holds a high relapse risk for you? _____. If so, why?

_____

Is that feeling helpful for your recovery? _____ Explain your answer:

Try to gain a healthy, realistic respect for the power of your drug/alcohol issue. If you imagine that its power is absolute, then recovery is impossible. But if you imagine its power is trivial, then it can surprise you and throw you into relapse. Somewhere between those extremes lies the reality. By choosing your battles, you show a healthy, realistic respect for the enemy and you live to fight and win another time.

Remember, the decision to avoid an activity isn't necessarily forever; it's just for now, while you're in early recovery.

You can in due time learn to go to cocktail parties and taverns and similar high-risk places and stay clean and sober, almost effortlessly. But you may also find that you have no desire to go there anymore because people are not at their best while under the influence, and they don't know it.

As time goes by and you string clean and sober days together, and as you learn to do more and more activities clean and sober, you will have reinvented yourself as a new person who has a full and rewarding life and who does not drink or use, no matter what.

 If you find yourself agonizing unduly whether to "avoid" or "learn" an activity, try making a Sobriety T-Chart about it (Chapter 1, Page 34).

D. Getting Satisfaction Another Way

For each item in your "Avoid" list, ask yourself whether there are substitute activities that would give you what you wanted from this particular activity, without so many risks. For example, if you crave being rowdy in a crowd, could you get this itch satisfied by going to hockey games with a sober friend or two, instead of to bars? Take a look at the activities in the long "My Activities Checklist" that you left blank, because they didn't apply to you, and see if there isn't something there that would give you satisfaction clean and sober.

Use the next worksheet to plan substitute activities that would give you some of the same satisfaction as the activities that you have opted to "avoid" for the time being.

Worksheet 12: Finding Substitutes for "Avoid" Activities

ACTIVITIES TO AVOID, AND SUBSTITUTES THAT GIVE SIMILAR SATISFACTION		
Activity to Avoid (Copy from worksheet on Page 79)	What satisfaction do I get out of this activity?	Substitute activity that will give me a similar satisfaction

1 Body   2 Exposure   3 Activities   4 People   5 Feelings   6 Life Style   7 History   8 Culture   9 Treatment

1 Body 2 Exposure 3 Activities 4 People 5 Feelings 6 Life Style 7 History 8 Culture 9 Treatment

E. My Clean and Sober Activities

Were there some activities in the *My Activities* checklist (starting on page 75) that generally found you clean and sober? If so, list those activities in the next worksheet (use an extra sheet if you need more space), and then consider the questions that follow.

Worksheet 13: Clean and Sober Activities

Activity that I generally did while clean and sober
(Third column in *My Activities* checklist)

How did you manage not to be drinking or using other drugs while doing this activity?

Was there something about this activity that was more important than drinking/using? If so, what was it?

What was the feeling (emotion) that motivated you to stay clean and sober while doing this activity?

Write your thoughts here:

_____

_____

_____

_____

_____

_____

Is there some way that you could capture the management ability that allowed you to do this activity sober, and apply it to other activities?

Is there some way that your sense about the importance of this activity, that allowed you to do it sober, could expand to cover other activities?

Is there some way that your emotion that motivated you to stay sober while doing this activity could be stretched or boosted to inspire you to do other things sober, as well?

Write your thoughts here, or on a separate sheet.

_____

_____

F. Questions about the Wobblers

Were there some activities in the *My Activities* checklist (starting on page 75) where you checked the middle column, "It depended"? These activities were your "wobblers" – they could fall in the A column or in the S column, depending. Copy those activities into this worksheet, and for each activity consider the questions that follow.

Worksheet 14: Activities that Depended

Activity that I sometimes did sober, sometimes not – depending (Middle column in My Activities Checklist)

What was the difference between the situations where you did the activity clean and sober, and where you used alcohol or other drugs while doing it?

In other words, what did the A or the S for that activity depend on? Try this checklist of possible factors:

___ The mood I was in
___ The feelings I was having
___ Who I was with
___ The time of day
___ The day of the week
___ The weather
___ The money in my pocket
___ Whether I had some
___ The place I was in
___ Some chance event
___ What I had had to eat
___ What else I'd been doing
___ How tired I was
___ How long it had been
___ Whether I had taken my meds
___ How much exercise I had

If not on this list, what other factors made the difference for you between doing an activity sober or doing that same activity under the influence?

_____

If you can see a pattern here, what could you do to get into the sobering circumstances more often? For example, if one of your "wobbler" activities was playing computer games, and if you did this activity sober when you felt connected, but you got high doing this same activity when you felt isolated, then what could you do to get more connected?

_____

_____

1 Body

2 Exposure

3 Activities

4 People

5 Feelings

6 Life Style

7 History

8 Culture

9 Treatment

1 Body   2 Exposure   3 Activities   4 People   5 Feelings   6 Life Style   7 History   8 Culture   9 Treatment

G. Questions about Your Work

The main "activity" that most people do is their work, the way they earn their living. If you have a job (or a profession or business), is this a source of strength for your addict tendencies (A) or for your sober self (S)?

___ My work mostly tends to reinforce my A (addict self)
___ My work mostly supports my S (sober self)
___ I'm not working, not applicable

If your work is a constant source of stress and negative feelings that drive you in the direction of relapse, give serious consideration to changing your work. That's a big decision. You may want to consider doing the same kind of work in a different setting, or changing into a different line of work altogether. Be sure to make a T-chart, see Chapter 1. On a separate sheet, write your thoughts about this issue, and raise it with your support group if you have one. There's more about this issue in the Sixth Domain, Life Style.

H. Finding Clean and Sober Passions

Getting clean and sober may suddenly leave you with a big hole in your free time. Were you surprised to realize how much time you used to waste drinking/drugging? What do you do with your newly found free time? You run a high risk of relapse if you just sit there, doing nothing, constantly thinking about what you used to be doing. You know the old proverb, "The devil finds work for idle hands." Your sobriety will be stronger and more fun if you find a new free time passion.

Have another look at the *My Activities* checklist (starting on page 75). Review the activities that you left blank because they didn't apply to you. Be sure to scan the activities under the "Hobbies and Recreation" subhead starting on page 76.

The list contains only a few of the thousands of pursuits that engage people's passions and allow them to find clean and sober thrills or clean and sober peace of mind, whichever they prefer. If your favorite is not on the list, add it.

Are there any activities here that you used to do before you started drinking, and that you dropped when you took up alcohol and/or other drugs instead?
- For example, were you once interested in learning the guitar, but let it slide? Now that you're sober, how about picking it up again? Since you'll probably have more money now, how about getting a better guitar and paying for lessons?
- Did you used to swim in water? How about joining a pool and working on your butterfly stroke?
- Always wanted to write a novel? Now that your head is clearing, get going!

Don't be afraid to experiment with different types of new activities, even ones that you never thought you might be interested in. You may have hidden talents that the veil of drinking/drugging concealed from you. Have you always had a secret desire to take up quilting or bungee-jumping or oil painting or raising chickens or rock climbing or translating the Dead Sea Scrolls? Now may be the time to go for it.

Make a list here of free time activities that you used to do but dropped, and other free time activities that seem kind of interesting now. Then make concrete plans to get started and try them out.

Worksheet 15: Possibly Interesting Free Time Activities

Activity	Did this before but dropped it	Never did this but looks interesting

55. Learning To Do One Activity Clean and Sober

After you have finished the *My Activities Worksheet* (it started on Page 75), look in Column 3 for checkmarks in the "Learn" column. For each activity that you have marked "Learn," make a photocopy of the *Learning To Do One Activity Clean and Sober Worksheet* that starts on Page 88.

You can use this worksheet any time that you feel you face a special challenge to your recovery. The example used here is for attending a wedding. You can make copies and use it to plan your sober survival for airplane trips, meetings with old friends, holidays, family events, and other situations where, in the past, you might have reached for your drug. You don't need to do that anymore! You can learn to live and enjoy life clean and sober.

Use this worksheet only for specific single activities such as the ones in the *My Activities Worksheet*. This worksheet is not designed for broad, compound categories like "have a life" or "improve my relationships." If you want to tackle broader issues like those, first break them down into smaller pieces.

No single worksheet will fit all activities, so experiment and modify to get what you need. Since work areas are all connected, it's likely that you'll find additional tools in the other domains.

Here is an example of one way to work this worksheet. Alex has been invited to attend a special activity, namely a wedding. Alex has tentatively decided to learn to participate in the wedding clean and sober, rather than to avoid going. Alex is aware that this is a high-risk activity. Here's Alex's worksheet:

1 Body   2 Exposure   3 Activities   4 People   5 Feelings   6 Life Style   7 History   8 Culture   9 Treatment

Worksheet 16: Learning To Do One Activity Clean and Sober (Example)

LEARNING TO DO ONE ACTIVITY CLEAN AND SOBER (EXAMPLE)	
The activity I want to learn to do clean and sober is:	Go to Dale's wedding
What is at stake for me with this specific activity?	My friendship with Dale – and my sobriety
Have I ever done this in the past without using drugs/alcohol?	Yes
How long ago was the last time I did this without using drugs or alcohol?	When I was about 14
How did I do it clean and sober then?	I hadn't started drinking yet
Can I recapture the skill or ability I had then, and do it sober again?	Can't remember what that felt like!
If I break this activity down into its elements, what are the most dangerous parts for my sobriety?	
Is there danger for my sobriety in the exposure to drugs/alcohol?	Definitely. I am concerned at being around so much free booze
Can I do the activity but avoid or minimize the exposure?	I could go to the wedding but skip the reception...
Can I confront the exposure without yielding?	Not without onsite support
Can I use a safe, non-drug, substitute for the risky substance?	I can keep my glass full of ginger ale and keep it in my hand at all times
Is there danger for me in the feelings I will have when I do this activity?	Yes, weddings stir up a lot of feelings and I'm not used to having strong feelings sober
What feelings give me the most trouble?	Probably feeling that I'm losing Dale, and will be more alone
Can I tolerate having these feelings for a limited time?	Not sure
Can I reduce my sensitivity to these feelings without using drugs?	Probably not, at least for a while; I will feel them no matter what I do
Can I change my attitude so that my feelings don't hurt so much?	I could talk with Dale beforehand and maybe that would make me feel less abandoned
Is there danger for me in the people that I have to deal with when I do this activity?	Definitely. Uncle Harry, and "Spoon"
Can I do the activity but avoid those people?	Yes, it is a big enough crowd where I might avoid running into them,
Can I say or do something so that those people will change their behavior?	Forget it, short of homicide

1 Body   2 Exposure   3 Activities   4 People   5 Feelings   6 Life Style   7 History   8 Culture   9 Treatment

LEARNING TO DO ONE ACTIVITY CLEAN AND SOBER (EXAMPLE)	
Can I change my attitude so that those people won't bother me?	Not enough time for that
Is there something else about the activity that is dangerous for my sobriety? What?	The reception is at Valley View where I've gotten plastered more than once
Is there some other way I can modify this activity so that I can handle it?	
Can I shorten my time in this activity so that I can handle it?	Yes! I could make a cameo appearance
Can I provide myself with an escape hatch so that I can bail out of this activity if I feel in relapse danger?	Yes! I can take my car (instead of riding with B.) and get out of there before I feel threatened in my sobriety
Is there someone who supports my sobriety who can do this activity with me?	Yes! I can take F. and L. and swear one of them to stay with me at all times!
Is there a written plan or some other physical thing I can take with me as a resource when I do this?	Yes. I can photocopy this worksheet and take it with me.
Is there some way I can change my attitude about it so that I can do it more easily?	Yes. It's just a wedding, it's not worth me blowing my sobriety over it.
Have I talked about this with my support group?	Not yet – will do
Have I talked about this with a professional?	Not yet – will do
Do I know anyone else who used to have trouble with this and now can do it OK?	M went to a wedding and survived but G went to one and relapsed …
Will someone else know how I do at this?	Yes, my family and my support group
Will someone else care how I do at this?	Ditto
Will someone give me strokes if I succeed at this?	My group will probably give me a round of applause
If I crash on this try, will I be too discouraged to try again?	No but I will be pissed at myself
Will I feel better if I learn to do this clean and sober?	Yes, I will be very happy, it will make me feel like a competent person
What else will I be able to do if I learn to do this?	I may learn to have a whole sober social life, what a concept!
After finishing this worksheet, am I still sure that I want to learn this activity now, rather than avoid it for the time being?	Yes, I think it can be done if I take all the precautions above

On the next page is the blank worksheet for you:

1 Body   2 Exposure   3 Activities   4 People   5 Feelings   6 Life Style   7 History   8 Culture   9 Treatment

Worksheet 17: Learning To Do One Activity Clean And Sober

LEARNING TO DO ONE ACTIVITY CLEAN AND SOBER	
The activity I want to learn to do clean and sober is:	
What is at stake for me with this specific activity?	
Have I ever done this in the past without using drugs/alcohol?	
How long ago was the last time I did this without using drugs or alcohol?	
How did I do it clean and sober then?	
Can I draw on that experience and do it sober again?	
If I break this activity down into its elements, what are the most dangerous parts for my sobriety?	
Is there danger for my sobriety in the exposure to drugs/alcohol?	
Can I do the activity but avoid or minimize the exposure?	
Can I resist the exposure ("white-knuckle" it)?	
Can I use a safe, non-drug, substitute for the risky substance?	
Is there danger for me in the feelings I will have when I do this activity?	
What feelings give me the most trouble?	
Can I tolerate having these feelings for a limited time?	
Can I reduce my sensitivity to these feelings without drugs?	
Can I change my attitude so that my feelings don't hurt so much?	
Is there danger for me in the people that I have to deal with when I do this activity?	
Can I do the activity but avoid those people?	
Can I say or do something so that those people will change their behavior?	
Can I change my attitude so that those people won't bother me?	

LEARNING TO DO ONE ACTIVITY CLEAN AND SOBER	
Is there something else about the activity that is dangerous for my sobriety? What?	
Is there some other way I can modify this activity so that I can handle it?	
Can I shorten my time in this activity so that I can handle it?	
Can I provide myself with an escape hatch so that I can bail out of this activity if I feel in relapse danger?	
Is there someone who supports my sobriety who can do this activity with me?	
Is there a written plan or some other physical thing I can take with me as a resource when I do this?	
Is there some way I can change my attitude about it so that I can do it more easily?	
Have I talked about this with my support group?	
Have I talked about this with a professional?	
Do I know anyone else who used to have trouble with this and now can do it OK?	
Will someone else know how I do at this?	
Will someone else care how I do at this?	
Will someone give me strokes if I succeed at this?	
If I crash on this try, will I be too discouraged to try again?	
Will I feel better if I learn to do this clean and sober?	
What else will I be able to do if I learn to do this?	
After finishing this worksheet, am I still sure that I want to learn this activity now, rather than avoid it for the time being?	

1 Body

2 Exposure

3 Activities

4 People

5 Feelings

6 Life Style

7 History

8 Culture

9 Treatment

56.   My Plan for My Activities

Summarizing all the detail work you have done in this domain, what is the main change (if any) you feel you want to make in your activities as part of your recovery?

The main change I intend to make in my activities is

_____

_____

_____

_____

_____

Today's date: _____

57.   Three-Month Review

Three months after your initial work in this area, what if any changes do you notice in your activities?

_____

_____

_____

58.   One Year Review

One year after working this domain for the first time, what if any changes do you notice in your activities?

_____

_____

_____

Chapter Five

Fourth Domain: My People

Staying clean and sober often involves reworking one's relationships with other people. For some people, recovery means overcoming isolation and learning to connect. For some, recovery means disconnecting from certain associates and spending some time alone finding oneself, or connecting with other kinds of people. For some, recovery will not bring major changes in the cast of characters, but the plot will change.

Dealing with peer pressure and establishing a new identity as a person who lives free of drinking and drugs can be a major challenge. Success here can bring major rewards.

This domain lets you explore issues that come up in re-establishing your social identity as a clean and sober person.

59.   People Say: How I Feel about Being Sober

__ It makes no difference to me whether people accept me as a sober person or not; they don't influence me one way or the other

__ When people pressure me to drink/use it weakens my resolve and creates a problem for my sobriety

__ I don't like being 'odd person out' when everybody else is drinking/using

__ I've been the only person not drinking in a crowd of 100 drinking and it doesn't bother me

__ I hate being called a party-pooper and being told I'm no fun. I just cave in when I hear that

__ If people don't respect my decision not to drink, the hell with them

__ It would be nicer to be with people who don't twist my arm or make me feel out of it for being sober

__ My sobriety is separate from anything else and it makes no difference where I am or who I'm with

__ Being with a bunch of drunks or druggies is really boring and I don't enjoy being there

__ I don't have any friends other than people who drink/use and I'd die of loneliness if I couldn't socialize with them

__ I slightly know some people who don't drink/use and I can approach them and become better friends with them.

__ Some people I know are really threatened by my decision to be clean and sober because they feel guilty about their own boozing/using

__ I can't stand to have people feel guilty about themselves because of my decision to be clean and sober

__ How people feel about their own drinking is their problem, not mine

__ If people are really my friends, they'll support my decision to be clean and sober

60.   Thinking about What People Say

To what extent did you pick your friends based on whether they drank/used, or not?

_____

_____

What other criteria really mattered in your choice of friends?

_____

_____

If there was nothing much else besides drinking/using holding your friendship together, what do you think will happen to your friendship when you get clean and sober?

_____

_____

Did you ever lose a friendship, or not get to first base, with someone whose opinion you valued, because that person saw you as a doper or a boozer?

_____

Now that you are clean and sober, do people under the influence seem as witty and brilliant as they think they are?

_____

Were you afraid to stick out like a sore thumb if you didn't drink/use in a "party" crowd? Yes No   Were you surprised that nobody noticed? Yes No

Why is it often easy to drink/drug alone, but usually hard to stay sober in isolation?

_____

_____

Now that you are not drinking/using, does it suddenly seem that you find less alcohol/drugs and fewer drinkers/users in your environment than there used to be? Yes   No   If so, why might this be?

_____

_____

61. Working with People – Introduction

On the next page is a table with three columns.   Make a mental list of the people in your life at this time. Then write their names into the table based on whether they support, are unaware of, or oppose your sobriety. If the people form a group, just put the group's name. Use initials or first names or pseudonyms for individuals if you prefer.

- In the first column, put the names of the people who support your sobriety – people who know that you used to drink/use, who know that you are starting a new life, and who are happy with the fact that you are clean and sober now.

- In the middle column, put the names of all the people in your life who, as far as you know, are unaware that you are now changing your life to be a clean and sober person.

- In the right column, put all the people who feel bent out of shape by the idea of you as a person who does not drink or use, and who put pressure on you (subtle or unsubtle) to go back to drinking/using. The behavior and attitudes of these people, well-intentioned or not, are obstacles to your recovery.

1 Body

2 Exposure

3 Activities

4 People

5 Feelings

6 Life Style

7 History

8 Culture

9 Treatment

Worksheet 18: Three Kinds of People

THREE KINDS OF PEOPLE		
1. People who support my sobriety	2. People who don't know about my decision to change	3. People who fight my sobriety

1 Body   2 Exposure   3 Activities   4 People   5 Feelings   6 Life Style   7 History   8 Culture   9 Treatment

62. Working with People Who Support My Recovery

Work these questions alone and/or take them to a meeting for discussion. Remember that there is no One True Answer to any of these questions. Different answers are true for different people. The important thing is to find out what works for YOU.

What defines a supporter of your sobriety?

___ A supporter of my sobriety has to be a person who is also in recovery
___ A person who has never used alcohol or other drugs can be a supporter
___ A person who drinks/uses lightly can be a supporter of my sobriety
___ A person who drinks/uses addictively can be a supporter of my sobriety
___ Someone who has no idea that this is an issue in my life can be a supporter
___ A paid professional such as a counselor can be a supporter
___ A supplier such as a bartender or dealer can be a supporter
___ A person who dislikes me personally can be a supporter of my sobriety
___ A rival or competitor can be a support person for my sobriety
___ A stranger can be a supporter
___ An imaginary person or a fictional character can be a supporter
___ A dead person can be a supporter
   A person who doesn't respond to me can be a supporter
___ A statue can be a supporter
___ An animal can be a supporter
___ A common object like a stone or a leaf can be a supporter

Are the degrees of supportiveness? Yes No
Would it make sense to think of primary supporters, second-line supporters,
   etc.? Yes No

In your own words, what are the qualities that make a person a good supporter of your sobriety?

_____

_____

_____

What kinds of things can you reasonably ask a supporter to do? For example:

___ I can ask a support person not to drink/use in my home
___ I can ask a support person not to drink/use in my presence outside my home
___ I can ask a support person to stop drinking/using, period
___ I can ask a support person to come over and keep me company if I feel in danger
      of relapse
___ I can ask a support person to answer my telephone call in the evening
___ I can ask a support person to answer my telephone call at work
___ I can ask a support person to answer my telephone call at 3 am
___ I can ask a support person to hang out with me and be sober company at social
      events

1 Body   2 Exposure   3 Activities   4 People   5 Feelings   6 Life Style   7 History   8 Culture   9 Treatment

__ I can ask a support person to read recovery literature to understand what I am
    doing
__ I can ask a support person to come to a recovery meeting with me

What other things can you reasonably ask a person to do by way of support
for your recovery?

_____

_____

_____

Do you feel that your sobriety support list has enough names on it?   Yes No

If your sobriety supporters are few in number, what could you do to increase
their ranks? Where would you be likely to find more supporters of your
sobriety? Think of some places or events to go where you are likely to find
such people. Think of activities that are likely to bring you in contact with
people who support you being a clean and sober person.

Ideas for getting more support:

_____

_____

_____

_____

Are your sobriety supporters close to you geographically, or are they fairly
remote?
Close Remote   If your supporters are remote, what could you do to be closer
with them?

_____

_____

_____

Do you spend most of your time with supportive people? Yes No If not, what
could you do to spend more time with people who support your sobriety?

_____

_____

_____

Are there major areas of your life where you see no one who supports your sobriety (e.g. work, home)? Yes No   If so, what could you do to get more support there?

_____

_____

_____

63. Working on Changes in a Continuing Supportive Relationship

Some of the people on your support list (Column 1 in the *Three Kinds of People* table, Page 94) may be people with whom you were already involved in a working or personal relationship when you were still drinking/using. In your support list, circle the names of these people, if any.

Just as learning to live sober now may mean considerable adjustment for you, it may require adjustments on their part, and changes in the relationship between you.

Here is a worksheet to help you and your continuing supporters transition your relationship to your new reality.

You might try working this worksheet alone the first time. Then discuss the issues with the other person, and revise your answers if appropriate.

Don't be surprised if the other person sees the issues somewhat differently than you do!

1 Body

2 Exposure

3 Activities

4 People

5 Feelings

6 Life Style

7 History

8 Culture

9 Treatment

Worksheet 19: Working on Changes in a Continuing Relationship

1 Body   2 Exposure   3 Activities   4 People   5 Feelings   6 Life Style   7 History   8 Culture   9 Treatment

WORKING ON CHANGES IN A CONTINUING RELATIONSHIP	
Name of Supportive Person In a Continuing Relationship With Me: _____	
Role this person plays in my life:	
How long has this person been a part of my life?	
How long has this person been aware of my drinking/using?	
Did my drinking/using create problems for this person?	__ No __ Yes, my drinking/using created the following problems for this person:
Do I owe this person an apology and/or a debt for the problems I created during the period when I was drinking/using?	__ No __ Yes, I owe the person an apology. I plan to deliver the apology as follows: __Yes, I owe the person money (or _____) to make them whole for the damage I did when I was drinking/using. I plan to repay them as follows: __ I feel that the harm I did them was so grievous that it can never be repaid. *[Do the Strong Trigger Feelings Worksheet, Page 136.]*
Am I being honest with this person now?	__ Yes, entirely __ Yes, but not about everything __ Not really …
Are there harmful things that I used to do to this person when I drank/used, that I will not do anymore?	__ No __ Yes, now that I am clean and sober I will no longer do the following things that hurt this person:

WORKING ON CHANGES IN A CONTINUING RELATIONSHIP	
Are there fun activities that I used to do with this person when I drank/used, that I had better avoid for the time being?	__ No. __ Yes, the following fun things we used to do together when I drank/used are activities I had better avoid for the time being: *[Check the My Activities Worksheet, Ch. 4]*
Are there other fun things I used to do with this person that we will keep doing, except I will do them clean and sober?	__ No __ Yes, we will keep doing the following, except I will do them sober: *[Check the My Activities Worksheet, Ch. 4]*
Are there new activities that we can start doing together now that I am clean and sober?	__ No __ Yes, we can now start doing the following: *[Check the My Activities Worksheet, Ch. 4]*
Are there any changes happening in our relationship now that I am clean and sober?	__ No __ Yes, I notice changes: I see some changes for the better: namely: I see some changes that concern me, namely:

1 Body

2 Exposure

3 Activities

4 People

5 Feelings

6 Life Style

7 History

8 Culture

9 Treatment

WORKING ON CHANGES IN A CONTINUING RELATIONSHIP	
Is my sobriety bringing up issues in our relationship that were buried when I was drinking/using?	__ No __ Yes. The following issues are coming up: To deal with these issues, we plan to do the following:

64.   Working with People Who Don't Know

Deciding what to tell people about the change in your life from drinking/using to living clean and sober can be a challenge.

One issue is deciding what words to use. Some people believe that it's very important to label yourself an "alcoholic" or "addict," and other people fiercely resist. Research suggests that people can make successful recoveries either way.*

It's not uncommon for people to change their minds about this issue as their recovery progresses.

As you consider your options, remember that the bottom line isn't what you label yourself; the bottom line is what you do or don't put in your body.

Still, knowing what to tell people about yourself makes life in recovery less stressful.

---

* Reid Hester and William Miller, Handbook of Alcoholism Treatment Approaches, Effective Alternatives, 2nd ed. 1995, p. 95: "Many treatment failures are quite willing to accept the label 'alcoholic,' and many people respond favorably to treatment without ever calling themselves 'alcoholic.'"

65. People Say: About "Coming Out"

__ The fact that I drank/used is my private business and nobody else's

__ I would buy from a different source each time to hide my habit

__ I would always buy groceries along with liquor to make my drinking seem casual

__ I would wrap my empties so the neighbors wouldn't see how much I drank

__ I would hide my bottles in the house so nobody would know how much I drank

__ I never made any secret of my drinking/using

__ I led people to see me as a casual drinker/user and hid my addiction from most people

__ I've flat out lied to people close to me about the extent of my drinking/using

__ I led a double life with two sets of friends and prayed they would never meet

__ I have successfully concealed my problem from the whole world, or almost

__ I was just about the only one in the world who didn't know how big a problem I had

__ I told everyone I was an alcoholic/addict when I drank/used and I was proud of it

__ Labeling myself an alcoholic/addict has helped me stay clean and sober

__ An alcoholic is a skid row bum and I'm not one

__ When I first came out to people as an alcoholic/addict, they were surprised

__ When I first came out to people as an alcoholic/addict, I was surprised they already knew

__ I've decided to start to label myself an alcoholic or an addict

__ I've decided not to label myself an alcoholic or an addict

__ I'll tell certain people that I'm an alcoholic or addict, not others

__ I'll label myself a recovering alcoholic/addict

__ I'll label myself a sober alcoholic/addict

__ I'll go along with the group I'm in right now regarding the labeling issue

__ I'll stay clean and sober for right now and postpone deciding what to label myself

66. Thinking about What People Say

Did you keep your drinking/drugging under wraps from certain people? Yes No

Did it cost you significant effort to cover up the extent of your drinking/using? Yes No

When you were drinking/using, were you ever embarrassed when someone found you out? Yes No

Now that you are not drinking/using any more, are people noticing that you're different somehow? Yes No

If so, what clues are they picking up on?

1 Body 2 Exposure 3 Activities 4 People 5 Feelings 6 Life Style 7 History 8 Culture 9 Treatment

Have you tried telling someone who (you think) didn't know about your situation that you have quit drinking/using? Yes No

Was the person surprised to hear that you used to drink/use? Yes No
If the person was not surprised, why do you suppose they never said anything to you about it?

_____

Was the person supportive of your decision to stop? Yes No

67. Telling People and Getting Their Support

Are there any people in your "Don't Know" column (middle column of the *Three Kinds of People Worksheet* on Page 94) who could become supporters of your sobriety if you told them that you used to drink/use and you have now quit? Yes No   If so, copy their names into the worksheet below. What specifically could you do to win these persons as supporters of your recovery? Outline a plan to let them in on what is going on in your life.

For example, your neighbor Sal has complained in the past that her husband drinks too much. Sal has no idea (you're fairly sure) that you used to do the same thing. Ask Sal to baby-sit your kids one evening so that you can go to a sobriety support group meeting. The discussion could be interesting.

Worksheet 20: Telling People and Getting their Support

TELLING PEOPLE AND GETTING THEIR SUPPORT	
Name of person who doesn't know yet what is going on with me (Copy from middle column of *Three Kinds of People Worksheet* on Page 94)	What I could do to win this person as a supporter of my recovery:

68. "Coming Out" – Looking at the Negatives

Are there any people in your "Don't Know" column (Page 94, Column 2) who would probably become opponents of your recovery and make your life more difficult if you told them that you used to drink/use a lot and have now quit? Yes No   If so, mark their names with an "x" in the table. Mentally outline a plan to keep them in the dark, if necessary. Use a separate sheet if you feel you need to make a more detailed, specific plan for these people.

If you say the phrase "I am an alcoholic/addict" out loud, what feelings does that arouse in you?

__ It makes me feel put down, as in "I am a skid row bum"
__ It feels like I have a disease, as in "I am a diabetic"
__ I feel burdened by the word
__ I feel relieved when I say the word

___ _____

_____

Do you feel stronger as a clean and sober person using this label, or do you feel less strong? Stronger   Less Strong   Why? Explain your reasoning:

_____

_____

Do you have any legal or financial issues that affect your decision whether to let certain people know that you used to drink/use and have now stopped? Use this checklist:

__ If my physician writes "alcoholic" or "chemical dependent" in my medical chart, I could be denied health insurance or life insurance
__ If I openly call myself an alcoholic or addict, I could lose custody of my children
__ If I get a diagnosis of alcoholism or addiction, it could affect my driving privileges
__ If I am classified as having a drug or alcohol problem, it could affect my probation, parole, immigration, or other legal status
__ I want more information about whether disclosing my past drinking/drugging would affect my legal rights

In general, if there are no legal consequences, do you think it is better for your recovery if people know, or if they don't know, that you have stopped drinking/using? Better if they know   Better if they don't know

Explain your reasoning:

_____

_____

_____

69.   Working with People Who Oppose My Recovery

You might think that the whole world loves someone who quits drinking/drugging, but it isn't necessarily so. One of the challenges that you will probably have to face in your recovery is handling people who try to undermine your recovery and get you to relapse. What are some of the subtle and not-so subtle ways that people let you know they aren't happy with the fact that you have quit drinking/drugging? Try this checklist for starters:

70.   How Some People Work on My Mind

__ They tell me I'm being a party-pooper
__ They tell me I used to be more fun when I drank/used
__ They don't invite me out anymore
__ They don't invite me in anymore
__ They tell me I can have just one, just one won't hurt me
__ If I ask them to not drink or use around me just this one time, they refuse and get mad
__ They offer me drinks or drugs even though they know I am in recovery
__ They don't respect my rule not to drink or use in my home
__ They pour alcohol in my non-alcoholic drink when I'm not looking
__ They make an exaggerated show of how good it feels to be high
__ They blow smoke in my face or pass a drink under my nose
__ They place bets on how long I'll last clean and sober
__ They won't take "no" for an answer when I refuse
__ They give me alcohol or drugs for presents
__ They don't treat me as well sober as they used to treat me drunk or high
__ They tell me I'm inevitably going to relapse
__ They talk dirt about my recovery behind my back or to my face
__ They complain about the amount of time I spend going to recovery meetings
__ They criticize my choice of treatment providers or recovery groups
__ They try to get me to dwell on the good times we used to have drunk or high
__ They invite me to revisit places that have strong drinking/using memories for me
__ They tell me I'm doing my recovery all wrong
__ They sabotage changes that I am trying to make in my life to strengthen my recovery
__ They tell me I have to go out and drink again until I'm ready to do recovery their way
__ They pick fights with me now over things that never bothered them when I drank/used
__ They make fun of my struggles to learn a different way of living than I used to
__ They lay unrealistic expectations of instant improvement on me
__ If I slip, they pounce on my mistake to make me feel worse
__ They tell me stories of terrible things that happened to people who stopped drinking/using

___

71. What to Do about People Who Work on My Mind

How do you feel when you face attacks on your sobriety?

_____

_____

_____

Do you find it's better to respond to attacks on your recovery, or to ignore them?

_____

_____

_____

Have you worked out any effective or witty responses to some of these attacks that you can share?

_____

_____

_____

Do you find yourself having these thoughts even though nobody else is talking this way to you? Yes No

72. "NO" Lines

Here are some lines that people have used to say "no" when they are offered alcohol or drugs. Check ones that you have used, and add your own. Try saying them out loud in front of a mirror, and rehearse them with your support group and/or other friends.

__ No, thanks.
__ No, thanks. If I got started, there wouldn't be enough here.
__ No, thanks. I don't want one. (I want 12!)
__ No, thanks. Doctor's orders.
__ No, thanks. I really can't today.
__ No, thanks. I don't drink at all.
__ No, thanks. Diet, you know.
__ No, thanks. I've had my quota.
__ No, thanks. I'd rather have a poke in the eye with a burning stick.
__ No, thanks. Alcohol and I don't get along.
__ No, thanks. I've quit.

Sidebar (vertical, right margin): 1 Body   2 Exposure   3 Activities   4 People   5 Feelings   6 Life Style   7 History   8 Culture   9 Treatment

1 Body   2 Exposure   3 Activities   4 People   5 Feelings   6 Life Style   7 History   8 Culture   9 Treatment

__ No, thanks. Could I have a (soft drink or mineral water) instead?
__ No, thanks. I got tired of being a drinker with a writing problem.
__ No, thanks. This is my "when."
__ No, thanks. I'm the designated driver.
__ No, thanks. I never drink on (day of week).
__ No, thanks. I'm a diabetic.
__ No, thanks. I gave myself the gift of sobriety.
__ No, thanks. Not this time of the month.
__ No, thanks. I'm trying to become pregnant.
__ No, thanks. It upsets my stomach.
__ No, thanks. It's against my religion.
__ No, thanks. It conflicts with medications I'm taking.
__ No, thanks. A dog ate my liver.
__ No, thanks. I plan to have sex later.
__ No, thanks. I don't want any right now.
__ No, thanks. I'm in recovery.
__ No, thanks. I'm an alcoholic in recovery.
__ No, thanks. Been there, done that.
__ No, thanks. I'm a non-drinker.
__ No, thanks. I haven't had a drink in ___ months (years).
__ No, thanks. I have to work tomorrow.
__ No, thanks. I have kids.
__ No, thanks. _____
__ No, thanks. _____
__ No, thanks. _____

73.   Wet-Weather Friends

Some people who were "the best of friends" when you were drinking/using may suddenly disappear when you stop. What does this tell you about them and the nature of their friendship? Try this checklist based on your own pattern when you were still drinking/using:

__ I had friends who drank/used with me
__ I had friends who I never drank or used with
__ I had friends who wouldn't drink or use when we got together even though I did
__ I would get together with friends who drank or used, but I would abstain
__ I basically selected my friends based on whether they were drinkers/users like me
__ I felt that my friends only liked me when I was high
__ I kept my place as a drug house or party house so that people would come over
__ I couldn't conceive of getting together with my friends and not drinking/using
__ I never drank/used with friends – I always did it alone
__ I couldn't wait for my clean and sober friends to leave so I could get loaded
__ If I had a choice between being sober with friends or drinking/using alone I'd dump my friends and go drink/use alone
__ When it comes right down to it, the bottle/drug was my only "friend"

74. Why Some People Fight My Sobriety

Why do you think certain people are unhappy with your being a clean and sober person now? For each person on your "opponent" list (Column 3), ask yourself:

- Is their problem just a matter of time until they get used to the change in you?
- Is their problem a case of ignorance about addiction and recovery?
- Are they being defensive about their own unacknowledged drug and/or alcohol-centered life style?
- Did they get some kind of personal benefit from your drinking/using in the past?
- Do they feel challenged by the new, more capable sober you that is emerging?
- What other explanation is there for their unhappiness with your sobriety?

Next is a worksheet that you can use to begin to think about these issues. A more detailed worksheet for working with people you are very close to and who oppose your sobriety comes later ("Working With Opponents At Close Range"). Put a checkmark in the appropriate column. If other explanations apply, write them on a separate sheet.

Worksheet 21: Why Some People Oppose My Sobriety

WHY SOME PEOPLE OPPOSE MY SOBRIETY						
Name *(Copy from Column 3 of People Table, Page 94)*	Just a Matter of Time	Ignorant About Addiction and Recovery	Defensive About Own Life Style	Got a Benefit From My Drinking/ Using	Feel Challenged by the New Sober Me	*Other

1 Body

2 Exposure

3 Activities

4 People

5 Feelings

6 Life Style

7 History

8 Culture

9 Treatment

1 Body　2 Exposure　3 Activities　4 People　5 Feelings　6 Life Style　7 History　8 Culture　9 Treatment

75.　Working with Opposition at Close Range

Is your life closely wrapped up with someone who undermines your sobriety? If so, work the *Close-Range Opposition* Worksheet on Page 109 for each such individual.

Reworking your connection with people in a long-term relationship with you can be among the most difficult problems in recovery. Unless there is an urgent need to stop the relationship immediately (for example, physical abuse), this is probably an area for patience, tolerance, and moving gradually, in small steps.

Remember that in many cases, these people were part of your support system for drinking/using when you were doing that. The main person who taught them to support your drinking/using was probably you. They may feel distrustful of what they see as your sudden about-face. They may not believe you are for real about sobriety. You may have treated them poorly and they may not be inclined to cut you slack. It may take time – quite a bit of time – before they make the adjustment to your new sober personality and life style.

Therefore, think nine times before you act to break off a long-term relationship with someone close to you based on their opposition to your recovery. Try for conciliation and compromise. Nevertheless, if after a long time and many attempts the person still will not support your recovery, then you will have to make a choice: your relationship, or your recovery. If you get to that fork in the road, make a Sobriety T-chart (Chapter 1).

Worksheet 22: Close-Range Opposition

WORKING WITH OPPOSITION AT CLOSE RANGE	
Name of Person Close To Me Who Undermines My Sobriety: _____	
What important role does this person play in my life?	
List of specific things this person has done to undermine my sobriety	1. 2. 3. 4. 5. 6.
Is this person just distrustful of my new direction, and will they probably come around in time?	__ No, I have already been clean and sober _____ (*time*) and the person's attitude has not mellowed __ Yes, the person is distrustful that I'm for real about my recovery. This lack of trust is / is not reasonable because:
Is this person just ignorant about addiction and recovery?	___ No. The person is well informed about the issues. ___Yes. What I can do to educate them is:

Is this person being defensive about their own unacknowledged alcohol/drug problem?	__ No. The person doesn't have a drinking/drug problem.
	 __ Yes. The person has a drinking/using problem and sees my recovery as an attack on their decision not to do anything about it at this time.
	     Short of relapsing, can I do anything to make the person more at ease with my recovery?
	     __ No
	     __ Yes, I can try the following:

1 Body   2 Exposure   3 Activities   4 People   5 Feelings   6 Life Style   7 History   8 Culture   9 Treatment

1 Body   2 Exposure   3 Activities   4 People   5 Feelings   6 Life Style   7 History   8 Culture   9 Treatment

WORKING WITH OPPOSITION AT CLOSE RANGE	

Did this person get some kind of payoff from my drinking/drugging?	__ No. The person had nothing to gain from my drinking/drugging.
	
	__ Yes. The person benefited from my drinking/using in the following ways:
	
	    __ Direct financial benefit
	
	    __ Indirect financial benefit, namely:
	        __ Distracted me from standing up for myself
	        __ Took my property
	        __ Sold my body
	
	    __ Psychological payoff, namely:
	        __ Had control over me
	        __ Felt superior to me
	        __ Could avoid being intimate with me
	        __ Could avoid commitment to me
	        __ Could rationalize abusing me
	        __ Other, namely:
	
	Short of relapsing, can I do anything to make this person less hostile to my recovery?
	__ No.
	__ Yes, I can try the following:

Is this person challenged by the new, more capable sober me that is emerging?	__ No. This person is not in competition with me in any way. __ Yes. This person is in competition with me (on the job, in business, in the family, for someone's affection, in sports, etc.) and senses that I am getting my act together and becoming a more formidable challenger. Now that I am clean and sober, this person can no longer control me. Short of relapsing, is there anything I can or should do about this problem? __ No. __ Yes. I can try the following:
Is there some other reason why this person is unhappy with my being clean and sober?	
Can I change this person's behavior and attitude toward me?	__ No. __ Yes. I have seen some positive changes already, namely:

WORKING WITH OPPOSITION AT CLOSE RANGE	
Is my involvement with this person more important to me than my sobriety?	__ No. My sobriety is more important than my involvement with this person __ Yes. I would rather be drunk/stoned if that's what it takes to keep my relationship with this person __ I don't know yet. I am going to give it _____ (*time*) before I make up my mind.
What is the worst thing that could happen to me if I ended my involvement with this person?	The worst thing that could happen if I ended my involvement with this person is: (Suggestion: You could also work this part of the exercise by making a T-chart with the topic: "Ending my involvement with X" See Chapter 1).

76.   Handling Uncertainty and Vacillation

Have you reviewed the *Working on Changes in a Continuing Relationship* Worksheet (Page 97) and the *Working With Opposition At Close Range* Worksheet (Page 109) and can't decide which one your Significant Other fits? Does the person sometimes seem like a supporter and other times like an opponent? Consider this: When you drank/used, did you tend to change from "friend" to "foe" depending on your level of intoxication? Don't be surprised if those who are involved in relationships with you display some of the same inconsistency now that you are clean and sober. Be patient and give it time. In time, as you yourself stabilize into your recovery, the other person will also commit – one way or another.

77.   Message Drinking and Message Sobriety

Did you ever find yourself reaching for a drink/hit so as to "send a message" to someone in your life? Yes No

Some people "drink at" people they are angry with. "I hate you – take THAT" (gulp). Some people use drinking/using as a way to say they find someone attractive. "You turn me on!" (gulp).

Think about drinking/using as a method of communicating your feelings about someone Does the other person usually even know that you are sending a message to them? Yes No   Is the message intelligible? Yes No   Is getting drunk/high an effective way to get your point across? Yes No

1 Body   2 Exposure   3 Activities   **4 People**   5 Feelings   6 Life Style   7 History   8 Culture   9 Treatment

1 Body   2 Exposure   3 Activities   4 People   5 Feelings   6 Life Style   7 History   8 Culture   9 Treatment

Sometimes your addiction sends the opposite message from the one you intended. Your words say, "I love you, I want you," but your actions say, "I love my drug more, I want my drug more." Been there? Yes   No
One possible counter to "message drinking" is "message sobriety." More than one person has started a successful recovery out of resentment at some authority figure who insulted their ability to stay clean and sober. "Unless you do it my way, you're going to drink." "Oh yeah? We'll see about that!"

If all else fails, the thought that this authority figure is going to say "I told you so!" may be the one thing that keeps you from relapsing. Sobriety may be the best revenge. After a period of sober time, more positive motivations will probably come into play to dissolve and replace the original spiteful impulse. Whatever works!

Sobriety can also be a powerful "come hither" message. "I find you more attractive than cocaine" is an opener that will get attention. If your conduct is consistent with it, it could be the start of something big.

78.   My Plan for My Relationships with People

Based on my work in this domain, I plan to make the following changes in my relationships with the people in my life:

Changes with my Column 1 people (supporters):

_____

_____

_____

Changes with my Column 2 people (uninformed):

_____

_____

_____

Changes with my Column 3 people (opponents):

_____

_____

_____

Today's date: _____

79.   Three-Month Review

In the three months since I first worked this section, I have noticed the following changes in my relationships with people:

_____

_____

_____

_____

_____

Today's date: _____

The changes in my relationships have affected my sobriety in this way:

_____

_____

_____

_____

80.   One-Year Review

In the year since I first worked this section, I have noticed the following changes in my relationships with people:

_____

_____

_____

_____

_____

1 Body

2 Exposure

3 Activities

4 People

5 Feelings

6 Life Style

7 History

8 Culture

9 Treatment

The changes in my relationships have affected my sobriety in this way:

_____

_____

_____

I have noticed the following changes in my ability to relate to people:

_____

_____

_____

_____

_____

_____

_____

_____

Today's date: _____

Chapter Six

Fifth Domain: My Feelings

Getting clean and sober often involves sorting out the relationship between the substance and one's feelings. This is not surprising; studies of brain anatomy show that addictive substances are active in the same brain circuits where our emotions run, particularly in our brain's pleasure systems.

Observation shows, however, that there is a great deal of individual variation in the way that people experience and handle the interplay between feelings and drugs. Some people got in the habit of using alcohol/drugs as a way to numb out painful feelings such as loneliness, anger, anxiety, or grief. For others, addictive substances were a way to try to rise above emotional numbness and to feel something, anything.

For some people, early recovery is an emotional roller coaster. Feelings that you struggled with before you started drinking/using can suddenly surface again. Whirlpools of bad feelings may temporarily trap a person, and emotional "cause" can get confused with emotional "effect." Probably no area of recovery is more complex than this one.

The good news is that there are many things you can do to help yourself in this area – you can often change your feelings just by talking about them. This domain outlines some "emotion" issues you may want to consider and start working on early in your recovery.

81.   People Say: Feelings and Drinking/Using

__ There are some painful feelings that I could only numb out by getting high
__ I would feel numb until I started drinking/using, and then I would feel more
   alive
__ When I started drinking/using, I would feel like a different person
__ People told me that I was a different person when I drank/used
__ I was the same old me when I drank/used, just me drunk/stoned
__ Whenever I felt angry/sad/stressed, I would start drinking/using
__ Whenever I was drinking/using, I would get angry, sad, or stressed.
__ I would drink/use to give myself a feeling of confidence to do things
__ Afterwards I would have this terrible insecurity about what I had said or done

Sidebar (right margin): 1 Body   2 Exposure   3 Activities   4 People   5 Feelings   6 Life Style   7 History   8 Culture   9 Treatment

__ When I was drinking/using I felt better but when I stopped I felt worse than before

__ All in all, drinking/using made me feel better about myself

__ All in all, drinking/using added to the negative feelings I had about myself

__ I drank because I felt bad and I felt bad because I drank

__ I drank because I was depressed and when I was drunk I got more depressed

__ I mostly used alcohol/drugs when I was down

__ I mostly used alcohol/drugs when I was happy

__ I mostly used alcohol/drugs when I was bored and not feeling anything

__ I used alcohol/drugs regardless of what I was feeling, it made no difference

__ I don't see how I can have fun in life without drugs/alcohol

__ I got to the point where drinking/drugging was very little if any fun

__ I crave to experience life again without drugs or alcohol

__ _____

82.   Thinking about What People Say

Do you think that you used alcohol/drugs as a way to change your feelings? __ Yes __ No.

If so, why did you try to change your feelings with alcohol/drugs instead of using some other way to change them? (For example, trying to change the situation that made you feel bad, or leaving and going somewhere else, or talking about it with someone who cares?)

_____

_____

While you were drinking/using, did the situation that made you feel bad get better? __ Yes __ No. Why or why not?

_____

What is the worst thing that could happen to you if you allowed yourself to feel your painful feelings without numbing them out?

_____

_____

Do you think that when you are under the influence you are less likely or more likely to harm yourself than when you are clean and sober? __ Less __ More

Do you think that you can't have fun without alcohol/drugs? __ Yes __ No. If so, think about what that means: "I need to use drugs/alcohol to compensate for a disability that I have when it comes to feeling pleasure."

If this describes you, have you always had this kind of disability? __ Yes __ No. Were you born with it? __ Yes __ No.

Do you drink/use to compensate for this disability – or did drinking/using create this handicap in the first place?

83.   Recapturing Pleasure

Most people would classify drugs/alcohol with the pleasures in life, like sex, food, and other joys of living. But then, most people are not addicted. One of the warning signs of addiction is that we continue to use the substances even though each dose brings less pleasure than the last, and sometimes we can't get high at all, but we still keep doing it.

Addictive drug and alcohol use typically invades and destroys our other natural pleasures.

Take sex, for instance. At first, a person may use alcohol or drugs as one way to get sex, and may look on alcohol/drugs as an option to enhance sexual pleasure. After a while, a subtle shift takes place: now alcohol/drugs seem to become necessary in order to have sex at all. As the addiction progresses, priorities get reversed: getting high becomes more important than having sex. A person at this stage may use sex to get drugs. Finally the addiction renders the person unable to perform sexually at all, or to experience sex consciously. The addiction starts out by enhancing sexual pleasure and ends up by killing it.

A similar destructive progression often happens with food, love, art, poetry, music and other human pleasures. As a result, many people emerge from addiction with seriously damaged pleasure systems.

An important part of recovery is recapturing the full range of pleasures that addiction has taken over or destroyed, and rebuilding one's basic capacity to experience pleasure in life.

Use the next worksheet (*My Pleasures*, Page 119) to begin to explore these issues. The worksheet includes only a few of the thousands of things that could make a person feel good. There are blank spaces for you to add your own.

Learning to enjoy yourself without alcohol/drugs can make a big difference in how you feel about your recovery and how easily you sustain it. Some people think that drinking/using = pleasure, and recovery = punishment. You'll turn recovery into more work than it needs to be if you believe in those false equations. Once you figure out that you can have fun clean and sober (and remember it afterwards) you'll find your recovery a much smoother ride.

- The tendency to remember only the pleasure and to forget the pain is natural. Psychologists call it "euphoric recall." In its absence, few women would give birth to more than one child and few enlisted personnel would sign up for a second tour of duty.

- When applied to drinking/using, euphoric recall is a harmful distortion that promotes relapse. The flipside of this coin is "awfulizing sobriety." If you remember only the highlights of your drinking/using career, you'll probably only see the shadows of your recovery.

In the *My Pleasures Worksheet* , you can challenge the image of recovery as punishment and build up your real-life capacity to say that recovery = pleasure.

1 Body   2 Exposure   3 Activities   4 People   5 Feelings   6 Life Style   7 History   8 Culture   9 Treatment

This can be a good topic to take to your support group: how to learn to have fun clean and sober.

Worksheet 23: My Pleasures (Example)

MY PLEASURES WORKSHEET		
Pleasure	How did my drinking/drugging affect this pleasure?	Am I able to enjoy this pleasure now while clean and sober?
Sex		
Anticipation	Usually got high thinking about it	Maybe
Pursuit	Always used liquor to get there	How do I get up the nerve to ask, without alcohol/drugs?
Sexual Contact	Never did it sober in 15 years	That would be a novelty!
Afterwards	Passed out. Next morning wondered who I was with.	Talk about what?
Reviewing it later	Worried about STDs ...	Would be a relief not to worry
Food		
Anticipation	Planned meals over cocktails	Sounds feasible
Selection	Shopped high	Can do, probably, with help
Preparation	Always with lots of wine & etc.	Would be an improvement to do it sober
Serving	Paid more attention to the wine than to the food	Would save $$$
Tasting	Tongue was pretty well numb by the time we ate	This tastebud's for me!

Worksheet 24: My Pleasures

MY PLEASURES WORKSHEET		
Pleasure	How did my drinking/drugging affect this pleasure?	Am I able to enjoy this pleasure now while clean and sober?
Sex		
Anticipation		
Pursuit		
Performance		
Afterwards		
Reviewing it later		
Food		
Anticipation		
Selection		
Preparation		
Serving		
Tasting		
Digesting		
Reviewing		
Love		
Kind words		
Kind deeds		
Warm smiles		
Really listening		
Being considerate		
Giving a gift		
Pat on back		

1 Body

2 Exposure

3 Activities

4 People

5 Feelings

6 Life Style

7 History

8 Culture

9 Treatment

Sidebar (left margin): 1 Body   2 Exposure   3 Activities   4 People   5 Feelings   6 Life Style   7 History   8 Culture   9 Treatment

MY PLEASURES WORKSHEET

Pleasure	How did my drinking/drugging affect this pleasure?	Am I able to enjoy this pleasure now while clean and sober?
Hug		
Friendly kiss		
Letter or card		
Compliment		
Friendly look		
Sharing a laugh		
Grooming		
Having a heart to heart talk		
Looking nice for someone		
Remembering a special day		
Relaxing with friends		
Respect		
Doing a good job		
Getting promoted		
Promoting someone		
Winning the game		
Getting beat but with honor		
Getting a pay raise		
Getting an award or trophy		

MY PLEASURES WORKSHEET		
Pleasure	How did my drinking/drugging affect this pleasure?	Am I able to enjoy this pleasure now while clean and sober?
Praising someone who deserves it		
Getting applause		
Getting published		
Helping somebody		
Thanking somebody		
Beauty		
Music		
Poetry		
Movies		
Books		
Photography		
Nature		
Drama		
Art		
Dance		
Philosophy		
Novelty		

Side tab (right margin, top to bottom): 1 Body   2 Exposure   3 Activities   4 People   5 Feelings   6 Life Style   7 History   8 Culture   9 Treatment

1 Body   2 Exposure   3 Activities   4 People   5 Feelings   6 Life Style   7 History   8 Culture   9 Treatment

MY PLEASURES WORKSHEET		
Pleasure	How did my drinking/drugging affect this pleasure?	Am I able to enjoy this pleasure now while clean and sober?
Invention		
Solving puzzle		
Making scientific discovery		
Travel		
Adventure		
Having a new idea		
Meeting someone interesting		
Risking my life		
Taking class in new subject		
Doing new volunteer work		

84.   My Pleasures Plan

After working the checklist above, are there any pleasures that alcohol/drugs have ruined for you? Make a plan to recapture at least one of those pleasures, clean and sober.

I will take back the pleasure of _____

_____

_____

_____

Are there any pleasures that you have never indulged in because you have been too busy (and perhaps too broke) with your drug/alcohol habit? Make a plan to try at least one such new sober pleasure as part of your recovery.

I will try and see whether I find a new sober pleasure in _____

_____

_____

_____

_____

What are you doing today that makes you feel good?   Write at least one sober thing you have done or will do today that will give you a good feeling.

_____

_____

What sober thing can you do every day that makes you feel good? Write at least one sober pleasure that you can build into your daily routine.

_____

_____

_____

_____

1 Body

2 Exposure

3 Activities

4 People

5 Feelings

6 Life Style

7 History

8 Culture

9 Treatment

85.   A Feelings Reference Chart

Here is a list of some common feelings or emotions. Please scan it. Put a check mark next to items that you have felt recently. Take your time.

Worksheet 25: Feelings Reference Chart

abandoned	destitute	hungry	old	smart
accepting	disdainful	ignored	one with the	stressed out
admiring	disgusted	illegitimate	universe	suicidal
adrift	distracted	impassioned	optimistic	surprised
afraid	distressed	impatient	out of control	taken for
alone	docile	impotent	out of gas	granted
amazed	doubtful	in control	outraged	tense
ambivalent	drained	in dread	overburdened	terrified
amused	dull	in love	overwhelmed	tired
angry	eager	inadequate	panicked	tough
antagonistic	ecstatic	incompetent	paranoid	traumatized
anxious	elated	indifferent	passionate	treated unfairly
aroused	embarrassed	infatuated	peaceful	unattractive
ashamed	emotionless	innocent	pensive	uncaring
assertive	empty	insane	pleased	uncertain
at ease	energetic	insecure	positive	unconcerned
attractive	enraged	insignificant	powerful	under attack
awed	enslaved	interested	powerless	unimportant
babyish	enthusiastic	intimidated	preoccupied	unloved
belligerent	evil	invisible	pressured	unloving
bewildered	exceptional	involved	protected	upset
blocked	excited	irresponsible	regretful	vengeful
bored	exhausted	irritated	rejected	victimized
boring	expectant	jealous	relaxed	victorious
brave	exploited	legitimate	relieved	violated
calm	fascinated	like a doormat	resentful	violent
cheated	free	like a failure	respected	vulnerable
cheerful	frightened	like God	responsible	weepy
clear-headed	frustrated	like shit	romantic	weird
comfortable	furious	loathing	sad	whiny
confident	glamorous	lonely	satisfied	wild
conflicted	gleeful	lost	scared	wise
confused	great	lousy	scorned	withdrawn
consoled	grief	loved	scornful	woeful
contemptuous	grouchy	loving	secure	woozy
content	guilty	malicious	self-confident	zany
cool	happy	mellow	self-destructive	(Other)
cowardly	hateful	mistreated	selfish	
crazy	healthy	misunderstood	sentimental	
cruel	heartsick	neglected	serene	
cynical	hopeful	nervous	sexy	
deceitful	hopeless	nostalgic	shy	
defeated	hostile	numb	sick	
depressed	humiliated	off-balance	silly	

(left margin, vertical) 1 Body   2 Exposure   3 Activities   4 People   5 Feelings   6 Life Style   7 History   8 Culture   9 Treatment

86. Catching and Identifying Feelings

If you used alcohol or other drugs to numb out your emotional life for a long time, you may have trouble sensing and identifying the feelings you are having.

What are you feeling right at this moment? How many different feelings are active inside you at this moment? Can you name them all?

You could ask a friend to play feel-check with you: at random intervals you ask one another what you are feeling. Or, if you have a wristwatch with a timer on it that beeps, try setting it for 5 or 10 minutes. Every time it beeps, name all the feelings you are having at that moment. (Use the Reference Chart if it helps.) Do this exercise daily until you are able to sense what you are feeling, and give each feeling its name, without much difficulty.

Try working your feelings into your conversation: "I feel this way about that," or "when I hear x, I feel y." Being able to sense, identify, express and communicate your feelings can be very useful in the control of cravings, not to mention that it's a mark of an emotionally intelligent, sociable person. For more on this topic, see *Stuffing Feelings and Letting Feelings Out Safely* on Page 132.

87. How Many Feelings Do You Feel?

As you scanned the *Feelings Reference Chart* on the previous page, did you find yourself drawing a blank on all but a small handful of the more than 200 feelings listed there? If so, consider whether the practice of frequent drinking/drugging may have limited your emotional range.

- Did you reach for alcohol/drugs in just about every emotional tough spot?

- Did you substitute the feeling of being high for almost every other kind of feeling?

If you used alcohol/drugs for a long time as a tool to suppress your feelings, you may find that it worked: you don't feel a lot of feelings. If this is your situation, life sober may feel gray and flat at first.

But, as your body begins to get used to functioning without alcohol/drugs and as you change the pattern of your activities, you may find that unexpected feelings start to surface within you.   Maybe you will have a sudden flash where you see the beauty of a street scene, even though you're not artistic. Maybe a random glance will send you off on a romantic fantasy about a complete stranger. Maybe you'll have moments of sudden enthusiasm, or attacks of the giggles, or a gush of tears, or feelings of love overflowing. Both awake and in dreams, you may feel all kinds of vivid feelings you didn't know you had in you. These resurgent feelings are evidence that despite all your hard work to kill it, your capacity to have feelings has survived. Congratulations!

1 Body   2 Exposure   3 Activities   4 People   5 Feelings   6 Life Style   7 History   8 Culture   9 Treatment

1 Body   2 Exposure   3 Activities   4 People   5 Feelings   6 Life Style   7 History   8 Culture   9 Treatment

Your recovery will have more colors and you will probably become more enthusiastic about it if you give yourself permission to feel more feelings, instead of looking for other ways to censor your emotions. A varied and changing emotional life, within limits, can be a great incentive to stay clean and sober.   Experiencing your own feelings naturally can be much more interesting and meaningful than getting high.

88.   Unfinished Emotional Business

Another side of this coin is that people may have a set of old feelings standing in line inside waiting to be processed. A frequent example is grief. Grief is a relatively well-defined emotion that generally needs to go through definite stages from onset to resolution. If the person was drinking/drugging during their bereavement, their neurochemistry probably was too blocked to do the processing necessary to resolve their grief. Result: they have unfinished grief stacked up. When they get clean and sober, their emotional processors start clearing up again, and suddenly out of the blue they find themselves grieving for someone who died years ago. Not only grief, but bits and pieces of all kinds of interrupted or unfinished emotional business may start coming up in unpredictable sequence.

Do you begin to see why some people say that early recovery was an emotional roller coaster for them? Fortunately, when you are a clean and sober and aware of what is happening to you, you can survive the ride, and you might even enjoy it.

If you have been experiencing "new" or stacked-up "old" feelings since you stopped drinking/using, describe them here:

_____

_____

_____

_____

_____

_____

89.   Spotting Trigger Feelings

For some people, certain feelings tend to set off urges to drink/use. These feelings act as triggers for them, much as the sight, sound or smell of "your" substance or paraphernalia (discussed in the Second Domain, Page 57) can be a trigger.
As you scan the *Feelings Reference Chart* on Page 124, are there any that you recognize as your trigger feelings? "Whenever I get mad, I feel I need a drink!"

"Whenever I get lonely, I want to get high." Perhaps as you read the item in the list, you have a reaction such as a slight tightness in your throat or chest, swallowing, frowning, sweating, knotting in your gut, etc. These could be clues to your trigger feelings. You might also spot your trigger feelings by reviewing your drinking/using history: what kinds of feelings led you into the drinking/drugging life? What kinds of feelings would set off your worst using/drinking sessions? (See Seventh Domain, My History, Page 165, for more on this.)

If you spot a trigger feeling, write a "T" next to it in the *Feelings Reference Chart* on Page 124 and then use the following worksheet to increase your alertness to these feelings and help you be prepared when they occur. Remember, this worksheet is about you the individual, not about some imaginary average person.

Sometimes just identifying your trigger feelings and becoming aware of the situations that tend to arouse those feelings is enough to get you out of trouble.

- Some very common feelings, such as being thirsty or hungry, may feel like cravings, when they're really not. Try drinking some water or another non-alcoholic drink you enjoy, or eating something, and watch the "craving" disappear. Fatigue also often masquerades as a craving. Rest a bit or go to bed, or just say to yourself, "I'm tired." Many women find that their cravings are linked to their menstrual cycle.

- In time you might unmask quite a few of your cravings as really just ordinary emotions you can learn to handle easily such as anxiety, loneliness, surprise, etc. Studying the *Feelings Reference Chart* on Page 124 may be helpful for this purpose.

Not everyone experiences emotions as a trigger. Many people feel emotionally numb most of the time, or feel out of touch with their emotions and unaware of what if anything is going on with them emotionally. If this describes you, you may want to inquire about methods that specifically address those conditions.

There is a large literature about understanding and connecting with one's feelings, and most counselors will be able to point you in the direction of readings and exercises. You may want to explore this area if you suspect that you have trigger feelings that operate without your being conscious of them, or if you just feel that it would be more enjoyable to experience a wider range and a more vivid palette of feelings in your life, now that you are clean and sober.

▶ If you feel so numb and remote from your feelings that you need to cut, hammer or burn your body in order to experience emotion, you will want to get professional help to supplement your self-help work.

People vary a great deal in the degree to which emotions set off their cravings and in the particular emotions that have this effect for them. For example, some people are vulnerable to "downer" feelings such as sadness, grief, stress. Other people handle those kinds of feelings easily, but fall prey to cravings when things are going well and they feel happy, esteemed, and loved. For some people, emotions are not significant triggers at all, by comparison to environmental cues (see Second Domain, Page 57).

1 Body   2 Exposure   3 Activities   4 People   5 Feelings   6 Life Style   7 History   8 Culture   9 Treatment

When you think about these issues, try to disregard sweeping generalizations you may have heard (for example "resentment leads to drink") and try to get in touch with the reality of your own personal emotional life. What feelings, if any, trigger *you* to want to drink/use?

Worksheet 26: Trigger Feelings Checklist

MY TRIGGER FEELINGS CHECKLIST	
Feeling that sets off urges to drink/use in me	Person, place, thing, thought, memory, or event that tends to raise up that particular feeling in me

90.   Working with the Trigger Feelings Checklist

Look at your list of people, places, things and events that tend to arouse your "trigger feelings," in the previous section. Suppose you wrote "lonely" in the first column and "when I get home after work" next to it. What can you do to avoid the situation that brings on that feeling?

- For example: *I can go to a gym after work where I won't feel so lonely.*

If you cannot avoid the situation, what can you do to change it?

- For example: *I can get a cat so when I come home from work I won't feel quite so lonely.*

If you can neither avoid the situation nor change it, what can you do to improve your ability to handle it without drinking/using?

- **For example**: *I can get online in the LifeRing chat room or social network or email lists right after work and connect with other people.*

Cross-reference your work in the Second Domain (My Exposure, Page 57), Third Domain (My Activities, Page 73), and Fourth Domain (My People, Page 91) for more ideas.

I can take the following actions to avoid some or all of the people, places, things and events on my *Trigger Feelings Worksheet*:

_____

_____

_____

_____

I can take the following actions to change some or all of the people, places, things and events on my *Trigger Feelings Worksheet*:

_____

_____

_____

_____

I can take the following actions to improve my ability to handle the people, places, things, thoughts, memories and events on my *Trigger Feelings Worksheet* without drinking/using:

_____

_____

_____

_____

1 Body   2 Exposure   3 Activities   4 People   5 Feelings   6 Life Style   7 History   8 Culture   9 Treatment

1 Body   2 Exposure   3 Activities   4 People   5 Feelings   6 Life Style   7 History   8 Culture   9 Treatment

91.   Breaking Vicious Circles of Bad Feelings

"I drink because I'm ashamed, and I'm ashamed because I drink."[*] This is one classic vicious circle of feelings. Do you beat yourself up when you have a craving? Do you give up on yourself if you have a relapse? Do you put yourself down when your recovery is not going according to expectations – yours or someone else's? These are all vicious circles where the addiction leads to bad feelings and the bad feelings lead back into the addiction.

People break out of these vicious circles in two main ways.

▶ One way to break out is by white-knuckling it. People grit their teeth and hold on to their chairs and stubbornly refuse to drink or use no matter how rotten they feel about themselves. White-knuckling is not a long-term solution, but it can work to get you over a bad spot because before very long the bad feeling goes away and a feeling of success for having stayed sober replaces it. Then you can unclench your teeth, relax your grip, and enjoy a more comfortable sobriety.

▶ Another way to break out of the vicious circle is to stop the bad feeling. There are many ways to do this. Discussing the feeling with supportive people online or face-to-face can be instantly effective. Pampering yourself can work; see the *My Pleasures Worksheet* at Page 123. Getting busy can work; see the Third Domain, My Activities, at Page 73. Be sure to try the *Working With Strong Trigger Feelings and Cravings Worksheet* on Page 136, later in this domain.

Once you're free of one of these vicious circles, like a kayaker on a river, you'll have learned an important lesson: how to recognize and steer clear of those situations in the future.

92.   Spotting Empowering Feelings

If there are some feelings that tend to set off your urges to drink/use, there may be other feelings that drive away the urges and make you feel stronger and safer in your recovery. Review the *Feelings Reference Chart* on Page 124 again and see if you can spot feelings of this kind. You may already know what they are, based on your experience. Or you may spot them if you get reactions such as subtle warmth in your gut, relaxation in your chest or throat, a smile on your face, or similar responses, as you consider the name of the feeling in the reference chart. If you have had periods of clean and sober time in the past, try to recall the feelings that sustained you during that time. Circle each such feeling in the chart.

After you have spotted and circled your safe or reinforcing feelings, do the *My Empowering Feelings Checklist* on Page 131. First copy each circled feeling from the reference chart into the left column of the checklist. Then briefly describe the people, places, things or events that usually arouse those empowering feelings in you.

---

[*] Based on *The Little Prince* by Antoine de Saint-Exupery (1943).

Again, people vary a great deal in this area. Some people find emotional refuge from cravings in a condition of meditative inner calm. Other people experience calm as boredom (which makes them want to drink/use) and they find reinforcement for their sobriety in excitement, adventure, novelty. Many are somewhere in between, and find safety in a moderate but varied diet of emotional states. It is not uncommon also for people to change over time in the things that make them feel that sobriety is good. As you work the worksheet, try to disregard sweeping generalizations you may have heard, and focus on the feelings that give *you* strength to lead *your* life clean and sober.

Worksheet 27: My Empowering Feelings (Example)

MY EMPOWERING FEELINGS CHECKLIST	
Feeling that drives away urges to drink or use and makes me stronger in my sobriety	Person, place, thing, or event that tends to raise up that particular feeling in me
When I feel connected with other people, it chases away my cravings	My League of Women Voters' meeting made me feel that way a couple of times; also when I volunteered in the library to teach literacy I felt this.

Worksheet 28: My Empowering Feelings

MY EMPOWERING FEELINGS CHECKLIST	
Feeling that drives away urges to drink or use and makes me stronger in my sobriety	Person, place, thing, or event that tends to raise up that particular feeling in me

1 Body 2 Exposure 3 Activities 4 People 5 Feelings 6 Life Style 7 History 8 Culture 9 Treatment

Body   2 Exposure   3 Activities   4 People   5 Feelings   6 Life Style   7 History   8 Culture   9 Treatment

93.   Working with the Empowering Feelings Checklist

If you have identified some feelings that tend to drive away your cravings to drink/use, and if you know the people, places, things and events that tend to arouse those safe feelings in you, then follow up with this exercise.

I could take the following actions to spend more time around the people, places, things and events that shield me from my cravings and make me feel more secure in my sobriety:

_____

_____

_____

_____

_____

_____

94.   "Stuffing" Feelings and Letting Feelings Out Safely

Sometimes people get in the habit of suppressing feelings, instead of experiencing them and processing them more or less consciously. People who have no drug/alcohol problem do this also, but suppressing feelings can hold particular relapse risks for some people in recovery.

Frustrations, resentments, disappointments and similar feelings are a normal part of life and can play a positive role, similar to the role that pain plays as a signal that your body has been injured. If you are cheated, mistreated or abused, it is natural to feel disappointed, resentful or frustrated. Such feelings can give you the initial energy to claim what is due to you, to stand up for your rights, and to make a better life for yourself and your children.

Many people were moved to action to get clean and sober in part out of frustration and resentment at what drugs/alcohol had done to their lives. Being in recovery does not mean becoming a doormat or giving up your dreams for a world with less unfairness and prejudice. On the contrary: becoming clean and sober can be an enabling experience that invigorates you to play a more active role as citizen and as a member of your community.

The problem comes when you consistently suppress feelings. Suppressing your natural frustrations and resentments does not make them go away. They continue to fester and gradually build up inside. Keeping them suppressed drains emotional energies that you need in order to resist cravings and to build a sober life style. The pain that you may feel inside comes not so much from the feelings themselves – which are generally natural and understandable – but from the effort to suppress them. The pain is the scream of your fatigued "suppressor muscles."

Stuffing our feelings also brings the additional risk that suppressed feelings are more difficult to release safely. Sometimes they seem to come bursting out explosively, occasionally with disastrous results. At such moments of emotional eruption, a person in recovery may be especially vulnerable to relapse.

In the worksheet that follows, try to identify any feelings that you are habitually suppressing.

This can be difficult, because we may suppress not only the feeling but also our awareness that we are suppressing it. Let your body give you hints here. Often suppression of feelings brings tightness or cramping in the abdomen, clenching of the jaw, grinding of teeth, and similar symptoms. Your friends may be able to see signs of which you are not aware; ask them. Write your stuffed feelings in Column 1.

Once you have spotted a consistently stuffed feeling, try to figure out a safe and constructive way to release it. Write your thoughts in Column 2.

For example, if a loved one consistently drives you crazy with lack of attention to your needs, and you consistently "stuff" your unhappiness at this treatment, what about writing the person a note to ask for what you need?

- How about taking the issue up with a mutual friend?

- How about suggesting counseling?

- How about leaving a book about the issue casually lying where your loved one will see it?

Or if someone at work is consistently harassing and mistreating you, and you consistently suppress your bad feelings about this, how about leaving them a memo to ask that it stop, or posting a news article about a similar case on the bulletin board, or going to their supervisor about it, or taking it up with your union steward (or contacting a union if there is none), or filing a grievance, or contacting a fair employment commission, or contacting a lawyer? These are good kinds of issues to bring to your support group, if you have one; you may start off a lively discussion about how people handle real-world frustrations while staying clean and sober.

It may also be helpful to describe extreme actions that this suppressed feeling wants to make you do, and that you will not do. For example: "String the S.O.B. up by his gonads." If you find it an emotional relief to express these fantasies that you will not do in reality, use Column 3 to write them down.

Many times, just venting your frustration to someone else provides immediate relief. Venting can be particularly helpful with feelings like guilt, shame and loneliness, which have isolation built into them. See Section 96 on Page 136, about working with strong trigger feelings.

Why do people suppress their feelings? There are probably many good answers, but one common reason is that they are taught and believe that certain feelings are "wrong" – immoral, unworthy, evil, weird, etc. Some people love the feeling of always being virtuous, correct and perfect, and are willing to pay a tremendous emotional price for this pleasant illusion.

1 Body   2 Exposure   3 Activities   4 People   5 Feelings   6 Life Style   7 History   8 Culture   9 Treatment

If you are able to accept yourself as a human being, a necessarily imperfect creature containing many mixed and contradictory elements, you will have an easier, less painful emotional labor and will have more energy for building a happy and fulfilling sober life.

Worksheet 29: Suppressed Feelings and Safe Release Worksheet

SUPPRESSED FEELINGS AND SAFE RELEASE WORKSHEET		
1. Feelings I Consistently Stuff	2. Safe Ways to Express This Feeling and Obtain Relief and Satisfaction	3. Fantasies of Extreme Actions That I Will Not Do

95. Passages I Came Through Clean and Sober

Sometimes it can be a source of strength to remember the difficult emotional situations in the past that you successfully handled clean and sober. If you had periods of sobriety in the past, you may have weathered some difficult passages, such as job changes, breakups, illnesses, births, arrests, bankruptcies, deaths, weddings, tornadoes, or big holidays and celebrations, without relapsing. Try to recall how you managed to do it. Perhaps you can get clues about how to do it again.

Sarah drank, smoked and used drugs except when she was pregnant. As soon as she felt she was pregnant, she immediately stopped smoking, drinking and drugging, and stayed clean and sober with little difficulty throughout the pregnancy. Not long after the baby was born, she slid back into her old ways. She did this four times. Could she somehow use this proven ability to help her stay clean and sober at other times also?

Dave had a daily crack habit going but when the earthquake of '89 hit the San Francisco Bay Area, he suddenly stayed clean and sober for six weeks. Could he use his ability to stay clean during this disaster as a source of strength to live clean in less stressful times?

In the following worksheet, describe any emotionally difficult or stressful experience that you survived clean and sober in the past. Try to figure out how you were able to handle your feelings under those circumstances without resorting to drugs/alcohol. If you were able to do it at that time, perhaps you can do it again. Try to recover the strength you had then as a resource for the challenges that face you today.

Worksheet 30: Emotional Passages I Came Through Clean and Sober

EMOTIONAL PASSAGES I CAME THROUGH CLEAN AND SOBER		
Approximate Date	Nature of the Emotional Passage	What Specifically I Did So That I Was Able to Survive This Crisis Clean and Sober

Right margin (vertical text): 1 Body   2 Exposure   3 Activities   4 People   5 Feelings   6 Life Style   7 History   8 Culture   9 Treatment

96. Working with Strong Trigger Feelings and Cravings

Some people sometimes experience intense emotions that can overwhelm their defenses and put their sobriety support systems to the ultimate test. Shame, guilt, anger, fear, powerlessness, and loneliness are probably high on the list of "killer feelings" for many people who are vulnerable in this way. If you suffer from frequent attacks of this kind of intense emotion, or if you feel locked into an emotionally crippling mind-set almost all the time, you may want to seek professional help. However, there is a great deal you can do for yourself.

Three main self-help techniques are in common use to deal with strong trigger emotions.

A. Sit through or surf the feeling

The first method is to disconnect the feeling from your behavior. When the feeling starts, you go sit down or lie down and let the feeling run its course. You can be like an outside observer watching the feeling happening inside you. In a few minutes the feeling will be over and you can resume normal activity. This is called "sitting through" or also "surfing" the feeling. The commonsense technique of taking a deep breath and counting to ten is an everyday example of this method.

The Japanese psychiatrist Shoma Morita, inspired by Zen Buddhism, pioneered a sophisticated therapy based on accepting emotions as they are but not permitting them to govern our actions. We take action based on an enduring purpose, such as sobriety, not on a momentary feeling; and when we do so, our feelings fall into place of their own accord. A popular Western approach based on a similar concept is Mindfulness; there is a considerable literature available for you to consult.

It may be helpful to have a supportive person with you the first time or two that you do this. Once you have experienced some success with this technique, you may feel a great boost in your confidence to stay sober in the face of all kinds of emotional challenges.

B. Argue with the feeling

A second approach is to change your feeling through inner argument. You listen for a factual-sounding statement that the feeling is throwing at you, such as "You're worthless." This is painful if you believe it. But instead of buying it, you argue with it. "I'm not worthless, I have two weeks of sobriety already." If you succeed in punching a hole in the statement, so that you no longer believe it, then its force will diminish.

There are many books written about this technique, termed Rational-Emotive Behavior Therapy, and there are professionals who specialize in teaching one or another variant of it. The American psychologist Albert Ellis is the leading exponent. The concept is applicable to an almost infinite range of psychological issues involving feelings.

C. Vent the feeling

A third approach is to deflate the feeling by venting the underlying concern before an understanding individual or group of people. The most burdensome part of many negative feelings is often the energy required to keep them locked up within you. Once you publish them, they may lose most of their intensity and readily submit to rational amendment. A support group environment in which you feel safe and protected is a good setting for this method.

Venting can be a simple matter of sharing a momentary feeling, or it may be a deep upwelling that releases long-suppressed feelings of shame or guilt about some incident in the past. Be aware that your disclosures in a self-help group are not legally confidential, and that some people gossip. But the relief of venting the matter may well be worth the price of having your life become an open book. In this era of TV shock shows, you're unlikely to have any secrets that will keep people fascinated for very long.

Venting can provide immediate relief, similar to the feelings of release some people get from confession or psychoanalysis. It is a very ancient device. Some people come out of the experience elated and report a diminished desire to drink/drug.

But the hours and days following an experience of deep release can also be times of great vulnerability to relapse. Some people feel drained of energy and disoriented at such times, and suffer acute pangs of regret at having "told" the secret they had protected so long. Instead of elation, they feel depression. The danger of relapse is particularly high if you or someone else forced the release prematurely, perhaps based on some therapeutic notion. It may be wise to arrange for extra support at such times.

The common purpose of all of these exercises is to allow you to live your emotional life without drinking/using. Feelings are inevitable. You can develop the ability to experience intensely powerful feelings completely clean and sober. You may be soaring in ecstasy, or plunged into the depths of madness, or mired in excruciating boredom, without yielding to – or even seriously considering – the use of alcohol or other drugs as an option.

People use one or all of these techniques to deal not only with strong negative emotions that may trigger a craving, but also directly with the craving itself. A craving is, after all, a feeling. Try it. You may (1) sit down and let the craving pass, (2) argue with the craving, and/or (3) talk about your craving to someone else or to your group. See which technique or combination works best for you.

You may also have other techniques that work for you; if so, by all means share them. Is there any reason you shouldn't learn all three of these techniques?

Make as many copies of the *Dealing With Strong Trigger Feelings and Cravings Worksheet* on Page 139 as you need.

1 Body   2 Exposure   3 Activities   4 People   5 Feelings   6 Life Style   7 History   8 Culture   9 Treatment

Worksheet 31: Dealing With Strong Feelings (Example)

DEALING WITH STRONG TRIGGER FEELINGS AND CRAVINGS		
Name of strong feeling (or craving): *I feel this intense feeling that I am worthless*		
Methods I have used to deal with it (circle all that apply) (1) (2) (3)		
(1) "Sitting through" or "surfing"	**Place and time when I sat down or lay down to let this feeling pass:** *It came on me Sunday evening. I felt it coming on and I lay down.*	
	What was going through my mind as this feeling was passing through me: *It felt like the end of a bad acid trip. I thought, "wow, my own body is producing these yucky chemicals that are making me feel really rotten right now." It was amazing to feel the physical sensation running through my system.*	
	How long it took before this feeling passed: *About 15 minutes and then it settled down and went away*	
	How I felt after the feeling was finished: *Really exhausted, and I napped for a little while. Then I got up and felt relieved and I did some cleaning and felt even better.*	
(2) Arguing with the feeling	**Place and time when I confronted the feeling:** *I was on the bus and seeing some ad set me off*	
	Rational-seeming argument that the feeling put up: *What came up was "These people in the ad are so successful and happy and I'm stuck in a shitty job ..." and like that.*	
	Counter-argument that I used to refute that argument: *"Why does everybody have to look like models in an ad?" I realized the people in the ad were just actors and probably were half-starving themselves between gigs, and I was doing pretty well to have a job at all compared to where I was two years ago ...*	
	How I felt after the argument was over: *I felt I had beat myself up over nothing and I determined to stop making myself feel miserable*	
(3) Venting the feeling to others	**Place and time when I vented the feeling to others** *At my Thursday night meeting I talked about it*	
	Who I vented it to: *To the group*	
	How I felt when it was over: *I told them I felt really worthless as a human being and didn't know why I was alive sometimes. Somehow just saying it in the group made me feel better. And then when other people responded to me and opened up that they had felt the same kind of thing I realized I wasn't alone in this, and that helped. Just having people respond to me in a caring way made me realize that we're alive to be there for each other, and I cried a little bit, and felt a whole lot better.*	

Sidebar (left margin): 1 Body   2 Exposure   3 Activities   4 People   5 Feelings   6 Life Style   7 History   8 Culture   9 Treatment

Worksheet 32: Dealing with Strong Trigger Feelings and Cravings

DEALING WITH STRONG TRIGGER FEELINGS AND CRAVINGS	
Name of strong feeling (or craving):	
Methods I have used to deal with it (circle all that apply): (1) (2) (3)	
(1) "Sitting through" or "surfing"	Place and time when I sat down or lay down to let this feeling pass:
	What was going through my mind as this feeling was passing through me:
	How long it took before this feeling passed:
	How I felt after the feeling was finished:
(2) Arguing with the feeling	Place and time when I confronted the feeling:
	Rational-seeming argument that the feeling put up:
	Counter-argument that I used to refute that argument:
	How I felt after the argument was over:
(3) Venting the feeling to others	Place and time when I vented the feeling to others
	Who I vented it to:
	How I felt when it was over:

If you use other methods, describe your experience on a separate sheet.

1 Body　2 Exposure　3 Activities　4 People　5 Feelings　6 Life Style　7 History　8 Culture　9 Treatment

1 Body   2 Exposure   3 Activities   4 People   5 Feelings   6 Life Style   7 History   8 Culture   9 Treatment

97.   Cravings "Out of the Blue"

People who have suffered serious trauma sometimes experience "flashbacks"– painful memories of the bad event that break into their consciousness at seemingly random times, without any apparent triggers in their current environment or in their conscious feelings at the moment. In a similar way, some people with a history of addiction to substances sometimes experience cravings "out of the blue," perhaps even in moments of tranquility long after they have stopped using/drinking.

If this happens to you, it may be useful for you to make a mental note that getting away from your environmental triggers and avoiding your emotionally stressful situations is no guarantee against the occasional strong craving. It may be necessary to put some extra effort into learning to recognize the feeling whenever it starts to come on, so as to be ready with your tools to handle it. Although these episodes can be intense, they usually pass in a few moments.

Have you had flashback-type cravings (cravings in the absence of obvious exposure or conscious emotional stress)? If so, describe the experience; use a separate sheet.

98.   A Checklist of Things to Do About Trigger Feelings

There are many things a person can do to address the issue of trigger feelings. Here is a short checklist:

___ I have tried "sitting through" my strong trigger feelings
___ I have worked exercises to argue with my "killer feelings"
___ I have vented my painful secrets to a group to obtain relief for my feelings
___ I have met some people who have the same "killer feelings" as I do
___ I have heard people in my group discuss these same feelings and learned from that
___ I have led a group meeting on the topic of this feeling and shared my experiences
___ I have asked members of my group for advice on my "killer feelings"
___ I have gone to a bookstore to look for books about my problem feelings
___ I have searched the Internet for web sites about the emotion that most bothers me
___ I have talked to a counselor one-on-one about my fear of this powerful feeling
___ I have inquired about classes, workshops or support groups about this feeling
___ I have learned about an exercise you can do that helps take the edge off this feeling
___ I have started a journal to keep track of when this feeling happens to me
___ I have asked my doctor whether there are medications to help with this feeling
___ Other: _____

99.   Working With What You Have

Sal was known as an exceedingly stubborn person. People had tried for years to get her to see that drinking/using was causing bigger and bigger messes in her life, but she obstinately refused to get help. When Sal finally got a wake-up call and got into recovery, this same character trait turned out to be very useful. Sometimes Sal's old drinking friends would descend on her and put the pressure on. But Sal was now even more stubborn in sobriety. They tried everything, but they couldn't get her to "pick up." The ability to feel very strongly and tenaciously about something, a quality that nearly killed her when enlisted in the service of addiction, became a great strength when she turned it around to serve her recovery.

Maurice had a chip on his shoulder about a lot of things, and "angry" could have been his middle name, particularly when he was drinking, which was every day. One day his counselor opined that Maurice just wasn't ready to stop drinking and that he would be a failure at recovery if he were to try it. Maurice deeply resented her remark and determined to "show her." He stopped drinking the same day. Whenever he had a craving or got into a problem situation where he was tempted to drink, he stopped himself with the thought that the counselor would say "I told you so" and he didn't want to give her that satisfaction. Five years later, Maurice is still sober. Additional, more positive motivations have arisen in him to support his recovery: he feels better all around, he is active in sports, his relationships are going better, and he has developed a much more positive outlook on life. He wants to stay sober for himself now, not just to spite the counselor. He laughs about the incident now and credits the counselor for doing him a favor.

Can you think of any emotional "baggage" that you could turn to good use to help you stay clean and sober?

- Fear might have driven you to drink/use once; can the fear of relapsing help you now to stay sober?

- Anger might have fueled your drunken rages in the past. Can anger at how low you had sunk then – the battle cry "Never Again!" – help you stay sober now?

- Having a high opinion of yourself might have delayed your seeking help for your problem in the past. Can the thought "I'm better than that" prevent you from picking up alcohol or other drugs today?

People get clean and sober using whatever they have. Ordinary people, with all the flaws and shortcomings of the human condition, manage recovery all the time. And that's a good thing, because if one had to become a perfect person before one could recover from addiction, nobody would.

Whatever feelings help you stay clean and sober today – even if those feelings may appear to some inner or outer critic as petty, childish, egotistic, vain, unworthy, etc. etc. – are helpful feelings. Ignore the critics and use what you have. As your sober time extends, other feelings, built on the positive experience of your clean and sober life, will rise alongside the old feelings to provide your recovery with a broader, more solid foundation.

1 Body   2 Exposure   3 Activities   4 People   5 Feelings   6 Life Style   7 History   8 Culture   9 Treatment

1 Body   2 Exposure   3 Activities   4 People   5 Feelings   6 Life Style   7 History   8 Culture   9 Treatment

Use the following worksheet to write about feelings that you have that could be turned to your advantage as sobriety tools. Check the *Feelings Reference Chart* (Page 124) for ideas.

Worksheet 33: Using the Feelings You Have

USING THE FEELINGS YOU HAVE TO HELP YOU STAY CLEAN AND SOBER		
Name of Feeling	How This Feeling Served My Addiction in the Past	How This Feeling Can Serve My Sobriety Now and In the Future

100. People Say: What It Feels Like Being Clean and Sober

___ I've been in a great mood from Day One and it hasn't stopped yet (years later)

___ I was euphoric from Day One and this lasted for a few weeks and now I feel about average

___ I have so little sober time I'm not sure yet how I feel about it

___ I felt wonderful for a while and then I plunged into a depression for a while, and back up again like a roller coaster, for several months, before it smoothed out

___ Day One felt like a root canal without Novocain but it gradually got better

___ I felt depressed from the beginning and I still do (years later)

___ I feel sort of normal most of the time but sometimes I am edgy and irritable

___ Most of the time I feel OK but occasionally I have these attacks of feeling really weird, as if I were still drinking or drugging

___ My days are like a kaleidoscope, always a new and different feeling

___ I don't notice much difference in how I feel now than before I got clean and sober

___ I noticed that I have a wider range of feelings and I enjoy having them more

___ I noticed that the feelings that used to give me trouble don't happen so often

___ I feel a lot less anger for some reason than I used to feel when I drank/used

___ I have feelings come up that I hadn't ever faced before and I had to get help

__ I have feelings come up that I used to drink over and now I feel "so what? What was the big deal?"

__ I know I have some long-term issues I want to deal with one of these days, and I feel confident now that I can handle them when I get ready

__ I have a lot less shame and guilt to process now and this has lightened me up

__ Generally I've been in a more positive mood

__ I've gotten more done in life and this has lifted my spirits and made me feel good

__ Since I've gotten sober my life has been a string of tragedies and disasters, but I'm glad I'm facing them clean and sober

__ Just the fact of being able to put a string of sober days together has helped my self-esteem tremendously

__ I've solved some of the real-life problems that I had, and this has eased up the stress on me

__ There's still the bills and the boss and runny noses and life is no rose garden but I'm coping, which is new for me

__ I don't feel so alone anymore, and this has picked me up

__ I feel like a more competent person

__ I've started dream projects of mine and I'm excited about that

__ I've found myself again – I felt like I was lost somewhere or dead and missing – it feels great to be here again

__ Sobriety rocks!

__ I've discovered I like myself. What a concept!

__ _____

__ _____

101. Thinking about What People Say

There's tremendous individual variation in how people feel in and about sobriety. There is no one "right" way that you "should" feel and there is no feeling that is abnormal. Books and studies about the subject can only deal in generalities. You are not a generality and you are not a statistic. You are you, and you have a right to feel how you feel, whether it's "correct" in somebody else's opinion or not.

Your expectations can powerfully color your feelings. If you expect early recovery to be like a punishment, it probably will be. If you look on it as a release from bondage, you probably will feel elated and energized.

How do you feel now about being clean and sober?

_____

_____

_____

1 Body   2 Exposure   3 Activities   4 People   5 Feelings   6 Life Style   7 History   8 Culture   9 Treatment

1 Body 2 Exposure 3 Activities 4 People 5 Feelings 6 Life Style 7 History 8 Culture 9 Treatment

102. Change What You Do, Change What You Feel

One of the most consistent experiences that people report – whether they are working on drug/alcohol issues or not – is that their feelings changed when their activities changed. Getting up and going for a walk, or brushing the cat, or cleaning the bathroom, or some other change in behavior, no matter how trivial it may seem, can sometimes bring about big changes in mood and feelings. Check out the My Activities (Third) Domain, Page 73, to get ideas for actions that can change your feelings. Sometimes if you feel very "stuck," almost any sober action will help, it almost doesn't matter what it is.   Do you know of sober activities that have worked to jolt you out of a stuck place emotionally? Write them here:

1)_____

2)_____

3)_____

103. Issues That Go Away By Themselves, and Issues That Won't

As you get more sober time and feel more solid on your sober feet, you may find that certain emotional issues that bothered you while you were drinking/using are dissolving and going away spontaneously. You may have thought that these were issues that "made you drink/use" and you are now learning that in reality your drinking/using either caused these bad feelings or magnified them out of proportion. For example, you may have felt a deep sense of shame, and believed that your shame made you drink. After a few months of sobriety, you feel better about yourself, and the things in your past that you felt ashamed about don't loom so large any more. Sobriety by itself can be a powerful solvent to reduce all kinds of emotional ailments.

However, sobriety itself can't solve every issue. You may find that you have persistent emotional concerns that won't go away – for example, problems arising from growing up in a dysfunctional family. What sobriety can do is to arm you with the clarity of mind and the courage to start tackling these issues. People often find that once they become clean and sober, the emotional issues that formerly seemed monstrous and insoluble now become manageable, and some end up seeming almost trivial in retrospect.

People differ a great deal in this dimension.

- Some alcoholics/addicts had average or normal childhoods, or they worked through their issues previously, and they don't have persistent unresolved emotional concerns on their recovery agenda.

- Most people have some issues, but find that there's no need to rush into them for sobriety's sake. They can live clean and sober without first solving those problems, just as one can usually learn to ride a bicycle or to debug a computer program without first resolving (for example) one's ambivalent feelings for one's parents.

- Some people encounter urgent emotional issues that trip up their recovery attempts time after time. For example, their self-image may be so profoundly shattered by unprocessed childhood traumas that they don't feel they deserve to recover, or even to live; or they may suffer from chronic clinical depression that leaves them powerless to get out of bed and work any kind of program to help themselves.

  Here's where a treatment team that includes not only a chemical dependency counselor but also a physician and a licensed professional with clinical training in psychology can be helpful in working out an individualized plan that fits your history and your needs. Refer to the First Domain, My Body, (Page 35) if you have not already done so, to get some clues whether you might have urgent collateral issues of this kind. You'll also find more material for working on these issues in the Seventh Domain, My History (Page 165).

The following checklist lets you identify your particular emotional concerns and think about whether these are issues that are (1) resolving spontaneously as you get more sober life experience, or (2) persistent but not urgent issues you may want to work on sometime in the future, or (3) urgent issues that you need to work on now in order to maintain your sobriety. Experience shows that a person's answers to these questions can change over time, so the worksheet has three different answer columns where you can return at different times.

Worksheet 34: My Issues Priority Checklist (Example)

ISSUES THAT RESOLVE BY THEMSELVES, AND ISSUES THAT WON'T									
Issue	Date: 3/12/06			Date:			Date:		
	(1) Resolving by Itself	(2) Work on Later	(3) Urgent Now	(1) Resolving by Itself	(2) Work on Later	(3) Urgent Now	(1) Resolving by Itself	(2) Work on Later	(3) Urgent Now
I'm shy around new people	✔								
Can't get out of bed for days on end			✔						
I'm chronically procrastinating		✔							

Worksheet 35: My Issues Priority Checklist

Issue	ISSUES THAT RESOLVE BY THEMSELVES, AND ISSUES THAT WON'T								
	Date:			Date:			Date:		
	(1)	(2)	(3)	(1)	(2)	(3)	(1)	(2)	(3)
	Resolving by Itself	Work on Later	Urgent Now	Resolving by Itself	Work on Later	Urgent Now	Resolving by Itself	Work on Later	Urgent Now

104. My Plan for My Feelings

Based on all my work in this domain, the most important change I would like to see in my feelings as I continue in my recovery is:

_____

_____

_____

_____

1 Body   2 Exposure   3 Activities   4 People   5 Feelings   6 Life Style   7 History   8 Culture   9 Treatment

_____

_____

_____

I plan to move toward this goal by doing the following:

_____

_____

_____

_____

Today's date: _____

105. Three-Month Review

How do you feel about your sobriety now?

_____

_____

_____

Today's date: _____

106. One-Year Review

How do you feel about your sobriety now?

_____

_____

_____

1 Body

2 Exposure

3 Activities

4 People

5 Feelings

6 Life Style

7 History

8 Culture

9 Treatment

Are there any issues arising from your family of origin, or other long-term emotional concerns, that you feel you want to work on with a professional? If so, how would you define your concern?

_____

_____

_____

Today's date: _____

Chapter Seven

Sixth Domain: My Life Style

After a while, the practice of heavy drinking/using tends to impact one's life style. To different degrees, the addiction can make its mark on the person's work, housing, social life, housekeeping, parenting, personal hygiene, sex life, finances, and other points. Recovery may mean working on changes in some or all of these life style areas.

In this domain you can explore these sorts of issues and make a plan for the changes you feel appropriate for your recovery. As part of your recovery planning, you may want to get information about, and make contact with, other social service providers besides those who are immediately involved in chemical dependency treatment, such as occupational rehabilitation, housing, public health, reproductive rights, legal aid, and others.

In some communities, there are agencies such as Drug Courts that specialize in connecting the person in recovery with related services, and that advocate on behalf of the recovering person to obtain access and fair treatment from service providers. However, you'd first have to be involved in the criminal court system to get access to this kind of service.

It's especially helpful in this work area to build a network of friends who have experience with various social services. Support groups can be very helpful in this regard. It's also helpful to have Internet access in order to explore available options.

107. My Work

I am:

    __ employed full time
    __ employed part time
    __ unemployed, living off savings
    __ unemployed, looking for work
    __ unemployed and unable to work
    __ disabled
    __ retired
    __ employed but at a job I hate
__ My current employment status is unrelated to my drinking/using

Side tab: 1 Body   2 Exposure   3 Activities   4 People   5 Feelings   6 Life Style   7 History   8 Culture   9 Treatment

1 Body   2 Exposure   3 Activities   4 People   5 Feelings   6 Life Style   7 History   8 Culture   9 Treatment

__ My drinking/using is related to my current employment status this way:

_____

_____

__ As a result of my drinking/using, my professional license has been suspended
__ I don't see any reason to change my employment situation in order to maintain
   or enhance my sobriety
__ It would be easier for my recovery if I were to change my employment picture in
   this way:

_____

_____

I need assistance with the following:
   __ Getting my professional license back
   __ Discovering what I am suited for
   __ Finding jobs I am qualified for
   __ Getting training or education to qualify me for a position I want
   __ Preparing a resume
   __ Learning interview skills
   __ Getting transportation to interviews and/or to work

   ___ _____

__ I have discussed this situation with my recovery support group

My recovery plan for change in my employment picture is:

_____

_____

_____

_____

_____

108. My Housing

I am:
   __ homeless (living on the street, in shelters, or staying with friends)
   __ renting in transient hotels (SROs)
   __ confined in prison or in a hospital or in the armed forces
   __ in a halfway house or recovery home
   __ living in a trailer or boat
   __ renting a house or apartment

___ living in a house I own
___ living in a drug-infested neighborhood
___ living in a neighborhood where everybody knows me as a user
___ living in a neighborhood that is "nice" except for my drinking/using here
___ constantly traveling

___ My housing situation has nothing to do with my drinking/using
___ If I had not been drinking/using, my housing situation probably would be
    different in this way:

_____

_____

___ I don't see any reason to change my housing situation for the sake of my
    recovery
___ My recovery would have a stronger chance of success if I made some changes to
    my housing situation, namely:

_____

_____

_____

___ If I moved to a different neighborhood, my addiction would move with me
___ If I moved to a different neighborhood, my addiction would stay behind
___ I believe that a change of neighborhood would improve my recovery because:

_____

_____

_____

I need help with the following:
    ___ Getting into a halfway house or recovery home
    ___ Getting public assistance for housing
    ___ Finding an apartment
    ___ Transportation
    ___ Deposit and first month's rent
    ___ Down payment
    ___ Cleaning up my credit to qualify for a loan

    ___ _____

___ I have discussed this situation with my recovery support group

My specific plan for changing my housing situation is:

_____

_____

1 Body

2 Exposure

3 Activities

4 People

5 Feelings

6 Life Style

7 History

8 Culture

9 Treatment

_____

_____

_____

_____

109. My Living Situation

I am:

    __ living alone and not in a relationship with anyone
    __ living alone but I am in a relationship with someone
    __ living with roommate(s)
    __ living together with a Significant Other
    __ living with an active alcoholic/addict
    __ living with my parent(s)
    __ living with relatives

__ _____

__ My living situation is not related to my drinking/using
__ My drinking/using did have something to do with my living situation, namely:

_____

_____

__ I see no reason to change my living situation for the sake of my recovery
__ My recovery would be more secure if I were to change my living situation in the following specific ways:

_____

_____

_____

_____

I need help with:

    __ finding compatible clean and sober roommates
    __ counseling to work on a troublesome relationship
    __ learning to be comfortable living alone
    __ finding an independent living situation

__ _____

__ I have discussed this situation with my recovery support group

My specific plan for changing my living situation is:

_____

_____

_____

110. My Social Life

I am

__ basically all alone in the world, without family or friends

__ alone here, but I am in regular contact with family/friends who live
     elsewhere

__ in regular face-to-face contact with family members

__ in regular face-to-face contact with friends

__ in contact with people at work, but rarely outside work

__ regularly invited over to visit other people socially

__ rarely if ever invited over to visit other people socially

__ frequently a host of social events at my place

__ a participant in organized group events such as dances, hikes, outings

__ active in a club, church, or association, other than a recovery group

__ active in a sports or athletic activity

__ active in a music, literary or other cultural group

__ active in a hobbyist association

__ active in a political group

__ _____

__ _____

__ I see no relation between the state of my social life and my drinking/using

__ There is some connection between my drinking/using and my social life,
     namely:

_____

_____

_____

__ I see no reason to change my social life for the sake of my sobriety

__ My sobriety would be improved if I made the following changes to my social
     life:

_____

_____

1 Body

2 Exposure

3 Activities

4 People

5 Feelings

6 Life Style

7 History

8 Culture

9 Treatment

1 Body   2 Exposure   3 Activities   4 People   5 Feelings   6 Life Style   7 History   8 Culture   9 Treatment

_____

_____

I want help with:

      __ meeting sober people and making friends

      __ improving my social skills

      __ overcoming shyness

      __ resolving old antagonisms that keep me separated from people I care for

      __ breaking the ice

      __ becoming more confident in social situations without drinking/drugging

      __ finding out about clubs, churches and associations I might be interested in

      __ finding a calendar of local events I might enjoy attending

      __ finding teams that play my sport at my level

      __ finding people to play music or do other cultural pursuits with

      __ finding political groups I sympathize with

      __ rearranging my schedule and finding time for activities

_____

_____

__ I have discussed this situation with my recovery support group

My specific recovery plan for my social life is:

_____

_____

111. My Parenting

__ My kids live with me and I'm their Number One caretaker

__ My kids live with me and I'm a backup caretaker for them

__ I have custody only some of the time

__ I don't have my kids but I have to pay child support

__ I'm owed child support

__ I'm a working parent – raise my kids and hold down a job

__ My kids are grown up and moved away; I have an empty nest now

__ I don't know where my kids are

__ I gave up my kids and I no longer have responsibility for them

__ They took my kids away and I want them back

__ My drinking/using is related to my parenting situation in this way:

_____

__ My drinking/using has nothing to do with my role as a parent
__ I have discussed my parenting with my support group
__ My plan for changing my role as a parent is:

_____

_____

_____

112. My Housekeeping

I am

    __ a neat and tidy person
    __ about average in my housekeeping and household management
    __ on the messy side when it comes to housekeeping and management
    __ definitely a slob and procrastinator
    __ embarrassed to have people come visit me because of my housekeeping

__ _____

__ I see no relation between my housekeeping and my drinking/using
__ There is some connection between my drinking/using and housekeeping,
    namely:

_____

_____

__ I see no reason to change my housekeeping for the sake of my sobriety

__ My sobriety would be improved if I made the following changes to my
    housekeeping:

_____

__ I have discussed this situation with my recovery support group

My specific recovery plan for my housekeeping is:

_____

_____

_____

1 Body

2 Exposure

3 Activities

4 People

5 Feelings

6 Life Style

7 History

8 Culture

9 Treatment

113. My Personal Hygiene and Appearance

I am

___ more careful than most people about my appearance and personal cleanliness

___ about the same as my friends and the people I work with in hygiene and dress

___ usually clean but somewhat careless about the way I dress

___ sometimes behind on my showering, shampooing and shaving, but I dress clean

___ too frequently out in public looking "somewhat the worse for wear"

___ too often dressed the wrong way for the situation

___ regularly without a bath or fresh clothing

___ embarrassed to go out because of the way I look

___ embarrassed to have people come visit me because of the way I look

___ other:_____

___ I see no relation between my hygiene and appearance and my drinking/using

___ There is some connection between my drinking/using and my hygiene and appearance, namely:

_____

___ I see no reason to change my hygiene and appearance for the sake of my sobriety

___ My sobriety would be improved if I made the following changes to my hygiene and/or appearance:

_____

_____

I would like help with:

___ access to a hot shower, bath, or tools and chemicals for cleanliness

___ haircuts, facial hair, body hair care

___ taking care of fingernails and toenails

___ concerns about body odor

___ access to laundry facilities and chemicals

___ access to more appropriate clothing and accessories

___ _____

___ I have discussed this situation with my recovery support group

My specific recovery plan for my hygiene and personal appearance is:

_____

_____

114. My Sex Life

I am:

    __ sexually active in a relationship with a steady partner
    __ sexually active with a few fairly steady partners
    __ sexually active with a number of casual partners
    __ sexually active as a sex worker
    __ not sexually active with other people
    __ not sexually active
    __ uninterested in sex because of low libido
    __ sexually frustrated on a regular basis

__ _____

__ There is no relationship between my drinking/using and my sex life
__ My drinking/using does have some relationship to my sex life, namely:

_____

_____

__ I don't see any reason to make changes in my sex life for the sake of my sobriety
__ My sobriety would be improved if I made some changes in my sex life, namely:

_____

_____

I want help with:

    __ counseling for me
    __ counseling for my sex partner(s)
    __ getting tested for Sexually Transmitted Disease
    __ getting condoms
    __ getting more variety and adventure in my sex life
    __ learning more about safe sex
    __ finding someone to get involved with
    __ getting support to break up with my current Significant Other
    __ reawakening my sexual desire
    __ cooling off my sexual desire
    __ dealing with a sexual addiction
    __ getting treatment for a STD

__ _____

During the first year of my sobriety, my plan is to:

    __ stay in my current relationship, even though my partner drinks/uses
    __ terminate my current relationship because my partner drinks/uses
    __ start a new relationship, provided the person is clean and sober
    __ start a new relationship, provided the person is also in recovery
    __ start a new relationship with a person who drinks or uses moderately
    __ start a new relationship with a person who is an active alcoholic/addict

Side tab (right margin, top to bottom): 1 Body | 2 Exposure | 3 Activities | 4 People | 5 Feelings | 6 Life Style | 7 History | 8 Culture | 9 Treatment

1 Body   2 Exposure   3 Activities   4 People   5 Feelings   6 Life Style   7 History   8 Culture   9 Treatment

___ stay out of any relationships and go to recovery meetings instead
___ have sex only with myself
___ abstain from any sexual activity, despite frustration I may feel
___ throw myself into some other kind of intense passion so I won't want sex
___ take medication to depress my libido so I won't want sex

_____

_____

Since I stopped drinking/using, I have noticed the following changes:
___ My sexual desire has dropped off
___ My sexual desire has increased
___ My sexual satisfaction has declined
___ My sexual satisfaction has improved
___ I have become more sexually frustrated
___ I have become less sexually frustrated
___ I have found myself attracted to different types of people
___ I have found that different types of people are attracted to me
___ I have noticed a change in my sexual orientation
___ I have noticed a change in the kinds of sexual activity I enjoy
___ I have noticed a change in my attitude toward safe sex
___ I have noticed a change in my sexual fantasies
___ Nothing has changed
___ I don't want to think about this

___ I have discussed this situation with my recovery support group

My specific recovery plan for my sex life is:

_____

_____

115. My Finances

I am

___ affluent and without financial concerns
___ financially stable, with savings
___ making ends meet, but with little or no savings
___ barely getting by and going into debt
___ broke and/or bankrupt

_____

___ There is no relationship between my drinking/using and my financial situation
___ There is some relationship between my drinking/using and my financial
    situation, namely:

_____

_____

___ My sobriety would be improved if my financial situation were to change, namely:

_____

_____

I need help with:

    ___ managing my investments
    ___ budgeting more realistically
    ___ supplementing my income
    ___ dealing with my credit card debt
    ___ paying bills
    ___ dealing with other debts I owe
    ___ dealing with back taxes I owe
    ___ rebuilding my credit
    ___ Feeding my family
    ___ Dealing with the welfare, disability, or housing agencies
    ___ Surviving until the end of the month
    ___ Getting some food today

I owe the following money debts:

    ___ mortgage company $ _____
    ___ state, federal taxes $ _____
    ___ landlord, for rent $ _____
    ___ car finance company $ _____
    ___ other installment loans $ _____
    ___ family members $ _____
    ___ friends $ _____
    ___ child support $ _____
    ___ spousal support $ _____
    ___ my dealer $ _____
    ___ Total $ _____

___ I have a plan for paying off my debts and I will gradually put this behind me

___ I need to talk to an advisor to see whether I should declare bankruptcy

___ My financial situation is so desperate that I have considered suicide

___ My family/friends don't know how bad my financial situation is and I am ashamed to have them find out

___ My family/friends know my financial situation and are doing what they can to help out

___ My family/friends know my financial situation but don't care and won't help

___ My financial situation is so hopeless I might as well spend what little I have left on alcohol/drugs

___ No matter how bad my finances are, drinking/drugging will only make them worse

___ I have discussed my financial situation with my support group

My specific recovery plan for my financial situation is:

1 Body   2 Exposure   3 Activities   4 People   5 Feelings   6 Life Style   7 History   8 Culture   9 Treatment

_____

_____

_____

116. My Health Insurance

___ I have adequate health insurance coverage for my needs at this time
___ I have no health insurance at all
___ My health insurance doesn't cover chemical dependency treatment
___ My health insurance doesn't cover psychological treatment
___ I have health insurance but it doesn't cover what I need (example: liver transplant)
___ I have some coverage, but it won't cover the length of treatment I feel I need
___ I have private health insurance but can't afford the deductible
___ My coverage has run out
___ I don't know the extent of coverage I have
___ There is no relationship between my drinking/drugging and my health coverage
___ As an indirect result of my drinking/drugging, I lost my health coverage
___ I was denied health coverage for a traumatic injury because I had been drinking/using
___ I am afraid to tell my doctor about my drinking/using because I fear loss of coverage
___ Thanks to having adequate coverage, I qualify for chemical dependency treatment if I want it
___ My health insurance requires me to undergo a type of chemical dependency treatment I don't care for
___ There is nothing I can do about my health insurance coverage situation
___ I feel I need to stay in my job and/or in my relationship in order to maintain my coverage
___ I want to get a job so that I can get health coverage
___ My health coverage situation has nothing to do with my recovery
___ I have discussed my health coverage situation with my support group
___ If I had adequate health coverage, I would:

_____

117. My Legal Situation

___ I have no legal problems at this time
___ I have warrants outstanding for my arrest
___ I am a runaway minor
___ I have a restraining order against me
___ I have a restraining order against someone who has been harassing me
___ I am awaiting trial

__ I am awaiting sentencing
__ I am considering a plea bargain
__ I am a witness against someone in a criminal case
__ I am on probation
__ I am incarcerated
__ I am on parole
__ I don't have a criminal problem but I am involved in a civil suit

_____

__ My legal problems have nothing to do with my drinking/using
__ My legal problems have something to do with my drinking/using, namely:

_____

__ I don't need to address my legal problems for the sake of my sobriety
__ My sobriety would be improved if I made the following moves as regards my
    legal problems:

_____

I want help with
        __ finding a private lawyer
        __ contacting my Public Defender
        __ getting into a drug diversion program
        __ establishing a good conduct record
        __ getting into vocational rehab
        __ getting into a drug treatment program
        __ getting more recovery literature to read
        __ _____
__ I have discussed my legal situation with my group

My specific recovery plan for my legal situation is:

_____

_____

_____

1 Body
2 Exposure
3 Activities
4 People
5 Feelings
6 Life Style
7 History
8 Culture
9 Treatment

118. My Life Style Plan

In the worksheet below, put a check mark in each life style area that you plan to work on, and write a short description of the changes you want to make, if any. You can also use this worksheet to check off areas where you want to get more information and areas where you want help.

Worksheet 36: My Life Style Issues (Summary)

MY LIFE STYLE SUMMARY WORKSHEET					
Life Style Area	OK as is	Needs to change	I want information	I want help	My plan in a few words
(1) My work					
(2) My shelter					
(3) My living situation					
(4) My social life					
(5) My parenting					
(6) My housekeeping					
(7) My hygiene and appearance					

Sidebar: 1 Body 2 Exposure 3 Activities 4 People 5 Feelings 6 Life Style 7 History 8 Culture 9 Treatment

(8) My sex life					
(9) My finances					
(10) My health insurance coverage					
(11) My legal situation					

Today's date: _____

119. Three-Month Review

I have accomplished the following changes in my life style:

_____

_____

_____

_____

_____

_____

Today's date: _____

1 Body
2 Exposure
3 Activities
4 People
5 Feelings
6 Life Style
7 History
8 Culture
9 Treatment

120. One-Year Review

I have accomplished the following changes in my life style:

_____

_____

_____

_____

_____

_____

_____

Today's date: _____

Chapter Eight

Seventh Domain: My History

This work area contains material that looks backward. The purpose of this material is to help you to disentangle the original sober you from the later drinking/drugging you, so that you can step forward freely in your new clean and sober identity.

We were born clean and sober. Even the unfortunate few who first got alcohol/drugs through the umbilical cord were detoxed at birth. Most people had at least a few years of clean and sober life at the beginning. Many people were practically adults before they began drinking/using heavily.   During those formative years, you learned most of the basic skills that you will need through adulthood.

There is a book with the semi-humorous title "All I Really Need to Know I Learned in Kindergarten."[29] This title makes a valid point. Your social skills, your sense of yourself, your capacity to handle stress, your personality, and much else, were all initially formed in your first five or six years – years while you were clean and sober.

The original "you" was a clean and sober person. This is why the word "recovery" has a real meaning: your project is to recover (to find again, to recapture) the clean and sober state in which you started out, and from which you were, somehow, sidetracked or separated.

121. Why Work on Your History?

In the first part of this domain you can try to refresh your memories of your first clean and sober life. Whether this earlier life was traumatic, or uneventful, or warm and sheltered does not fundamentally matter. Although many people who suffered childhood trauma later try out heavy drinking/drugging, not all go there; and many people who drink/drug too much and become addicted had "normal" or "average" childhoods, whatever those terms may mean. Addiction can happen to anyone who puts alcohol and/or drugs into their body – and your reasons for starting to drink/drug could span a broad range of motives.

---

[29] All I Really Need to Know I Learned in Kindergarten, Uncommon Thoughts on Common Things, by Robert Fulghum.

1 Body   2 Exposure   3 Activities   4 People   5 Feelings   6 Life Style   7 History   8 Culture   9 Treatment

The important thing for purposes of your recovery now is that you had an earlier clean and sober life. You are not living drug-free now for the first time. Sobriety is not a brand new concept that has to come to you from the outside; it has always been there inside of you all the time. You are returning to your clean and sober origins. You are reclaiming your birthright.

In the second part of this domain, you will find material that reviews your detour into drinking/drugging. These exercises have several purposes. One is to help you settle your accounts with the drinking/drugging period of your life, so that you can get a sense of closure and put it behind you. Another – seemingly contradictory – purpose is to preserve the memory of the negative consequences of your drinking/drugging, in case you should forget and be tempted to return there. A final purpose is to help you gain additional insight into life situations that may pose particular relapse dangers for you, because these were times in your history when alcohol and drugs carved their first impressions into your brain. As with My Exposure (Second Domain) and My Feelings (Fifth Domain), forewarned about these situations is forearmed.

▶**Caution:**

The past can be an uncomfortable place to revisit. For some people, thinking about their early lives brings up painful memories that they are tempted to "medicate" with alcohol/drugs. For many people, reviewing their own drinking/using histories, or listening to other people's, can wake up strong cravings, or may stir up intense guilt, shame or similar negative emotions that overwhelm their current coping skills and support systems.

Therefore, *enter with caution into this domain.* At the first sign of a reaction that might unbalance your sobriety, back off and do something safe. (There are exercises in My Feelings (Fifth Domain) to help deal with strong trigger feelings; see Page 136.) Do not force yourself – or permit anyone else to force you – to work in any part of this domain with which you are not comfortable. It is not the purpose of treatment or self-treatment to push you to the brink of relapse. Sooner or later in your recovery, perhaps much later, you may feel interested and motivated to look at these issues. That will be the right time to do it.

122. My First Life

The term "then" in this checklist refers to the years before you started drinking/using at all. If you also had a period in your life when you were still drinking/using in a very occasional and insignificant way, include that also here for purposes of this particular checklist.

Defining the boundary between early "occasional and insignificant" drinking/using and a later, deeper involvement can be difficult to do in retrospect. For some people there is a large gray zone. Your judgment about this may change as you progress in your recovery. Just do your best for right now. There is more on this issue starting with Section 129 on Page 175.

__ I started my life with _____ years clean and sober
__ I had _____ years of schooling during my first clean and sober life
__ My life then was pretty much average
__ There were some awful things that happened to me then
__ I had a happy childhood
__ My childhood was miserable
__ My childhood was boring and uneventful
__ I was very sheltered as a child
__ My life as a child was interesting and unusual
__ There were times then when I coped with intense emotional pain
__ There were times then when I experienced great joy
__ I was shy and awkward in social situations then
__ I experienced stress then
__ I had good friends then
__ I was often alone then
__ I knew how to enjoy myself then
__ I like the person I was then
__ I was very unhappy then
__ I had a dream for myself then
__ I can't remember what I was like then
__ I'm uncomfortable thinking about that time in my life

__ _____

__ _____

__ _____

Do you have a clear picture of who you were then, or is the image fuzzy and remote?

_____

Do you feel a connection with this earlier self, or does that person feel like a stranger now?

_____

How do you feel about the pre-drinking/drugging you?

_____

_____

If you met your earlier self now, would you give it a hug? Or a kick? Or what?

_____

_____

Did your earlier, pre-addicted self have any dreams, plans, projects or visions that you feel are valid and worthwhile? If so, what were they?

1 Body   2 Exposure   3 Activities   4 People   5 Feelings   6 Life Style   7 History   8 Culture   9 Treatment

1 Body   2 Exposure   3 Activities   4 People   5 Feelings   6 Life Style   7 History   8 Culture   9 Treatment

_____

_____

Are those plans still alive in you somewhere? Yes No If so, might this be a good time to pick them up again and start working on them? Refer to the *My Activities Worksheet* beginning on Page 75 for ideas.

123. Early Coping Skills

If you can remember how you dealt with stressful feelings and situations in your first sober life, write your memories here. For example, maybe you handled loneliness by drawing fantasy pictures; maybe you handled anger by kicking a tree; maybe you handled boredom by picking fights with your siblings. Maybe these weren't model responses – but they were a lot smarter than drinking/using, weren't they?

I handled _____ by doing: _____

_____   _____
(feeling)   (how I handled it then)

_____   _____
(feeling)   (how I handled it then)

Can you get any clues from these early responses about how to handle similar issues in a clean and sober manner today? For example:

- If you handled loneliness as a child by drawing fantasy pictures, and if loneliness bothers you now, how about signing up for an art class?
- If you kicked trees then, how about playing soccer or taking kick boxing lessons to work off your anger now?
- If you picked fights with your siblings when bored, how about going to the gym and challenging people to shoot hoops with you? Or going bowling with a sober friend?

You may have had more wisdom as a kid than you give yourself credit for.

124. People Say: My Parents

__ Neither of my parents drank or used "drugs" at all ever, to my knowledge
__ My father drank occasionally, but I never saw him drunk
__ My father drank regularly, but never so much that he seemed impaired to me
__ My father would get drunk around me from time to time
__ My father would get drunk and then he would be mean
__ My father would get drunk and be violent
__ My father was drunk a lot of the time or practically all the time that I knew him

__ My father was an alcoholic
__ My father was a drug dealer
__ My father used drugs around me from time to time
__ My father was often stoned on drugs around me
__ My father was a drug addict
__ My mother drank occasionally, but I never or rarely saw her drunk
__ My mother drank regularly, but never so much that she seemed impaired to me
__ My mother would get drunk around me from time to time
__ My mother was drunk a lot of the time or practically all the time that I knew her
__ My mother would get drunk and be mean
__ My mother would get drunk and be violent
__ My mother was an alcoholic
__ My mother used drugs around me from time to time
__ My mother was often stoned on drugs around me
__ My mother was a drug addict
__ My mother was a drug dealer
__ Other people besides my parent(s) drank/used in the home where I grew up
__ I have strong reason to think that my own drinking/using was at least partly hereditary
__ I have little reason to think that my own drinking/using was hereditary to any significant degree
__ When I was growing up, it bothered me that my parent(s) would drink/use
__ When I was growing up, I never paid my parent(s)' drinking/using much attention
__ When I was growing up, I swore never to drink like my parent(s) because I did not want to end up like him/her/them
__ When I was growing up, it seemed natural to me that I would drink/drug the same as my parent(s) did
__ My parent(s) introduced me to drinking/using
__ When I started drinking/drugging I had to hide it from my parent(s)
__ My parent(s) encourage(d) me to drink/use with them
__ I have never talked with my parent(s) about their drinking/using
__ I have tried to get my parent(s) to stop drinking/using
__ My parent(s) tried to get me to stop drinking/using
__ My parent(s) used to drink/use but stopped _____ years ago
__ My parents are/were active in a recovery organization

__ _____

__ _____

1 Body   2 Exposure   3 Activities   4 People   5 Feelings   6 Life Style   7 History   8 Culture   9 Treatment

125. Thinking About My Parents

If your parents drank/used heavily, does that mean you have to follow their example? Yes No

Do children have to do everything their parents did? Yes No

Don't children have the right to rebel if their parents set a bad example? Yes No

If you have a hereditary predisposition to alcoholism (you got it in your genes), does that make it your parents' fault that you became an alcoholic? Yes No

Where did your parents get *their* genes?

_____

If your parents' drinking/using was an issue for you, did you ever try to stop them?
  Yes No   If so, what was the result?

_____

_____

If your parents started you on drinking/drugging, what do you suppose were their motives?

_____

_____

If you have a lot of alcoholics in your family, do you also have family members who don't drink or use at all? Yes No If so, why don't they?

_____

_____

If there are no drinkers/users in your family, did you have other adult role models who drank/used when you were growing up? Yes No   Who?

_____

Are you able to talk with your parents about your decision to become clean/sober?
  Yes No   Why or why not?

_____

_____

_____

126. Thinking About My First Life

Try to remember the quality of your life before you first began to put alcohol/drugs into your body at all, or before you did that in more than an occasional and insignificant way, if you had such a period in your life. (There is more about this issue starting with Section 129 on Page 175.)

What were some of the good, positive things you did, or things that were going on in your life at that time? What made you happy, or proud, or otherwise feel good, without drinking/using?

_____

_____

_____

_____

Can you recreate any of these feel-good situations today? Yes No Can you recapture the attitudes or feelings that allowed you to be happy in your earlier life, without putting drugs/alcohol into your body? Yes No   Why or why not?

_____

What were some of the things you did or that happened in your earlier life that you handled at that time without drinking or using, but that you now have negative feelings about, such as sadness, hurt, anger, shame, guilt, etc.? (Back off this exercise and do something safe if going down this particular memory lane is an emotional trigger to drink/use.)

_____

_____

_____

_____

Can you recapture your former ability to handle hard situations and to survive emotional pain without drinking/using?   Yes No Why or why not?

_____

_____

Pretend a time machine has carried you back to your first life, and you can alter your future by changing what you do. Would you start drinking/drugging this time, knowing what you now know?   Yes No

1 Body   2 Exposure   3 Activities   4 People   5 Feelings   6 Life Style   7 History   8 Culture   9 Treatment

What if anything would you have lost in your life if you had never started to drink/drug?

_____

_____

_____

How would you be different today if you had not started drinking/ drugging?

_____

_____

_____

_____

127. Later Clean and Sober Times

Many people's drinking/drugging career had significant interruptions when they were sober, or nearly so. Did you have times like that? If so, then use this next worksheet. Write down any periods of time after you first started drinking/using heavily (but before you got into recovery) when you stopped completely, or almost so – zero drugs, zero alcohol, or only on rare occasions. Describe what was going on in your life during this period. Ignore periods that were only short breathers between binges.

Worksheet 37: Later Clean and Sober Times (Example)

LATER CLEAN AND SOBER TIMES		
Start Date: Jan 1979	**Duration:** 4 yrs 2 mos	**What was going on in my life then:** I was sky-diving and hang-gliding regularly; I never gave drinking/using a thought during this time
End Date: March 1983		
Start Date: June 1989	27 mos	Married to G. My daughter and son were born. I was into them and put alcohol/drugs out of my life.
End Date: September 1991		

Worksheet 38: Later Clean and Sober Times

LATER CLEAN AND SOBER TIMES IN MY LIFE		
Start Date: End Date:	Duration:	What was going on in my life then:
Start Date: End date:	Duration:	What was going on in my life then:
Start Date: End Date: End Date:	Duration:	What was going on in my life then:
Total Sober Time:		

1 Body
2 Exposure
3 Activities
4 People
5 Feelings
6 Life Style
7 History
8 Culture
9 Treatment

128. Working with the Later Clean and Sober Times Worksheet

What is your longest single stretch of time clean and sober in the worksheet above? _____

In your recovery at this time, have you exceeded your previous longest time clean and sober?   Yes No

What is the average duration of your clean and sober periods in this table? _____

Worksheet 39: Adding up the Sober Time in my Life

ADDING UP THE SOBER TIME IN MY LIFE	Years	Months
What is the total amount of my clean and sober periods in the table on the previous page (copy bottom line from worksheet)?		
How many years was I completely clean and sober from birth until I ever took a drink or did a drug?		
How long have I been clean and sober now?		
My lifetime accumulated experience with living clean and sober amounts to:		

Based on the worksheet above, approximately what percentage of your life so far have you lived clean and sober?

_____ %

What conclusions do you draw from this calculation?

_____

_____

Does the table suggest any patterns in your life – recurring situations where you are able to stay clean and sober? If so, what are they? What was the secret to your being able to stay clean and sober at those times?

_____

_____

_____

_____

_____

129. Why I Drank/Used and Why I Became Addicted

In the following sections you can explore your drinking/drugging career from the beginning. This material may help you answer the question "Why did I start to drink or use?" But no recovery workbook exercises can help you answer the very different question, "Why did I become addicted?"

People become addicted when the dosage of drink/drug that they put into their body exceeds an invisible threshold. The cumulative overdose breaks a limiting circuit in the brain, and thereafter, people cannot reliably stop after just one or a few. They are hooked.

Current technology cannot foretell when a person's drinking/using career will cross the boundary line into addiction. There is no test for it. The next drink or dose might be that one too many, or it might not. You can't see the boundary line in the headlights, only in the rear view mirror.

Laboratory experimenters can readily convert ordinary wild-type monkeys, dogs, rats, hamsters, and mice, among other species, into alcoholics/addicts simply by saturating their systems with high doses of alcohol or other addictive drugs for a long enough period of time.   Once hooked, laboratory rats will press a lever thousands of times to get another dose of drug, and will ignore food, water, sex and sleep. This fact suggests that the cause of addiction does not lie in human psychology, personality, character or other specifically human issues. The why of addiction lies in neurobiology, in the structure and electro-chemistry of basic brain structures shared by many species.

For this reason, unless you're a neurobiologist it's usually uninteresting and a waste of time to try to figure out "why I became addicted." Addiction is a consequence of the action of addictive substances on the brain.

Since we generally can have no knowledge that we are approaching our boundary, we can normally have no specific intention of crossing it. Rare is the individual who sets out to use alcohol or other addictive substances with the intention of becoming addicted.

People start using alcohol or other addictive drugs for a wide variety of motives. We may be drinking/using because we are isolated and maladjusted, or we may be carousing in cheerful harmony with our friends, or for any of dozens of other reasons, good, bad, and indifferent.

Deep down in our brain, below the level where high-order concepts such as emotional adjustment or social intention have any meaning, the chemicals that we have been putting into our body reach a critical concentration and cause the neuronal equivalent of a blown fuse. The next time we start to drink/use, we don't get an "enough" signal. Our thirst or craving becomes unquenchable. The brakes are gone. We're hooked.

This is probably all-too familiar territory for you, or you would not be reading this workbook.

For more than five decades, researchers have been trying to find out whether there is anything distinctive about the human beings who become addicted to alcohol/drugs. The clear answer is that there is no particular personality type that is especially liable to become addicted. There is as much diversity of

1 Body   2 Exposure   3 Activities   4 People   5 Feelings   6 Life Style   7 History   8 Culture   9 Treatment

personalities and psychological types among alcoholics/addicts as among the general population.

As you work these exercises about the start of your drinking career, try to look clearly at who you really were and what really happened to you. Remember that becoming addicted is not an indictment of your personality or character. If you spend time in treatment or in a recovery support group, you will see for yourself that alcoholism/addiction strikes all kinds of people – kind as well as mean, brilliant as well as dim, empathetic as well as egotistical.

130. People Say: How I Got Started

___ I started drinking/using alone

___ I started drinking/using to fit in with my friends

___ I started drinking/using to impress older friends

___ I started drinking/using to impress a certain particular individual

___ My parents were the ones who turned me on to drinking/drugging

___ I started drinking/using as a rebellion against my parents

___ I started drinking/using just to see what it was like, out of curiosity

___ Sex was on my mind when I started drinking/using

___ I started on the spur of the moment

___ I had been thinking and planning it for some time before I started

___ I had resisted doing it for a long time but then came a moment where I gave in

___ I paid for my first drink/hit of drugs with my own money

___ Someone else paid for my first drink/hit of drugs

___ I gave something other than money for my first drink/hit of drugs

___ I came by my first drink/hit of drugs by shady means

___ I started out in the open, not hiding from anybody

___ I started by sneaking it

___ I started drinking in the military service

___ I was basically pressured to start it, against my will

___ When I started, I intended to stop almost right away

___ When I started I intended to keep on doing it

___ When I started, I never intended to become an alcoholic / drug addict

___ When I started, I knew people who were alcoholics / addicts and I wanted to be like them

___ The first drink/hit of drug I had, I had a strong feeling of pleasure

___ The first drink/hit of drug I had made me sick and I had to work at going back to it

___ I can't remember how or why I started

131. Thinking About How I Got Started

How important in your starting was the desire to please or to make an impression on other people, or to belong? Very Partly Not important

If pleasing others was an important motive for you when you started, is pressure from drinking/using friends an important trigger for you still today? Yes No

If so, how important might it be for your sobriety to acquire clean and sober friends?
Very important   Maybe   Not important

Did you start drinking/using because you felt somehow that you should?   Yes No

Did you believe that you have to drink or use drugs in order to be normal? Yes No

Do you (still) believe this today?   Yes No

Did/Do you think that people who never use alcohol/drugs are defective or substandard?   Yes No

If so, what is the source of this belief?

_____

_____

If another person was influential in getting you started drinking/using, what do you think was their motive in doing that?

_____

Was your very first experience with alcohol/drugs pleasurable?   Yes No

If not, what made you go back for more?

_____

When you started out, did you visualize that alcohol/drugs would take over your life and that they might one day define you as a person? Yes No

Did you intend that to happen?   Yes No

Did anyone make a profit, directly or behind the scenes, from getting you started drinking/using?   Yes No

If so, who or what were they and how did they influence you?

_____

_____

1 Body   2 Exposure   3 Activities   4 People   5 Feelings   6 Life Style   7 History   8 Culture   9 Treatment

1 Body   2 Exposure   3 Activities   4 People   5 Feelings   6 Life Style   7 History   8 Culture   9 Treatment

132. People Say: My Education about Drugs/Alcohol

___ I learned what drugs were available and how to use them from a drug education program at school

___ My parent(s) taught me how to drink

___ My parents taught me how to use drugs

___ I learned about drugs on the Internet

___ I learned about beer being good to drink by watching television commercials

___ I got the idea that people should drink and smoke by watching movies and shows

___ A particular individual gave me my education about drugs/alcohol

___ I got my drug and alcohol education from my friends generally

___ I learned about drugs/alcohol from reading books and magazines

___ We had a regular class in school where we learned about alcohol/drugs

___ When I started, I did not know that people could get hooked on it

___ Before I started drinking/using, I had learned that some people could get addicted

___ Before I started drinking/using, I knew that becoming addicted was common

___ Before I started drinking/using, I knew the words "alcoholic" and "addict"

___ I knew about alcoholism and addiction but I didn't connect it with myself

___ I saw "scare" movies about drugs but I laughed at them

___ Before I started, I had heard speakers talk about their recovery from drugs/alcohol

___ _____

___ _____

___ _____

133. Thinking About Drug/Alcohol Education

At the time you were starting to drink/use, do you think you were given an adequate education about drugs and alcohol? Yes No

Have you seen "drug education" programs that actually influence kids to start using drugs?   Yes No

If the "you" as you were on your last day of drinking/using could have appeared to you in a vision while you were still in school, do you think it would have made a difference in your life? ___ Yes ___ No

If you could design an education program to teach kids the true facts about drinking/drugging, what points would you stress? How would you deliver your message?

_____

_____

What do you think is a good age for kids to start being taught in school about alcohol/drugs?

_____ Why:

_____

Do you think that people who used to drink/drug and who have now successfully quit do a good job as educators about drinking/drugging?   Yes No

Once you get some years of sobriety under your belt, would you like to volunteer to give educational talks about drinking/using to young people?   Yes No

134. People Say: My Drinking/Using Patterns

__ When I first started out, I only drank/used very occasionally and it didn't have any significance in my life

__ At first I was a social drinker, only drinking at events when everybody else did

__ For a time, unless they handed it to me I wouldn't do any; I'd not go looking for it

__ There was a time when I never thought about it; I only did it when the situation came up where people did it

__ Earlier on we would just do it for giggles and then forget about it

__ There was a time when I would go months between doing any, and then only do a little bit

__ At first I only did it to keep my friend company, I'd never do any by myself

__ There was a time when I never kept any in the house, I'd only do it if I went out

__ There was a time when I had no problem saying "no thanks" after one or two, and sticking to it

__ I mainly always used the same substance all of my drinking/using career

__ At different times I have had different main drugs

__ I have used alcohol together with other drugs at the same time

__ If I couldn't get my "drug of choice," I wouldn't get high at all

__ If I couldn't get my "drug of choice," I'd use whatever was available at the time

__ I have used the following at least once:

_____

_____

_____

__ I have never used the following even once:

_____

_____

__ I'd mainly get high when together with groups of people

__ I mainly drank/used with a particular drinking/using partner, rarely in groups

__ I was mainly a solitary drinker/user; I'd mainly drink/use by myself

1 Body   2 Exposure   3 Activities   4 People   5 Feelings   6 Life Style   7 History   8 Culture   9 Treatment

__ In my drinking/using career, I started out social and drifted toward solitary
__ In my drinking/using career, I started out solitary and drifted toward social
__ It didn't matter whether people were around or not, it made no difference to me

__ My main pattern was to drink/use every day
__ My main pattern was to binge; namely, I would typically go _____
    (*time*) without drinking/using and then binge for _____ (*time*)
__ At different times in my drinking/using career, I would have different patterns,
    namely:

_____

_____

_____

__ I would start drinking / using first thing after getting up
__ I had a rule about no drinking/using until _____ (*o'clock*)
__ I had a rule about no drinking / using in certain places, namely:

_____

_____

__ I had a rule about no drinking / using on certain occasions, namely:

_____

_____

__ I had a rule about no drinking / using in front of certain people, namely:

_____

_____

__ I generally stuck to my rules
__ I had all kinds of rules but ended up breaking most of them and making new
    ones
__ I would usually drink/use all day long and try to keep a constant high all the time
__ I would usually not drink/use on weekdays until _____ o'clock
__ I would usually drink/use more on weekends, holidays and vacations
__ I could go without for weeks or months and then I would head out on self-
    destructive binges
__ I usually only drank a certain kind of alcoholic beverage, namely
_____

__ If I couldn't drink my favorite kind of drink, I wouldn't drink at all that day
__ I drank/used whatever happened to be available
__ I tried to buy my alcohol/drugs from a different source every time, because:

_____

_____

1 Body   2 Exposure   3 Activities   4 People   5 Feelings   6 Life Style   7 History   8 Culture   9 Treatment

__ I always bought some groceries along with my bottles, because:

_____

_____

__ I bought a new supply of alcohol/drugs every day, because:

_____

_____

__ I usually kept enough alcohol in the house to keep me going for _____ (*time*)
__ For illegal drugs, I usually kept enough supply to last me _____
      (*time*)
__ For illegal drugs, I had one steady connection
__ For illegal drugs, I would score from dealers on the street
__ If for some reason I couldn't get my usual supply of my drug, I would just go
      without
__ If my usual drug supply failed, I would make an extra effort to get some
__ The most money I ever spent in one day for drugs/alcohol is: $_____
__ The longest distance I have traveled to get a drug supply is _____
      (miles)
__ Some of the risks I have taken to get a drug supply include:

_____

_____

_____

135. Thinking About Drinking/Using Patterns

How do you feel inside as you review the details of your drinking/using history? Are you OK in your sobriety remembering this material? If you feel triggered to drink/use, stop and do something else (sober) immediately. For example, do the *Working With Strong Trigger Feelings and Cravings Worksheet* at Page 136. Don't continue with your drinking/using history until you feel OK.

Try to discuss this material with a group, face to face or online. Do you find that everyone has the same drinking/using patterns or do you see variety?

Did you have a period in your life when you drank/used infrequently and when it meant nothing in your life? Yes No

If so, were you conscious of a change in your pattern after a time? Yes No

If so, was the change gradual, or sudden? _____

1 Body   2 Exposure   3 Activities   4 People   5 Feelings   6 Life Style   7 History   8 Culture   9 Treatment

1 Body   2 Exposure   3 Activities   4 People   5 Feelings   6 Life Style   7 History   8 Culture   9 Treatment

How did it make you feel when you became aware of the change?

_____

In your experience, is it more common for people to use only one drug (including alcohol) all their lives, or to use a variety of drugs (either together or one after the other)? ___ Only one ___ More than one.

Have you ever had the experience of starting out to use one drug, and then moving on to another? Yes No

Do you agree that using any drug (including tobacco and alcohol) tends to break down your resistance to using another? Yes No

Why or why not?

_____

_____

Do you think of people who used different drugs than you as being "better" or "worse" than you? Yes No

Why or why not?

_____

_____

Do you (or did you) have stereotypes in your mind about "the alcoholic" and "the crack addict" and "the heroin addict"? Yes No

Have you actually met such people, and did they conform to your stereotypes? Yes No

Would you refuse to associate in recovery groups with people who used different drugs than you? Yes No

Why or why not?

_____

_____

If your pattern was to drink/use every day, would you reasonably expect that you might experience cravings every day, at least at the start of your sobriety? Yes No

If so, might it be a good idea to do some kind of recovery exercise every day (see My Daily Do, Page 70)? Yes No

If your pattern was to start drinking/using at a certain hour each day, would you reasonably expect that you might experience especially strong cravings at that hour (at least at the start of your recovery)? Yes No

If so, might it be a good idea at the beginning to get to a "safe place" before that hour begins? (See My Safe Space, Page 67.) Yes No

If you bought a new supply every day, why did you do that, instead of purchasing in big quantities?

_____

_____

If you bought every day, are trips to the store strongly wrapped up in your mind with drinking?   Yes No

If so, would it be helpful to take someone sober with you on shopping trips for a while?   Yes No   (See also My Exposure (Second Domain), Page 57 and My Activities (Third Domain), Page 73.)

If you concealed your purchases and your consumption, you were probably ashamed of your drinking/using. Do you agree? Yes No

If you were ashamed of your drinking/using, do you feel better now that you are sober? Yes No

Is your life simpler now that you don't have to do all this hiding and deception? Yes No

Or are you hiding your recovery work now with the same energy as you used to hide your drinking/using? Yes No

If so, why?

_____

_____

Were you a binge drinker/user? Yes No

Would you go for days, weeks or months without drinking/using at all, and then hole up somewhere and drink/use until your money ran out or you ended up in the hospital? Yes No

If so, did you keep a calendar to chart your binges?   Yes No

Was there a predictable pattern to your timing?   Yes No.

Did you become aware ahead of time that you were headed for another binge? Yes No

136. People Say: My Tolerance

___ From the start of my drinking I seemed to be able to drink more than most
       people
___ My tolerance (the amount it took before I passed out) increased over the years
___ My tolerance increased for a while and then hit a plateau and stayed there
___ I could not get really high any more no matter how much I drank/used
___ My tolerance collapsed suddenly and a small amount would get me very drunk
___ Early in my drinking/using career it was more interesting than later on

1 Body   2 Exposure   3 Activities   4 People   5 Feelings   6 Life Style   7 History   8 Culture   9 Treatment

___ I kept drinking/drugging even though I didn't especially want to any more

___ I kept wanting to recapture the first "high" and never could

___ I felt trapped in the alcohol/drug and it terrified me that I couldn't find a way out

___ I only drank/used when it got me high and felt good

___ I only drank/used as much as I planned to each time, and then stopped

___ After I started, I'd change my plan and would have more

___ I could walk away from half a drink or half a dose of my drug

___ If somebody left half a drink or half a hit laying unattended I'd finish it for them

___ I kept drinking/using even though I didn't like the high and it didn't feel good

___ I believe that I can reduce, moderate, or control my drinking/using at any time, I just don't want to right now

___ I know from experience that I can always cut down, moderate, or control my drinking/using at any time

___ I have tried to cut down, moderate, or control my drinking/using, and my experience was that I could not sustain the effort

___ I was able to cut down, moderate, or control my drinking/using for a while, but eventually I lost control again

___ Once I had the first drink/hit each time I would keep going until the supply was gone or I would pass out, whichever came first

___ I never felt that I was hooked on alcohol or drugs

___ At some point I began to suspect I might be getting hooked, so I stopped immediately

___ I never had a sense that I was getting hooked, but one day I knew I was

___ At some point I felt I might be getting hooked, but I didn't try to stop

___ At some point I was certain I was now hooked, and this made me feel terrified

___ I felt I was hooked from the very first drink/use in my life

137. Thinking About Tolerance

Again, are you OK thinking about this material? If you feel triggered to drink/use, stop immediately.

Studies have shown that many sons of alcoholic fathers have a lower than ordinary responsiveness to alcohol at an early stage in their drinking career. It takes more alcohol to get them intoxicated than the average person.

Did you find early in your drinking career that you could out-drink other people?
Yes No

Did you know at the time that this is a danger sign that you may have a genetic predisposition toward alcoholism? Yes No

Or did you misinterpret it as a sign that it was OK for you to drink since you could "handle it" better? Yes No

If you had classes about alcohol use, did they discuss this issue? Yes No

If people relapse after a period of sobriety, they typically go back to their old level of consumption in a very short period of time. They may have spent years building up to, say, a liter of vodka per day; but if they relapse it may take only days or weeks before they are back again to that level. It seems that the body permanently remembers its last tolerance level. Have you experienced this phenomenon in your own recovery, or do you know someone who has?   Yes No

Sometimes people who are very heavy drinkers find that their tolerance collapses and very small amounts get them drunk. Has this happened to you? Yes No (If this has happened to you, strongly consider getting medical attention promptly for your liver; this can be a sign of advanced alcoholic disease.)

If you have ever tried to control your drinking (to stop after 1 or 2 drinks a day), did this work for you?   Yes No

If this has consistently worked for you, and you can still do this, you probably don't need this workbook. If you have tried to control your drinking in the past, how many times did you repeat the experiment before you realized this was not going to work for you?

_____

Some researchers make the controversial claim that a certain percentage of people who become addicted to alcohol/drugs can learn to regain control over their drinking/using.   Unfortunately there is no test to predict who, if anyone, may be able to do this. If you were a doctor, which do you think would be the more harmful error: (a) Prescribing abstinence for a person who could do controlled drinking, or (b) Prescribing controlled drinking for a person who needs to do abstinence?

___ It would be more harmful to prescribe abstinence to someone who can drink in
      moderation
___ It would be more harmful to prescribe moderation to someone who needs to do
      abstinence

Why?

_____

_____

_____

Most people who have tried both report that abstaining (having zero drinks/doses of drug) is easier than trying to control or moderate (having 1 or 2 drinks/doses of drugs a day). Do you agree that abstinence is easier to maintain?   Yes No

Why or why not?

_____

_____

1 Body   2 Exposure   3 Activities   4 People   5 Feelings   6 Life Style   7 History   8 Culture   9 Treatment

(Left margin vertical text:) 1 Body   2 Exposure   3 Activities   4 People   5 Feelings   6 Life Style   7 History   8 Culture   9 Treatment

If you were able to stop after just 1 or 2 drinks/hits each day, would you be satisfied? ___ Yes ___ No.   Why or why not?

_____

_____

Some people report that only the first high of their drugging career felt really wonderful, and that they spent the rest of their years trying to recapture that feeling, but never could. Does this apply to you? Yes No

How would you feel about a barber who gave great first haircuts but only shoddy ones thereafter? A lover who was wonderful the first night but short and inconsiderate ever afterward?

_____

Do you remember realizing at some point that you had become hooked on alcohol/drugs? Yes No

If so, did you at first block out or fight the knowledge ("denial")? Yes No

If you blocked it out, why?

_____

_____

How much time do you feel, in retrospect, you spent being addicted without admitting it to yourself?

_____

Some people feel comfortable or even proud in an upside-down way about being active alcoholics/addicts. They even brag about it. Does this describe how you were? Yes No

Do you feel that the people who openly admitted being alcoholics/addicts while they were drinking/using were somehow healthier than those who were "in denial"?
Yes No

Why or why not?

_____

If there had been a test that could have told you ahead of time when to stop so that you would not become addicted, would you have stopped then? Yes No

Why or why not?

_____

_____

138. People Say: About Blackouts and Personality Changes

__ I drove drunk/high and do not know how I got home
__ I drove drunk/high and don't know whether I hurt somebody or what I did
__ I drove drunk/high and had no idea the next morning where the car was
__ I would hear about things I supposedly did at a party and not remember anything
__ People showed me a video of me at this event and I swear I do not remember it at all
__ When I had my first few blackouts I got scared and I changed my drinking/using pattern to try to avoid them
__ In my blackouts I would do things I secretly wanted to do while sober but couldn't work up the nerve
__ In my blackouts I would do things that would never occur to me in my right mind
__ I never had blackouts
__ People told me that I turned into a different person when I got drunk/high
__ I was conscious of changing into a different person as I got drunk/high
__ It never bothered me having these two different parts of my character
__ It worried me that I would go through those personality changes
__ I drank/used in order to take on a different personality
__ I was a funner, more likeable person when I was drunk/high
__ I was an asshole when I was drunk/high
__ I never went through personality changes when I drank/used

139. Thinking about Blackouts and Personality Changes

If you feel unsettled in your sobriety when thinking about this topic, skip it and do something else. Come back when you feel secure about dealing with it.

If you had blackouts, do you think that deep down inside you intended to do the things that you did during blackouts? Yes No

Why or why not?

_____

_____

If you "turned into a different person" when you got drunk/high, do you think the alcohol/drugs created that person, or did they just give that person permission to come out?

_____

_____

If you experienced personality changes, do you value your "drunk/high" personality more highly than your sober personality? Yes No

1 Body   2 Exposure   3 Activities   4 People   5 Feelings   6 Life Style   7 History   8 Culture   9 Treatment

1 Body   2 Exposure   3 Activities   4 People   5 Feelings   6 Life Style   7 History   8 Culture   9 Treatment

If so, what is it you like better about your drunk/high self?

_____

_____

Why are those particular qualities so important to you that you would accept all the consequences that come with drinking/drugging?

_____

_____

Did other people prize the "drunk/high" edition of your personality as highly as you did? Yes No

If you believe that your blackouts and/or personality changes prove that you were or are crazy underneath, do you think that taking alcohol/drugs was the appropriate treatment for your craziness? Yes No

Why or why not?

_____

_____

Have you considered talking with a mental health professional about your blackouts or personality changes to get a second opinion? Yes No

Why or why not?

_____

_____

Now that you are clean and sober, do you find the "drunk/high" personalities of your drinking/using friends and acquaintances as charming and interesting as they find themselves? Yes No

Why or why not?

_____

_____

Most people want to be someone else sometimes. Look at the popularity of Halloween. If you feel that you used alcohol/drugs to give yourself permission to become someone else, have you considered clean and sober ways of going there? Yes No

If so, why not consider joining an amateur theatrical group, or helping out with a puppet theatre? Or why not try being a different person in real life?

140. Alcohol/Drug Intake Worksheets

Use these worksheets to estimate how much alcohol / drugs you have put into your body over your lifetime, and to estimate the dollar cost and the time involved. Use a separate line for each substance. For example, in Part 1 (Money) you might have:

Worksheet 40: Lifetime Alcohol/Drug Intake: Money (Example)

Start Date	End Date	Dura- tion	Substance and unit cost	Quantity per Session	Frequ- ency	Total Quantity	Total Cost
1989	1999	10 yrs	Beer, $5 per six-pack	1 six-pack	daily	3650 six-packs (21,900 cans)	$18,250

And in Part 2 (Time) you might have:

Worksheet 41: Lifetime Alcohol/Drug Intake: Time (Example)

Start Date	End Date	Dura- tion	Substance and Frequency	Time Getting	Time Using	Time Recovering	Total Time
1989	1999	10 yrs	Beer, daily (3,650 days)	½ hour per day, total 1825 hours	3 hours a day, total 10,950 hours	2 hours hung over next day, total 7,300 hours	20,075 hours (about 2 years, 3 months)

The blank worksheets are on the next page:

Worksheet 42: Lifetime Alcohol/Drug Intake: Money

1 Body

2 Exposure

3 Activities

4 People

5 Feelings

6 Life Style

7 History

8 Culture

9 Treatment

1 Body   2 Exposure   3 Activities   4 People   5 Feelings   6 Life Style   7 History   8 Culture   9 Treatment

MY ALCOHOL / DRUG INTAKE WORKSHEET – PART 1: MONEY							
Start Date	End Date	Dura-tion	Substance and unit cost	Quantity per Session	Frequency	Total Quantity	Total Cost
						Total Money Cost:	

Worksheet 43: Lifetime Alcohol/Drug Intake: Time

MY ALCOHOL/DRUGS INTAKE WORKSHEET – PART 2: TIME							
Start Date	End Date	Dura-tion	Substance and Frequency	Time Getting	Time Using	Time Recovering	Total Time
		Totals:					

1 Body

2 Exposure

3 Activities

4 People

5 Feelings

6 Life Style

7 History

8 Culture

9 Treatment

1 Body　2 Exposure　3 Activities　4 People　5 Feelings　6 Life Style　7 History　8 Culture　9 Treatment

141. Following Up After the Intake Worksheets

These questions follow up on the work you started in the Intake Worksheets:

Besides the money I spent on alcohol/drugs directly, I had the following additional dollar costs from my drinking/using:

$ _____ for paraphernalia/equipment/literature
$ _____ for travel and other costs of getting a supply
$ _____ for lost wages or other income due to missed work
$ _____ money or things stolen from me while under the influence
$ _____ money or things that I have no idea what happened to
$ _____ money or things I gave away while I was drunk/stoned
$ _____ things I bought under the influence I wouldn't have sober
$ _____ money I spent to buy drinks/drugs for other people
$ _____ for property damage caused while under influence
$ _____ for medical bills for injuries while under influence
$ _____ for legal bills due to things I did under the influence
$ _____ interest or service charges on loans or overdrawn accounts
$ _____ other dollar costs, namely: _____
$ _____ Total of these other costs
$ _____ Total cost of substances, copied from intake worksheet
$ _____ Grand total (total from worksheet plus total of other costs)

My total take-home income during my drinking/drugging life was approximately

$ _____. Thus, I spent approximately _____ per cent of my take-home income on drugs and alcohol.

The total dollar cost of my drinking / drugging comes to about the same as a
__ vacation cruise
__ economy car
__ midrange car
__ luxury car
__ down payment on house
__ house payments for _____ years
__ _____ shares of stock in _____
__ _____ years of retirement income

__ _____

I distributed my alcohol and drug money approximately this way:
_____ per cent to alcoholic beverage companies and distributors
_____ per cent to bar, restaurant and tavern owners
_____ per cent to illegal drug growers, labs and dealers
_____ per cent to prescription drug companies and pharmacies
_____ per cent to other, namely: _____

The total time I spent getting, using and hung over from alcohol/drugs is approximately the amount of time it would take to:

__ raise a family
__ finish high school
__ finish community college
__ finish four year college
__ get a certificate in _____
__ write a book
__ build a _____
__ learn to _____

__ _____

142. People Say: My Feelings about Drinking/Using

__ I have never questioned my drinking/using or had any doubts about doing it
__ I had bad feelings about drinking/using occasionally but I suppressed them
__ I would argue with myself occasionally about drinking/using but not often
__ I knew that my drinking/using were really bad for me but I kept on anyway
__ I had arguments in my head about my drinking/using most of the time
__ I felt terrified that I was continuing to drink/use even though I knew it was bad for me
__ I had fights with myself about my drinking/using just about every day
__ Some voices in my head said go ahead and use, other voices said stop, don't; it was a kind of war in my head and it was torture
__ I'd look at ads that showed how glamorous drinking was, and I'd want to puke
__ I felt really depressed about my continuing to drink/use
__ I felt that I would kill myself if I continued to drink/use and that was OK with me
__ I felt that alcohol/drugs had not kept their promise to me, that I'd been had

__ _____

__ _____

__ _____

1 Body

2 Exposure

3 Activities

4 People

5 Feelings

6 Life Style

7 History

8 Culture

9 Treatment

1 Body   2 Exposure   3 Activities   4 People   5 Feelings   6 Life Style   7 History   8 Culture   9 Treatment

143. Narrowing Uncertainty about Credit and Blame in My History

Prolonged drinking/drugging creates insecurity about where the credit and the blame in life belong: to me or to the bottle/drug? Many active alcoholics/addicts had careers and some achieved distinction in various fields.

For example, Gen. Ulysses Grant was frequently drunk while directing the victorious Union armies during the American Civil War. Did Grant's inebriation contribute to or detract from his military triumphs?

Conversely, misfortune and failure strike people who are clean and sober as well as people who are addicted. Were the disasters and failures in your life due to your drinking/using, or would they have happened anyway?

Why does it matter? If you are Gen. Grant and you are considering getting sober, you may mentally link drunkenness with winning battles, and you may fear that sobriety spells military defeat. Or if you have suffered much misery while drinking/using, you may harbor the expectation that sobriety will turn your life into a rose garden, in which case you will be disappointed.

Because we only live this life once, we can never answer what-if questions about our history with complete certainty. But you can constrain the range of your self-doubts and get a more sharply focused image of yourself if you break the issue down into smaller pieces and give it some sober reflection. This is the purpose of the following two worksheets, Pages 196 and 199, and of the *General Ledger Worksheet* that follows them at Page 204.

144. My Positive Achievements Worksheet

This next worksheet (it starts on Page 196) is a tool to help you separate your positive qualities from your use of alcohol/drugs. No one is without good qualities, but after years of drinking/drugging it can be hard to remember this.

Interpret "positive achievements" here in the broadest sense, including not only the usual material advancements, promotions, achievements, honors, and awards, but also other ways in which the world gave you strokes, or would have, had it known.

For example: finished school, got award, got out of service alive, fell in love with wonderful person, cooked great ribs, got a smile from Ms. L., landed good job, fixed motorcycle, helped motherless kitten survive, got promoted, got compliment on quilt I made, bought house, got married, debugged P.'s program, had loving children, designed a new product, published a novel, ran a marathon, climbed Mt. Kilimanjaro, etc.

List each such item in the worksheet. Make copies and continue on additional pages if necessary. Be thorough. Your positive achievements are part of the wind that lifts the wings of your recovery from addiction.

Then, for each achievement:

Check Column 1 if you now feel that your drinking/drugging was a *brake* on this achievement.

- For example, during your drinking/drugging career you placed third in a local running club's annual 10K race. Your feeling in retrospect is that you got this far despite your drinking/drugging – you might have placed first or second if you had been clean and sober during your training. You check Column 1.

- While stoned you wrote a play based on Romeo and Juliet, but your conclusion in retrospect is that the play would have been more intelligent and might have been published if you had not been stoned while writing it. You check Column 1.

Check Column 2 if you feel that your drinking/drugging *facilitated* or made possible this achievement.

- For example, if you feel that by drinking/drugging you ran a more relaxed race, and if you had been sober you would have probably pulled a hamstring and not finished the race, you check Column 2.

- Or if you feel that you would not have had the originality to write a play based on Romeo and Juliet at all unless you had used marijuana, then you again check Column 2.

If you're not sure or the question doesn't apply, do the following short checklist to see whether the achievement might belong in one of the first two columns. Otherwise, check Column 3.

__ There was never any indication in my clean and sober earlier life that I had ability of the kind that this achievement was based on

__ All my education, preparation and training for this activity were under the influence

__ I never spent time in this activity clean and sober; I was always drunk or stoned while pursuing this

__ If I had not been drinking/using I would never have commenced the activity in which I had this achievement

If you checked all of these items, consider moving this achievement to Column 2 in your Positive Achievements Worksheet. Otherwise, it probably belongs in Column 1. Leave it in Column 3 if the above checklist still doesn't resolve the issue.

In the second worksheet (*Worksheet 45: Negative Events* , starting on Page 199), you'll be asked to make similar decisions about the negative side of your life story. In the concluding exercises of this domain, you'll be asked to reflect on your decisions in more detail and then to sum them up in a *General Ledger Worksheet* , Page 204.

1 Body   2 Exposure   3 Activities   4 People   5 Feelings   6 Life Style   7 History   8 Culture   9 Treatment

Worksheet 44: My Positive Achievements

MY POSITIVE ACHIEVEMENTS WORKSHEET			
My Lifetime Positive Achievements	(1) Drinking/ using was a brake on this achievement	(2) Drinking/ using facilitated this achievement	(3) Can't decide or N/A

1 Body   2 Exposure   3 Activities   4 People   5 Feelings   6 Life Style   7 History   8 Culture   9 Treatment

145. My Negative Events Worksheet

In the next worksheet, list the negative things that had an impact on your life during the time that you were drinking/using.

Don't do this exercise if thinking about the bad things in the past stresses you out and makes you feel like drinking/using. Come back when it feels safe to look at these issues.

"Negative events" means, for example: dropped out of school, got dumped by person I loved, didn't get promotion, got fired from job, got evicted from apartment for nonpayment of rent, shacked up with a loser, had children who hate me, was arrested for drunk driving, caught serious illness, fell off cliff, etc.

You may want to refer back to the Life Style Domain (Sixth Domain), Page 149, for completeness in doing this exercise. You might also review the Activities Domain (Third Domain), Page 73, at this time.

When you are ready to do this worksheet, then:

For each item on your list:

Put a checkmark in Column (1) if your drinking/using was a cause of this negative event.

> For purposes of this worksheet, "cause" means that the event would not have happened but for your drinking/using, or your drinking/using made this bad thing worse.

- For example, if you contracted the HIV virus during your drinking/drugging career, and you feel in retrospect that you got it from an infected partner, and that you would not have been with this person or you would not have failed to protect yourself but for the fact you had been drinking/using, then you check Column 1.

- If you were going to get laid off from a job for economic reasons (unrelated to your drinking) but on your last day you got drunk and sent the boss an email filled with obscenities and got fired for cause instead, making you ineligible for unemployment compensation, you check Column 1.

Check Column 2 if your drinking/using was unrelated to this negative event either as a cause or as an aggravating factor.

- For example, you caught the HIV virus when your dentist accidentally used an infected tool while you were having a routine tooth cleaning.

- You lost your job when your company was merged into its chief competitor and everyone was laid off.

If you're unsure where an event belongs, try this short checklist:

(Right margin tabs: 1 Body   2 Exposure   3 Activities   4 People   5 Feelings   6 Life Style   7 History   8 Culture   9 Treatment)

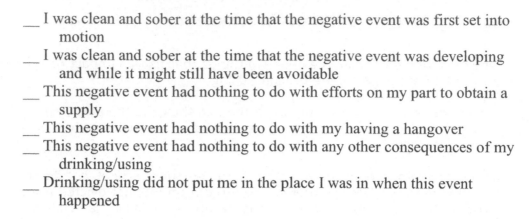

__ I was clean and sober at the time that the negative event was first set into motion

__ I was clean and sober at the time that the negative event was developing and while it might still have been avoidable

__ This negative event had nothing to do with efforts on my part to obtain a supply

__ This negative event had nothing to do with my having a hangover

__ This negative event had nothing to do with any other consequences of my drinking/using

__ Drinking/using did not put me in the place I was in when this event happened

If you checked any of these items, consider moving this event to Column 2 in the *Negative Events Worksheet*. Otherwise, it probably belongs in Column 1. If the above checklist still doesn't resolve the issue, check Column 3.

1 Body   2 Exposure   3 Activities   4 People   5 Feelings   6 Life Style   7 History   8 Culture   9 Treatment

Worksheet 45: Negative Events Worksheet

MY NEGATIVE EVENTS WORKSHEET			
Negative Events in My Life	(1) Drinking/ using was a cause of this	(2) Would have happened regardless	(3) Not sure or N/A

1 Body

2 Exposure

3 Activities

4 People

5 Feelings

6 Life Style

7 History

8 Culture

9 Treatment

146. Thinking About Credit and Blame in My Life

If you cannot think of any positive achievements and you are quite convinced you have no good qualities, or if you cannot think of any negative events in your life that were caused or aggravated by your drinking/drugging, try working the worksheets with someone who knows you, or with a group. Sometimes four or more eyes can see better than two.

Do you believe that you drank/used in order to dumb yourself down to the level of other people? Yes No

If you feel this way, why do you think it was necessary for you to carry this excess weight? What bad things would have happened if you had let your full abilities shine?

_____

_____

If you have superior abilities, do you feel that you still have to suppress them now that you are clean and sober?   Yes No

If so, why?

_____

_____

Do you think that while people are under the influence, they are good judges of how well they are performing at a task?   Yes No

Why or why not?

_____

_____

Do you think that you were a good judge of your own abilities while you were drinking/using?   Yes No

If not, which way did you tend to err – overestimating or underestimating yourself?
I overestimated   I underestimated

Why?

_____

_____

Do you feel that drinking/using made you smarter or more talented than you naturally are? Yes No

If so, how do you explain this, since intelligence and talent do not actually come in bottles, powders, herbs, or potions? (Or do they?)

_____

_____

Do you believe that the chemicals in drugs/alcohol, taken in repeated large doses, activated some creative part of your brain that otherwise lay latent? Yes No

Do you believe that large repeated doses of alcohol/drugs switched off some part of your brain that inhibited your creativity? Yes No

What if any is your scientific basis for such beliefs?

_____

_____

Is or was your performance under the influence actually better than otherwise?

_____

_____

In whose opinion?

_____

How do you explain that people are able to be creative without using addictive chemicals?

_____

_____

 Could you devise non-destructive ways of stimulating or disinhibiting your brain?

_____

_____

If you believe that some of your achievements should be credited to alcohol and drugs, rather than to you, how does that make you feel about yourself?

_____

_____

Have you considered that your sense of unworthiness may be the reason why you believe that something coming from outside yourself (alcohol/drugs) deserves the credit for your achievements rather than you? Yes No

Have you considered that your drinking/drugging may have caused or aggravated this sense of unworthiness? Yes No

If you are unalterably convinced that certain of your achievements were due to alcohol/drugs and not to your innate ability, hard work and/or good luck, are you prepared to abandon those pursuits, at least for a while, in order to maintain your sobriety? Yes No   Make a T-chart on the question (Chapter One).

Some people feel that they are responsible for all their achievements, but someone or something else is at fault for all the bad things that happened to them. Other people feel that they are responsible for everything bad that

1 Body   2 Exposure   3 Activities   4 People   5 Feelings   6 Life Style   7 History   8 Culture   9 Treatment

1 Body   2 Exposure   3 Activities   4 People   5 Feelings   6 Life Style   7 History   8 Culture   9 Treatment

happened to them and that credit for anything positive belongs to something outside them. Can you find a middle ground between these two extremes? Yes No

Explain your reasoning:

_____

_____

Can you use some entries from your *Negative Events Worksheet*, Page 199, in your *Daily Do* exercise, Aversion Flavor (Page 70)? Yes No

Can you use some entries from your *Positive Achievements Worksheet* (Page 196) in the Affirmation Flavor of your *Daily Do* exercise? Yes No

In reviewing the *Negative Events Worksheet*, do you see any instances where other people did you wrong? Yes No

If so, does it make any difference to your sobriety whether or not they apologize and pay compensation for the harm they caused you?   Yes No

Why or why not? Refer to the Feelings Domain (Fifth Domain) beginning Page 115 if you have not already done so.

_____

 In reviewing both the *Positive Achievements* and the *Negative Events Worksheets*, do you see any instances where you did harm to someone else? Yes No

If so, does it make any difference to your sobriety whether or not you apologize and pay compensation for the harm you caused? Yes No

Why or why not?

_____

Do you feel that some of the negative events in your life were the cause of your drinking/using? Yes No

If so, why do you think so?

_____

_____

147. Summing Up My Drinking/Using Career

This worksheet pulls together your previous work in this domain as a General Ledger. A General Ledger in bookkeeping is the master sheet that summarizes all the details in the underlying accounts. This worksheet has four compartments. Fill it in by copying the appropriate items from the previous worksheets, as follows.

- In the upper right corner, copy out the main items from your *Positive Achievements Worksheet* (Page 196) that represent or point to your own good qualities – qualities that did not "come out of a bottle." These would be the *Positive Achievements*, Column 1 items.

- In the upper left corner copy out the main items from your *Negative Events Worksheet* (Page 199) that represent harm caused in your life, or aggravated, by your drinking/drugging. These would be the *Negative Events*, Column 1 items.

- In the lower left corner, copy out the main items from your *Positive Achievements Worksheet* that represent good things that your drinking/drugging has brought into your life. These would be the *Positive Achievements*, Column 2 items.

- In the lower right corner, copy out the main items from your *Negative Events Worksheet* that represent harm that has come into your life unrelated to your drinking/drugging. These would be your *Negative Events*, Column 2 items.

1 Body

2 Exposure

3 Activities

4 People

5 Feelings

6 Life Style

7 History

8 Culture

9 Treatment

Worksheet 46: Summing Up My Drinking/Using Career

THE GENERAL LEDGER OF MY DRINKING/USING CAREER	
Negative Events That My Drinking/Drugging Caused in My Life	Positive Qualities That Belong to Me and Not to Alcohol/Drugs
Positive Things That My Drinking/Drugging Has Done For My Life	Negative Events That Happened In My Life Unrelated to Alcohol/Drugs

(left margin) 1 Body   2 Exposure   3 Activities   4 People   5 Feelings   6 Life Style   7 History   8 Culture   9 Treatment

148. Thinking About the Drinking/Using Life

Would you recommend to your children or your friends that they take your drinking/using life as a model to follow? __ Yes __ No. Why or why not?

_____

_____

_____

Do you know any people who are still drinking/using despite negative consequences and who have no thoughts about quitting? __ Yes __ No. If so, how do you feel about people who are in that situation?

_____

_____

_____

Do you know any people who say that they want to quit but who are not making any actual moves to quit? __ Yes __ No. If so, how do you feel about people who are at that point?

_____

_____

_____

_____

149. Saying Good-Bye

You are probably aware that some people experience termination of their drinking/using careers like the loss of a friend or loved one, and they go through a period of mourning or grief. The traditional exercises on this page help a person process grief and move on. Use a separate sheet of paper for these exercises.

- Pretend your drink/drug is a person you had a relationship with. Write a "Dear John/Jane" letter to it, explaining why you are breaking off the relationship. Write a response from "John/Jane" to you. Reply to the response.

Or:

- Pretend your drink/drug is a pet cat, dog or some other animal. Write a letter to the Animal Society why you are giving up this animal for adoption even if it means its destruction. Write a plea from the animal wanting to be saved. Respond to the plea.

1 Body   2 Exposure   3 Activities   4 People   5 Feelings   6 Life Style   7 History   8 Culture   9 Treatment

1 Body   2 Exposure   3 Activities   4 People   5 Feelings   6 Life Style   7 History   8 Culture   9 Treatment

Or:

- Pretend your drinking/using experience is a car you owned and that you are now taking to the junkyard. Write a letter to the junkyard owner explaining why you are dropping the car off. Write a reply from the junkyard owner refusing it (or from the car wanting you to take it back). Respond.

Or:

- Pretend that you are the sober Dr. Jekyll and that when you drank/used, you turned into the maniacal Mr. Hyde. Write a letter to Mr. Hyde saying why you don't want to see him – or be him – anymore. Write a reply from Mr. Hyde. Answer the reply.

150. **My Plan for Moving Forward from My History**

As a result of my work in this domain, I am going to start thinking more positively about the person I used to be before I took up using alcohol and/or other drugs. In particular, I am going to keep uppermost in mind the following good qualities I had as a sober young person:

_____

_____

_____

_____

After reviewing how I got started using alcohol and/or other drugs, I am going to forgive the people involved, including myself, because:

_____

_____

_____

_____

After reviewing my *General Ledger Worksheet* (page 203), I realize that I probably owe some people an apology and that I may have messes to clean up and unpaid debts that I need to settle, if possible. My specific plan in this regard is:

_____

_____

_____

_____

Now that I no longer spend my money using alcohol or other drugs, I plan to spend my money instead on:

_____

_____

_____

_____

Now that I no longer spend my time using alcohol or other drugs, I plan to spend my time instead on: (Cross-refer to the *My Activities Worksheet*, Page 74.)

_____

_____

_____

_____

After reviewing my *General Ledger Worksheet* (page 203), I realize that I have a number of good qualities, some great, some small. In this next period of my life, I am going to do the following specific things to develop my good qualities, bring my good qualities to the forefront, and let my good qualities govern my behavior:

_____

_____

_____

_____

_____

_____

_____

_____

_____

_____

_____

1 Body

2 Exposure

3 Activities

4 People

5 Feelings

6 Life Style

7 History

8 Culture

9 Treatment

1 Body   2 Exposure   3 Activities   4 People   5 Feelings   6 Life Style   7 History   8 Culture   9 Treatment

[Chapter Nine]

Eighth Domain: My Culture

Recovery takes place in a setting filled with messages that tend either to reinforce or to undermine an individual's sobriety. Literature and the media are major sources of persuasion about alcohol, tobacco, and other drugs. Having been exposed to these messages all of our lives, we tend to adopt them as if they were our own, and we may be unaware of their sources and sponsors.

Alcohol and drugs have been political, economic, and military issues in the histories of many cultures, and have been used as weapons of cultural domination and conquest. In some cultures, there are powerful economic and political interests – legitimate and otherwise – in support of alcohol and drug marketing. In turn, cultures contain powerful recovery values and can supply important emotional support for shaking off addiction and leading a drink- and drug-free life style. *La cultura cura* – culture can cure.

It may be useful in recovery to become aware of and to tune out the cultural messages that promote drinking and drugging, on the one hand, and to recognize and resonate with the cultural values that promote recovery, on the other. Participation in activities and movements that strengthen recovery messages in the culture can be a useful personal recovery tool for some individuals.

This work area points to some of the key issues in recognizing positive and negative cultural influences and allows you to begin to define yourself as a drink- and drug-free actor in your particular cultural setting.

You may get more value out of this domain if you work it in a culturally diverse group, so that you have the benefit of a broad range of experiences and perspectives.

1 Body

2 Exposure

3 Activities

4 People

5 Feelings

6 Life Style

7 History

8 Culture

9 Treatment

1 Body   2 Exposure   3 Activities   4 People   5 Feelings   6 Life Style   7 History   8 Culture   9 Treatment

151. General Attitudes

__ In my culture, drinking and using drugs is prohibited, period

__ In my culture, using drugs in any amount is looked down on but drinking in moderation is tolerated

__ In my culture, using certain drugs is tolerated, but using alcohol is prohibited

__ In my culture, children are allowed to drink wine or beer with meals

__ In my culture, children are allowed to inhale marijuana smoke

__ In my culture, parents and educators teach children to use marijuana, crack, heroin, speed and other drugs

__ In my culture, men and women are held to different expectations about drug and alcohol use

__ In my culture, people are not allowed to drink until they reach a certain legal age

__ In my culture, people can drink or use whatever they want, whenever they want

__ In my culture, the issue of drinking or using drugs is never discussed

__ In my culture, alcoholism and other drug addiction are very common and a large proportion of my people have died or are dying from this cause

__ My culture has used alcohol since the dawn of its recorded history

__ The use of alcohol is part of my religion

__ The use of certain drugs is part of my religion

__ In my culture, alcohol was unknown until relatively recent historical times

__ In my culture, drugs and alcohol were unknown until outsiders brought them in

__ In my culture, drugs and/or alcohol were only used on ceremonial occasions, within strict limits, and never for individual recreation

__ Drugs and alcohol have disabled and killed a large proportion of the people in my culture

__ Drugs and/or alcohol were/are used by outsiders as a weapon to oppress and destroy the culture of my people

__ There is reason to believe that the government deliberately introduces drugs into my community in order to divide and control my people

__ In my culture, many people cannot physically tolerate alcohol, at least at first

__ I would like to learn more about the history of alcohol/drugs in my culture

―― ――

152. Thinking About General Cultural Attitudes

Have you had the experience of transitioning from one culture to another, or do you know someone who did? Yes No

Did the cultural transition involve a change in attitudes toward drinking/using? Yes No

If so, how and why?

_____

_____

Use of alcohol was mostly unknown in Native American cultures until the European conquest. Can you see how a return to traditional values would be a means of counteracting alcoholism and addiction in Native American cultures today? Yes No

Native Americans in the 1700s formed the earliest known self-help alcoholism recovery groups in North America. Can you see why this might have happened?
Yes No

In many European cultures, drinking beer and wine was much more widespread before the Industrial Revolution, when public water supplies were nonexistent or polluted, than it is today. Can you see how a return to "traditional values" might not be helpful to overcoming alcoholism among descendants of European settlers?
Yes No

What cultural values would be more helpful?

_____

_____

British gunboats introduced opium into China as a means to undermine China's resistance to Western domination, and for the lucrative revenue to be made in the opium trade. Can you think of other instances in the past or in the world today where drugs and alcohol have been used as weapons of conquest and domination? Yes No

If so, give an example:

_____

_____

Malcolm X was a drug dealer, among other pursuits, before he straightened himself out and became a spokesman for the liberation of the African-American people. Can you see how drug use and drug dealing form an obstacle to the advancement of a people? Yes No

If so, explain how drug use and drug dealing are an obstacle to advancement of a people:

_____

_____

Can you find cultural values in African-American history that are useful in achieving freedom from drugs and alcohol? Yes No

If so, give an example:

_____

_____

The Conquistadors brought alcoholism to South America, along with smallpox and venereal diseases. Can you think of cultural values in the pre-conquest

1 Body   2 Exposure   3 Activities   4 People   5 Feelings   6 Life Style   7 History   8 Culture   9 Treatment

1 Body   2 Exposure   3 Activities   4 People   5 Feelings   6 Life Style   7 History   8 Culture   9 Treatment

and indigenous traditions that promote living a life free of alcohol and drugs? Yes No

If yes, give an example:

_____

_____

Can you identify sources of support for recovery in traditional Latino cultures, or in contemporary Hispanic-American cultures? Yes No

If yes, give an example:

_____

_____

_____

Can you see ways in which the culture treats women who are alcoholics/addicts differently than men? Yes No

Can you identify recovery needs that are specific to women in your culture? To men? If so, give examples:

_____

_____

_____

_____

_____

153. Models, Heroes and Villains

__ In my culture, there are celebrated heroes or geniuses who were addicted to
    drugs
__ In my culture, notorious villains or demons were known to use alcohol or drugs
__ In my culture, there are celebrated heroes or geniuses who are or were alcoholics
__ In my culture, people who do not use drugs or alcohol are held up as models
__ In my culture, people who use alcohol and smoke cigarettes are held up as
    models
__ In my culture, the role of "alcoholic" is a familiar one in literature and the arts
__ In my culture, the role of "drug addict" is a familiar one in literature and the arts
__ In my culture, the role of "family member" or "lover" or "friend" of an alcoholic
    or addict is a familiar one in literature and the arts
__ I personally know people in my culture who are active drug addicts
__ I personally know people in my culture who are active alcoholics
__ I know of people in my culture who are drug addicts and have done well in life
__ I know of people in my culture who are alcoholics and have done well in life

__ Most of the people I have known in my culture who are addicts have ended
   badly
__ Most of the people I have known in my culture who are alcoholics have ended
   badly
__ I have admired people in my culture who are/were alcoholics/addicts and wanted
   to live like them
__ I always despised people in my culture who are/were alcoholics/addicts and it
   troubles me to see that I have things in common with them

In my culture, people who are hooked on drugs/alcohol are considered
__ contemptible
__ sinners
__ criminal
__ psychologically defective
__ ill
__ suspect
__ stupid
__ misguided
__ normal
__ above average
__ geniuses
__ heroes
__ saints
__ all of the above

__ _____

154. Thinking About Models, Heroes and Villains

Can you think of famous people in your culture who were or are drunks or
addicts? Name some:

_____

_____

_____

When you think about these people, do you feel that their achievements
legitimize and excuse drug and alcohol addiction? __ Yes __ No.

Do you feel that their addiction was a source of their creativity? Or do you feel
sorry for them and see their addiction as a burden on them, without which they
would have lived longer and achieved more?

_____

_____

_____

1 Body   2 Exposure   3 Activities   4 People   5 Feelings   6 Life Style   7 History   8 Culture   9 Treatment

Most people don't intend to become alcoholics or addicts. However, a few people may have deliberately chosen this role for themselves, based perhaps on some early exposure to alcoholics/addicts whom they considered role models. When you were growing up, did you have role models who were active, obvious alcoholics/addicts? Yes No

If yes, what did you admire about such people?

_____

_____

Some characters in literature/movies/television give the role of alcoholic or dope addict a comic twist. Can you think of examples?

_____

_____

_____

Do you think that these funny characters make drinking or dope smoking more acceptable as a life choice, or do they make drunks/addicts seem ridiculous and unacceptable? More acceptable   More ridiculous

When you review your own drinking/drugging history, does it help you to see humor in it and to laugh at how you used to be? Yes No

In many movies and television shows, the principal characters appear with a cigarette in one hand and a drink in the other. Tobacco and alcoholic beverage companies typically pay the movie studios for these product placements. To what extent do you think the movies foster the belief that putting addictive substances like alcohol and tobacco into your body is normal behavior?

_____

_____

_____

Where do you think society spends more money: for advertising cigarettes and alcoholic beverages, or for educating people about the health hazards of smoking and alcohol consumption?   Advertising   Educating

155. Expectations

__ In my culture, teenagers are expected to experiment with drugs
__ In my culture, teenagers are expected to get drunk at social occasions
__ In my culture, teenagers using drugs or getting drunk is looked down upon
__ In my culture, drinking to excess at certain seasonal occasions is expected of
    grownups and you're an outcast if you don't do it
__ In my culture, drinking to excess is expected as part of one's working life and is
    necessary for career advancement

___ In my culture, drinking to excess is considered a bad mark and counts against a
　　person's reputation

___ In my culture, doing wild things while under the influence is expected and is
　　generally forgiven afterward

___ In my culture, being drunk or drugged is not considered an excuse for doing
　　things that are harmful to others or oneself

___ In my culture, it's expected that people under the influence will say what they
　　really believe

___ In my culture, it's expected that people under the influence will tell lies and say
　　things they don't mean

___ _____

___ _____

___ _____

156. Thinking about Cultural Expectations

How much of your excessive drinking/using scratched an itch inside of you, and
how much of it felt more like the performance of a social duty?

_____

_____

_____

Have you been in situations where you were expected to do heavy
drinking/drugging whether you felt like it or not? If so, give an example or
two:

_____

_____

Can you identify some cultures and/or subcultures where drinking/drugging to
excess were or are more or less mandatory behavior?

_____

_____

What purpose do you think such cultural pressures (to drink to excess) serve?

_____

_____

Some people believe that getting drunk relieves social tensions because it
creates a space ("time out") where people can say what they really feel about
each other, and then excuse themselves on the grounds of intoxication. Do you
believe that when people are drunk/stoned they are likely to be more truthful
than at other times?
Yes No

1 Body 2 Exposure 3 Activities 4 People 5 Feelings 6 Life Style 7 History 8 Culture 9 Treatment

1 Body   2 Exposure   3 Activities   4 People   5 Feelings   6 Life Style   7 History   8 Culture   9 Treatment

Do you believe that drunkenness/drug use promotes social harmony? Yes No

Or do customs that encourage excessive drinking promote violence and conflict that would not otherwise occur? Yes No

Can you think of cultural methods other than drunkenness that can relieve social tensions and allow people to speak their feelings without suffering harmful consequences? If so, give an example:

_____

_____

157. Stigma

__ In my culture, the person who admits to having a drug/alcohol problem can be denied employment or promotion

__ In my culture, the person who admits to a drug/alcohol problem can be denied health and/or life insurance

__ In my culture, the person who admits to a drug/alcohol problem can be denied security clearance

__ In my culture, the person who does not admit to their drug/alcohol problem and does not try to deal with it suffers less stigma than the person who does admit to it and who tries to do something about it

__ In my culture, the people who control jobs, insurance, security clearances and other benefits don't really believe that a person can ever recover from an alcohol/drug problem, no matter how long they have been clean and sober

__ In my culture, people who have stopped drinking/using don't believe themselves that they can ever recover, no matter how long they have been clean and sober

__ In my culture, people who are in recovery from an alcohol/drug problem hide their faces unless they are celebrities

__ _____

158. Thinking about Stigma

Have you experienced discrimination as a result of admitting to an alcohol/drug problem? Yes No

Do you know someone else who has? Yes No

In the U.S., the Americans with Disabilities Act (ADA) is supposed to protect alcoholics/addicts against discrimination based on their status as alcoholics/addicts (although not, of course, against consequences of their drinking/using). Were you aware that this legal protection exists? Yes No

Do you think that the public is sufficiently informed about the availability of this protection? Yes No

Which do you think is a greater security risk: (1) a person who drinks or uses drugs and does not admit to having a problem, or (2) a person who has admitted a problem, gone through treatment and stopped drinking/using?

Explain your answer:

_____

_____

After how much time clean and sober should an employee be considered fully recovered for purposes of employment? _____

Do you believe that you should always be considered a greater employment risk than the average person because you used to drink/drug too much in the past? Yes No

Why or why not?

_____

_____

Do you think that you are a better employee, a worse one, or no different, as a consequence of your having stopped drinking/using? Better Worse Same

Do you see any advantages or lessons that your recovery experience has brought you, besides the fact that you no longer drink/use? Yes No

Why or why not?

_____

_____

What methods have other social groups used to overcome unfair discrimination in recent decades? Has concealing their faces been a generally successful tactic for oppressed minorities? Or have such groups made more progress against stigma by being open and in-your-face about their distinctness? Discuss:

_____

_____

_____

_____

1 Body   2 Exposure   3 Activities   4 People   5 Feelings   6 Life Style   7 History   8 Culture   9 Treatment

1 Body   2 Exposure   3 Activities   4 People   5 Feelings   6 Life Style   7 History   8 Culture   9 Treatment

159. Consistency

__ In my culture, the issue of drinking and drug use is handled in an honest, consistent manner

__ In my culture, how people view drunken behavior depends on who the drunk is

__ In my culture, people who use some kind of deadly addictive substances are viewed with approval while those who use other deadly addictive substances are punished

__ In my culture, there are big differences in the way that wealthy alcoholics/addicts and poor alcoholics/addicts are treated

__ In my culture, there are big differences in the treatment of alcoholics/addicts of different nationalities and ethnic backgrounds

__ In my culture, there are big differences in the way that men and women are treated as regards alcohol/drugs

__ In my culture, very large sums of money are spent to promote the use of approved lethal addictive substances and other very large sums are spent to prohibit the use of unapproved lethal addictive substances

__ In my culture, there is a big gap between preaching and practice as concerns drugs and alcohol

__ _____

__ _____

160. Thinking About Cultural Consistency

Cultures rarely follow logic, but few areas display such formidable challenges to logic as the drug and alcohol issue in the U.S. today. Currently, the drugs that cause by far the greatest mortality and illness in society (tobacco and alcohol) are legal, readily available, and widely promoted, whereas billions are spent to interdict and punish a fraction of the users of other drugs whose impact on society's life and health is comparatively minor. Do you think that this type of inconsistency is helpful or not helpful to a culture's legitimacy?

_____

It has been said that whether addiction is handled as a disease meriting treatment or as a sin and crime deserving of punishment depends on the person's social class and ethnic background. Do you agree? Yes No

Do you know instances where the society's response to addiction has been influenced by considerations of the addict's wealth, color, nationality, celebrity status, or other extrinsic factors? Yes No

Have factors of this type played a role in your own addiction and/or recovery? Yes No

If you feel that the society's policies on drugs and alcohol have little consistency, how does this awareness impact your own recovery?

_____

Do you feel your recovery is better served by ignoring the cultural and political issues? Yes No

Or do you feel that at some point you might want to join in organized efforts to bring greater consistency to the way the society handles the drugs and alcohol issue? Yes No.
Explain your thinking.

_____

_____

161. Economics

___ In my culture, the production and distribution of alcohol was/is mainly a local homebrew affair

___ In my culture, production and distribution of alcohol is mainly in the hands of big businesses and/or government

___ In my culture, the production and distribution of drugs was/is mainly a small homegrown affair

___ In my culture, the production and distribution of drugs involves big money and government

___ In my culture, the bulk of the alcoholic beverage market consists of people who are excessive drinkers or alcoholics

___ In my culture, some people get very rich by supplying alcohol to alcoholics

___ In my culture, some people get very rich by supplying drugs to addicts

___ In my culture, some people who supply alcohol to alcoholics go to jail

___ In my culture, some people who supply drugs to addicts go to jail

___ In my culture, liquor companies pay large sums of money to put on sports evcnts

___ In my culture, liquor companies pay large sums of money to film companies and TV companies to have actors drink their brand on camera

___ In my culture, many newspapers and magazines depend on liquor company money for a substantial part of their revenue

___ In my culture, liquor companies and cigarette companies are owned by the same conglomerates

___ In my culture, liquor and cigarette companies make big political contributions and are a powerful force in government

___ I would like to learn more about the economics of alcohol, drugs and tobacco in my culture

_____

_____

1 Body

2 Exposure

3 Activities

4 People

5 Feelings

6 Life Style

7 History

8 Culture

9 Treatment

1 Body   2 Exposure   3 Activities   4 People   5 Feelings   6 Life Style   7 History   8 Culture   9 Treatment

162. Thinking About the Economics of Addiction

In the U.S., ten per cent of the drinkers drink about three quarters of all the alcoholic beverages, and five per cent of the drinkers drink about half. In other words, alcoholics and other heavy drinkers form the alcoholic beverage industry's main source of revenue.

If a pill or other method were invented tomorrow that took away the craving to drink, do you think that it would meet with universal acclaim, or do you foresee powerful economic interests working to undermine it and oppose it?

_____

_____

What, besides legality, is the difference between the owners of alcoholic beverage and tobacco companies and the heads of drug cartels?

_____

_____

How does it make you feel when you realize that there is big money being made from addiction – that powerful economic interests need people to be addicted, for their profit?

_____

_____

Do you see yourself blocking out and not thinking about the cultural, political and economic framework of addiction, or do you believe that greater awareness about these issues would be helpful to your recovery? Block out Think about Why?

_____

_____

Do you see yourself becoming involved in advocacy about drug and alcohol issues as part of your personal recovery plan?   Yes No

163. Definitions and Solutions

___ In my culture, people choose alcoholism/drug addiction as a life style or a
      philosophical statement, sort of the way people choose vegetarianism or
      getting tattoos or growing beards
___ In my culture, people drift into alcoholism or addiction because they neglect
      their health, the way some people become diabetics or develop high blood
      pressure or gout
___ In my culture, people become alcoholics/addicts because they were reckless in
      the amount and type of substances they used, like playing Russian roulette
___ In my culture, people become alcoholics/addicts because they were ignorant
      about how much and what type of drugs they could safely use

__ In my culture, people become alcoholics/addicts because they fall prey to the illness of addiction

__ In my culture, people become alcoholics/addicts because they are hedonists and put their own selfish pleasure above everything else

__ In my culture, people become alcoholics/addicts because they were genetically or physically predisposed to it

__ In my culture, people become alcoholics/addicts because they are evil and given to the ways of sin

__ In my culture, people believe any or all of the above, depending on how they feel about the person they're analyzing

__ In my culture, people believe that alcoholics/addicts should be punished until they repent

__ In my culture, people believe that alcoholics/addicts should be shown the error of their ways and reformed

__ In my culture, people believe that alcoholics/addicts should get medical treatment and be restored to health

__ In my culture, people believe that alcoholics/addicts should be shown the irrationality of their behavior and be reprogrammed

__ In my culture, people believe that alcoholics/addicts should be cast out, ignored and left to die

__ In my culture, people believe that alcoholics/addicts should be allowed to live but should not be allowed to have children

__ In my culture, people believe that alcoholics/addicts who refuse or fail at treatment should be executed

__ _____

__ _____

__ _____

164. Thinking About Definitions and Solutions

If addiction is defined as no problem, then the addict is left alone. Do you think that addiction is no problem and that the addict should be left alone? Yes No

Or do you agree that addiction is a problem and that something has to be done about people who are addicted? Yes No

What would happen if there were no treatment and no consequences of any kind for people who drink/drug without limit? Explain your reasoning.

_____

_____

One purpose of definitions is to assign ownership. Defining addiction as a medical disease puts doctors in charge of it. If addiction is stupidity or bad thinking, then the solution lies with educators. If addiction is a sin, then religious leaders own the solution. If addiction is defined as a crime, then judges make the diagnosis and prison guards administer the treatment. If

1 Body

2 Exposure

3 Activities

4 People

5 Feelings

6 Life Style

7 History

8 Culture

9 Treatment

1 Body   2 Exposure   3 Activities   4 People   5 Feelings   6 Life Style   7 History   8 Culture   9 Treatment

addiction is defined as mainly genetic, then some people will call for eugenics or sterilization. When addiction is defined as a many-sided problem – a biopsychosocial disorder – then several groups of professionals have joint ownership.

If you had a choice, which set or sets of professionals would you prefer to have in charge of the society's drinking/drugging problem? Whom would you want in charge of your own drinking/drugging issue? Why?

_____

_____

_____

In recent decades, Democrats and Republicans have tended to differ on whether addiction is a disease meriting treatment (Lyndon B. Johnson, 1960s) or a moral deviation deserving punishment (Ronald Reagan, 1980s). In some states, addiction issues involving a clash between the medical and the penal definitions of drug use (treatment v. incarceration) have been on the ballot (e.g. Prop. 36 in California, November 2000). How does it make you feel that basic concepts of your self-definition and your recovery path have become partisan political issues? Do you feel that your personal recovery is better served by shutting your eyes to the political football game, or by becoming involved in it? Why?

_____

_____

As you look back on it, to what extent do you believe your own drinking/drugging was (check all that apply):

    __ a life style choice
    __ a career decision
    __ a marriage or relationship choice
    __ a philosophical/ideological decision
    __ a religious conversion
    __ an accident
    __ a result of ignorance on your part
    __ a result of negligence on your part
    __ a result of recklessness on your part
    __ a scientific experiment
    __ a disease you contracted
    __ a result of a selfish, hedonist streak in your character
    __ a result of a weakness in your personality
    __ an inevitable expression of your genetic makeup
    __ a piece of wickedness and malice on your part
    __ all of the above to some extent
    __ none of the above

Which explanation or set of explanations (in the short checklist above) makes you feel like relapsing, if any?

_____

_____

Which explanation or set of explanations, if any, makes you feel stronger in your personal recovery?

_____

_____

Do explanations and definitions of this type matter to your personal recovery? Yes   No

Why do they or don't they?

_____

_____

Does everyone define their drinking/drugging involvement in the same way? Yes No

What is your basis for your answer?

_____

_____

165. Take Apart an Ad or Commercial

If you feel safe doing so, have a sharp, detailed look at a print ad or a billboard for an alcoholic beverage, or record a TV beer or wine commercial and play it back scene by scene. Then ask yourself:

- What is the ad saying about the social status of people who drink the product?
- What is the ad saying about the health of the people who drink the product?
- What is the ad saying about the sexual desirability of the people who drink the product?
- What is the ad saying about the emotions that go along with drinking the product?
- What is the ad saying about the kind of situation where people drink the product?
- What is the ad saying about the social acceptability of drinking the product?

1 Body   2 Exposure   3 Activities   4 People   5 Feelings   6 Life Style   7 History   8 Culture   9 Treatment

To what extent are the ad's messages explicit? To what extent are they implied? Do the implied messages go beyond, or contradict, some of the explicit messages? Discuss:

_____

_____

Is the ad pushing any of your personal triggers? (Refer to the Exposure, People and Feelings Domains (Second, Fourth and Fifth Domains).

_____

In your real life experience, are the ad's messages about the status, health, sexual desirability, emotions, situations, and acceptability of drinking the beverage fair and accurate?

_____

Do you see in the ad any direct or indirect endorsement of:
___ under-age drinking
___ driving under the influence
___ unsafe sex
___ alcoholism
___ other public health concern, namely:

_____

_____

If celebrities appear in the ad, what is your feeling about the fact that they were paid big money to appear in the ad?

_____

_____

If you became a celebrity, would you appear in an ad that promotes alcoholic beverages? Yes No   Does it depend on how much they offered? Yes No

The famous 1950s Brooklyn Dodgers pitcher Don Newcombe, a recovering alcoholic, sued a major beer company for using his picture in a beer ad, and won. Do you think he did the right thing? Yes No

Cigarette packages are required to carry warning labels about the hazards of smoking. Would you find it helpful to your recovery (or do you think you might have been helped at an earlier stage) if alcoholic beverage containers carried similar kinds of labels?   Helpful   Not helpful

Explain your thinking:

_____

_____

Would you find it helpful to your recovery (or do you think it might have helped you at an earlier stage) if there were public service print and TV ads educating people about the dangers of alcohol addiction? Helpful Not helpful

Explain your thinking:

_____

_____

_____

166. Helpful and Burdensome Elements in My Cultures

The worksheet on Page 226 gives a starter list of a few of the many cultures and subcultures that you may have experienced. ("Culture" is used very broadly here to mean the traditions, customs and values of any group or organization.) For each culture or subculture of which you have knowledge, name the traditions, customs, values or beliefs of that group that you find supportive of your recovery, and those that you don't.

For example:

- You may find the tradition of extended family ties in many Latino cultures helpful to support your recovery. There may be other elements that you do not find so helpful to you.

- In Japanese culture, you may find that the tradition of self-control is helpful to your recovery, but the custom of heavy drinking at company events is a hazard.

- In African-American culture, the struggle for freedom may be a powerful model for your personal liberation from addiction. Other elements in the culture may not be helpful to you.

- In Western (US regional) culture, you may have experienced the custom of outdoor living as helpful to your recovery, but the tradition of barroom brawling less so.

- In the culture of the labor movement, you may look on the tradition of solidarity as a source of strength for your recovery, but you may find the sentimentality about the worker's beer less inspiring.

- In the NASCAR culture, the emphasis on the drivers' need for alertness, precision, and quick reflexes may be helpful to maintain your sobriety, but the heavy barrage of beer and tobacco advertising may contradict that message.

1 Body   2 Exposure   3 Activities   4 People   5 Feelings   6 Life Style   7 History   8 Culture   9 Treatment

Worksheet 47: Analyzing Cultures for Harmful / Helpful Values

ELEMENTS OF CULTURE THAT HINDER AND ELEMENTS THAT HELP MY RECOVERY		
Culture or Subculture	Parts that Hinder My Recovery	Parts that Help My Recovery
African-American cultures		
Art and sculpture scene		
Body-building culture		
Car culture		
Chinese culture		
Classical music scene		
Computer programming worlds		
Cuban culture		
Culture of churches, synagogues and temples		
Culture of contractors and building trades people		
Culture of corporate management		
Culture of fishermen and women		
Culture of gardening		
Culture of hiking and the outdoors		
Culture of hospitals		
Culture of party politics		
Culture of poverty		
Culture of professional sports		
Culture of salespeople		
Culture of schools and education		
Culture of the 60s and 70s		
Culture of the entertainment industry		
Culture of the environmentalist movement		
Culture of the Internet		
Culture of the stock market		
Disney world		
Dot-com subculture		
English culture		
Farming and agricultural world		
Filipino culture		

1 Body   2 Exposure   3 Activities   4 People   5 Feelings   6 Life Style   7 History   8 Culture   9 Treatment

ELEMENTS OF CULTURE THAT HINDER AND ELEMENTS THAT HELP MY RECOVERY		
Culture or Subculture	Parts that Hinder My Recovery	Parts that Help My Recovery
Folk music scene		
French culture		
Friends TV program		
Gay / Lesbian / Bisexual / Transgender cultures		
German culture		
Ghetto culture		
Gourmet culture		
Hillbilly culture		
Hip Hop Culture		
Hunting culture		
Irish culture		
Italian culture		
James Bond movies		
Japanese culture		
Jazz music scene		
Labor movement culture		
Life Styles of the rich and famous		
Mexican culture		
Military culture		
My family culture		
Native American cultures		
New England culture		
Porn subculture		
Prison culture		
Puerto Rican culture		
Rave and club culture		
Reality TV show culture		
Rock music scene		
Runners' world		

1 Body   2 Exposure   3 Activities   4 People   5 Feelings   6 Life Style   7 History   8 Culture   9 Treatment

ELEMENTS OF CULTURE THAT HINDER AND ELEMENTS THAT HELP MY RECOVERY		
Culture or Subculture	Parts that Hinder My Recovery	Parts that Help My Recovery
Russian culture		
Science and research subculture		
Security guards' world		
Southern (US regional) culture		
Suburban culture		
Survivors TV program		
Television industry culture		
The Simpsons TV program		
Vietnamese culture		
Western (US regional) culture		
Working class cultures		
World of high fashion		
World of lawyers		
Yoga scene		
Zen culture		

1 Body   2 Exposure   3 Activities   4 People   5 Feelings   6 Life Style   7 History   8 Culture   9 Treatment

167. Analyzing Your Cultural Values Worksheet

If a particular culture or subculture doesn't have any significant elements that you find supportive for your recovery, and many that you find burdensome, what would be a sensible thing for you to do with regard to that world?

_____

If there is a subculture that has a lot of strong, supportive elements for your recovery, what specific moves could you make to become more closely connected with that world?

_____

When you look at the various things that you find supportive in various subcultures, what do they have in common? What, in general, are the cultural messages that help you progress in your recovery?

_____

_____

What, in general, are the cultural messages that burden your recovery work?

_____

_____

If you could design a subculture that would contain the maximum support and the minimum burden for your personal recovery, what would it look like? (Use a separate sheet.)

168. My Cultural Plan

__ Sometimes individuals can change their whole culture, and I may be one of those individuals and this may be one of those times

__ I can't change my whole culture, but I can do something to change my little world around me

__ I can't change anything or anyone but myself

__ I can't even change myself, so why worry about my culture

__ If I could change my little world around me I would have more support for continuing to change myself

__ By becoming active in changing my culture I will reinforce my personal sobriety program

1 Body   2 Exposure   3 Activities   4 People   5 Feelings   6 Life Style   7 History   8 Culture   9 Treatment

1 Body   2 Exposure   3 Activities   4 People   5 Feelings   6 Life Style   7 History   8 Culture   9 Treatment

For the sake of my recovery from drugs/alcohol, I will actively oppose certain parts of my culture, namely:

_____

_____

_____

For the sake of my recovery, I will consciously filter out and ignore certain parts of my culture and not let them affect me, namely:

_____

_____

_____

_____

For the sake of my recovery, I will consciously adopt certain parts of my culture and work to strengthen these, namely:

_____

_____

_____

_____

___ I will work my cultural plan by myself
___ I want to link up with other people as part of my cultural plan, namely with:

_____

_____

Write your three-month review and your one-year review on a separate sheet.

[Chapter Ten]

Ninth Domain: My Treatment and Support Groups

A small minority of people who suffer from alcohol/drug problems obtain treatment. The quality of treatment for those who are able to obtain it varies widely. Some patients come out of treatment programs with new insights into their situation and with strong motivation to rebuild their lives. Others feel confused and abused, and drop out and relapse, or relapse shortly after discharge. Which outcome holds for you will depend in part on what you bring to the treatment experience, and in part on the quality of the treatment program and staff.

Probably more important than the treatment experience will be your experience with support groups. Treatment rarely lasts more than a few weeks and insurance restrictions often cut treatment to much shorter periods – sometimes just days. You may have spent quite a few years building your current alcohol/drug involvement, and it is unlikely that you will shake it off completely during the average treatment period. Support groups are likely to be the major source of outside "people" help available to you after treatment is over.

In this work area, you can get oriented to the world of treatment and support groups so that you can form realistic expectations and make a plan to get what you need from them to help your recovery.

169. People Say: How I Got Into Treatment

__ This is my first time in treatment
__ I have been in treatment _____ times before
__ I have done outpatient treatment before
__ I have done inpatient treatment before
__ I have participated in therapeutic communities
__ I graduated successfully from treatment before and then relapsed
__ I dropped out of treatment early and then relapsed
__ I was thrown out of a previous treatment program
__ I checked myself into this program voluntarily

Sidebar (right margin, top to bottom): 1 Body　2 Exposure　3 Activities　4 People　5 Feelings　6 Life Style　7 History　8 Culture　9 Treatment

__ I am here at the strong suggestion of someone close to me
__ I am here because a spouse told me "or else"
__ I am sent here by an Employee Assistance Program
__ I am here because a judge or probation officer gave me a choice of this or jail
__ I was picked up and sent here after a psychiatric emergency
__ I was sent here from the Emergency Room after an alcohol/drug overdose
__ I selected this treatment program from among several alternatives
__ I had no choice about where I ended up for treatment
__ I thought about treatment for some time before going in
__ The decision to enter treatment came about rather suddenly

__ _____

170. Thinking About How I Got Into Treatment

If you were forced to go into treatment, you may be resisting the whole experience like a turtle in its shell. If so, you could be making a strategic error. The first thing to be learned from treatment is how to avoid having to go to treatment a second time.

If you entered treatment voluntarily, you may be put off by some staff attitudes that assume you were forced into treatment, like other patients. Try to appreciate that treatment staff are typically overworked and underpaid.

Are you in treatment to pacify a Significant Other? Your S.O. may be very uncomfortable with the responsibility of having sent you there. The sooner you can find some motivation within you to be in treatment for reasons of your own, the easier things will go for your strained relationship – and for you.

Is this your first treatment experience? If so, try to learn from the repeat visitors. They can often explain the ropes to you more quickly than any staff lecture or handout. The fact that a patient comes back for treatment can mean a variety of things; try asking the individual why they are back.

Are you back for a second or third time? Assuming the program and its staff have not materially changed, what makes you think the outcome this time will be different than the last time(s)? If you have made sincere efforts to practice what the program instructed, but this has not worked for you, perhaps you should try a different kind of program. Consider asking staff or looking on the Internet for referral to a program with a different therapeutic approach.

Were you sent to treatment after a psychiatric or medical emergency? If so, be sure to maintain contact with your psychiatrist or regular physician, or establish a relationship if you had emergency treatment only. Few substance abuse counselors also have credentials to do psychiatric or other medical treatment. You will almost certainly want to have follow-up contact with a physician after treatment is over.

171. People Say: About Treatment Staff

__ The treatment staff helped me to understand my problem better
__ The staff pressured me to admit to problems I don't feel I had
__ I felt safe to talk about what was really going on with me
__ I never developed a feeling of trust for the staff to where I would open up
__ The staff helped me feel more motivated to stay clean and sober
__ The staff made me feel more determined to drink and use as soon as I could
__ I felt that staff and I were mostly pulling in the same direction
__ I felt that staff and I were too often pulling in opposite directions
__ The staff helped me survive as a sober person after discharge
__ The staff set me up to relapse as soon as I got out
__ The staff treated me in a professional manner
__ The staff berated me and humiliated me
__ The staff respected my confidences
__ I felt that the staff used my confidential information against me
__ I felt that staff really made me think and I am grateful for that
__ I felt that staff were basically doing a brainwash and I didn't go for it
__ The staff seemed up on the literature and knew what they were talking about
__ The staff seemed pretty ignorant and unread and just repeated slogans
__ The staff respected our intelligence and tried to get us to use it to help ourselves
__ The staff called us stupid and asked us to stop thinking and trust them on faith
__ I felt the staff were my friends and were working alongside me
__ I felt the staff were like Nazis ordering me around
__ I felt the staff were good educators, sharing useful knowledge with me
__ I felt the staff were basically guards checking that I was still there
__ The staff appreciated that we had done a smart thing to come into treatment
__ The staff told us that our being there was proof we were dumb
__ The staff made an effort to understand me as an individual
__ The staff treated me like just another widget on their assembly line
__ The staff took pleasure in helping me and watching me get stronger in my sobriety
__ The staff got off on humiliating me and watching me fall apart
__ When I asked a question, staff answered it thoughtfully
__ When I asked a question, staff didn't know the answer and said I was "in denial"
__ The staff helped us patients to get along with each other
__ The staff tried to divide us patients and set us against each other
__ When I tried to complain about a staff member I was punished for it
__ My complaint about a staff member was heard impartially and handled fairly
__ The staff offered me choices
__ The staff said I had no choices and had to follow their "suggestions" or else
__ The staff has followed up after discharge to see how I am doing
__ I have never heard from the staff after my discharge
__ I liked some of the staff, and I hated others
__ I decided to stay clean and sober because of what I learned in the treatment program
__ I used the shortcomings of the program as an excuse to relapse
__ I decided to stay clean and sober to spite an arrogant counselor who said I couldn't

Sidebar (top to bottom): 1 Body   2 Exposure   3 Activities   4 People   5 Feelings   6 Life Style   7 History   8 Culture   **9 Treatment**

___ Some of the counselors are my friends today and I send them holiday cards
___ I didn't feel moved by the program one way or another
___ I feel very grateful to the program and everything it did for me
___ I was so glad to get out of there and would never go back
___ I would gladly go back there if I ever needed to
___ I would not recommend the experience to my friends
___ I have referred people to the program and will continue to do so

___ _____

172. Thinking About Treatment Staff

One indication of the quality of a treatment program is the professional qualifications of its staff. Look near the door for a listing of staff, if there is one, or else ask reception to show you a paper that lists staff qualifications. The better programs tend to show MD and PhD degrees in supervisory positions, and graduate degrees such as MA, MSW (Master in Social Work), MFCC (Master of Family and Child Counseling) and LCSW (Licensed Clinical Social Worker) – the equivalent of Master's degrees plus several thousand hours of supervised clinical training – in all counseling positions.

At the lower end of the scale, program staff will consist basically of recovering addicts and alcoholics who have taken a correspondence course or a weekend seminar. You may find some excellent individuals there, but don't expect them to rise above the limits of their personal experience. How does your program rate?

_____

For at least a hundred years people have been debating whether staff who have a personal background as alcoholics/addicts are more effective than staff who do not. The most recent research suggests that it makes no difference. What makes a recovery counselor effective is, first of all, empathy – the ability to listen and to care.

The place to look for the advantages of being with someone who has "been there" is in your self-help support groups. High quality counselors are supportive, non-threatening, available, and have wisdom broader than their personal experience. Have you had the good fortune to work with such a counselor?

A few counselors have a confrontational, authoritarian, in-your-face style. Frequently, these counselors are accountable for the bulk of the program's dropouts and relapses. If your counselor humiliates you, ridicules you, or otherwise makes you feel like you want to leave the program and/or relapse, consider asking for a reassignment to a different counselor. If there are no procedures to obtain a reassignment or you are punished for asking, consider lodging a complaint with the state licensing authorities. Have you known this type of counselor?

Staff work with people who have alcohol/drug issues all day, every day. You are guaranteed to be able to learn something from them. Even if staff members may have some wrong ideas or poor attitudes, they have a tremendous amount of valuable experience and insight. It might be the case that the counselor who annoys you the most has the most to teach you. You can learn from every staff member, including the nurses, orderlies, receptionist, clerical staff, kitchen workers, security guards, and custodians. You will not help yourself if you are rude to anyone. If you listen and ask questions, you may learn a lot. What would be your opinion of a patient who on the first day claimed to know everything better than staff?

If you lie back and expect that staff will perform some kind of miraculous recovery surgery on you as you sleep, metaphorically speaking, you will be disappointed. Treatment is more like school: what you get out of it depends on how much effort you put into it. The sooner you understand that your progress mainly depends on you, the more helpful staff can be and the happier and more successful the treatment experience will be for you.

173. Taking What You Can Use From the Treatment Program

Patients come into treatment with a great variety of histories and with ever-changing needs, but many treatment programs are structured around a narrow, unchanging curriculum. If that curriculum happens to match your needs, you're in luck. If not, you're going to have to do some extra work in order to get what you need.

In many programs, the main purpose of the curriculum is to accustom you to attending AA, NA or other 12-step meetings after your discharge. The program may be designed to prepare you mentally to do the "first step" of AA (to believe that you are powerless over alcohol and that your life has become unmanageable). Or the program may take you deeper into the world-view of the 12 steps, such as "surrender to a Higher Power" and "ask God to remove your character defects." You may also be introduced to AA rituals such as holding hands and saying prayers and slogans together. Frequently the only reading to which you will have access in programs is AA or NA literature.

If this type of content appeals to you and motivates you to stay clean and sober, you don't have a problem. But if this atmosphere fails to inspire you with confidence, makes you uncomfortable, and causes you stress, as it does many people, you may have a difficult choice to make. If you voice your discomfort freely and honestly to the group, you may be criticized, ostracized, and made to feel like a troublemaker. If you suppress your honest feelings so as to avoid rocking the boat, you may feel false inside and your self-esteem may plunge.

If the 12-step approach does not resonate with you, you are not alone. Out of 100 people who try AA, only five stick with it for as long as a year.[30] And if you choose a different path, you are not doomed. The majority of alcoholics (60 per cent) who achieve long-term sobriety do it without using AA.[31]

Sidebar (right margin, top to bottom): 1 Body   2 Exposure   3 Activities   4 People   5 Feelings   6 Life Style   7 History   8 Culture   **9 Treatment**

---

[30] Don McIntire, "How Well Does A.A. Work? An Analysis of Published A.A. Surveys (1968-1996) and Related Analyses/Comments," *Alcoholism Treatment Quarterly* 18, No. 4 (2000):1-18.

[31] George Vaillant MD, "Interview: A Doctor Speaks." A.A. Grapevine, May 2001, p. 36.

If you feel uncomfortable with the slant of your treatment program, make a Sobriety T-Chart (Chapter One). What is better, or less bad, for your personal sobriety: speaking your mind honestly, or keeping quiet and pretending to agree? It depends on your background and on the specific circumstances.

Are you confident enough to speak your feelings honestly in front of a group, even if you are attacked for it? If so, speak out.

Do you feel too shaky to speak up and feel safer putting up a protective false front? If so, be silent, at least for now.

Among the staff there is probably at least one to whom you can express your feelings of discomfort in confidence. Tell that person frankly what you feel and believe. The program will never raise its level of patient services unless patients speak to someone about it.

In a modern, quality treatment facility, counselors will be skilled in a variety of treatment approaches, and will endeavor to find one that matches your individual characteristics, culture, history, and other particular needs. Professionally qualified counselors will respect your religious beliefs or lack thereof and will show you tools to help you stay clean and sober either way.

A quality treatment facility will offer a choice of support groups – 12-step and alternatives to 12-step – and will encourage you to investigate and to select the option that best helps you maintain your Sobriety Priority.

As a consumer of chemical dependency treatment services, you have the same rights as any other consumer. You have the right to form opinions, develop concerns, lodge complaints, and to advocate for your issues concerning the quality and quantity of treatment. There may be advocacy groups already formed in your community, or you may want to form one after you return from treatment.

When talking to a group or to a counselor about your feelings, remember always the Sobriety Priority. A thing is good or bad depending on whether it helps you or hinders you in staying sober and off alcohol and other drugs. Try to avoid making sweeping generalizations, especially ones that are confrontational. Avoid rhetorical questions and speeches.

Helping patients stay clean and sober is the only legitimate reason for a treatment facility to exist. If you can demonstrate that some aspect of the program works counter to that purpose for you, you will have made a legitimate point. But, on the other hand, if you cannot find a substantial, credible relationship between your concern and your Sobriety Priority, then maybe this particular concern should take a back seat for the moment. (Does your sobriety really depend on a pass to go home and get your blue sweater?) Any kind of social or organizational setting requires individuals to make some compromises and concessions.

Next is a worksheet to help you become a more effective advocate to get what you need from your treatment program. In the left column, describe your initial gut reaction when you find something in the program that makes you uncomfortable. In the right column, examine the need that underlies your reaction in terms of the Sobriety Priority. Use the first person singular ("I feel" or "I need" or "for me" etc.).

Here are some examples:

Worksheet 48: Getting What You Need in the Treatment Context (Example)

EFFECTIVE ADVOCACY TO GET WHAT YOU NEED IN A TREATMENT CONTEXT	
Less effective: Gut Reaction	**More effective: Sobriety Priority**
I'm not powerless! I came here on my own two legs, didn't I?	For me, the feeling of being powerless is a strong trigger to drink or use. It's essential for me to feel that staying sober or relapsing is my decision to make. I want to be active and in charge of my own recovery. That's why I decided to come here.
What do you mean, unmanageable? I manage a department of 23 employees and that's how come I can afford to be here in the first place!	I feel I'm successful at my job but I feel stressed by it also, and I've gotten into the bad habit of using drugs to unwind. I would appreciate learning some tools to help me face my professional and personal challenges clean and sober.
Why should I surrender to something that doesn't even exist, as far as I know?	I feel more energized if I believe that the responsibility for staying clean and sober lies in my hands.
Since when is prayer a cure for allergies?	I feel that I need to take positive action to solve my medical problems, instead of wishing and waiting for someone else to solve them.
The _____ Anonymous meetings make me want to relapse.	When I hear people talk at length about their past drinking exploits I get strong cravings to drink or use. Being asked to participate in prayers that I don't believe in drives a wedge between me and the others. I feel that I would rather be in a group that has more inclusive practices. Can you please tell me about the alternative recovery support groups so that I can have a choice?

1 Body 2 Exposure 3 Activities 4 People 5 Feelings 6 Life Style 7 History 8 Culture 9 Treatment

Worksheet 49: Getting What You Need in the Treatment Context

EFFECTIVE ADVOCACY TO GET WHAT YOU NEED IN A TREATMENT CONTEXT

1 Body   2 Exposure   3 Activities   4 People   5 Feelings   6 Life Style   7 History   8 Culture   9 Treatment

Less effective: Gut Reaction	More effective: Sobriety Priority

174. People Say: The Company of Peers

Even in lower quality treatment programs, you can often get something useful out of the offerings, if you make an effort. At the very least, the facility is providing you with two valuable resources that you would not otherwise have: time clean and sober, and the company of peers.

___ After I got over my initial fright, it was just a good warm feeling to be in the company of people who understood and who didn't judge me

___ After telling the others about my resolve to be clean and sober, I felt more deeply committed to really do it

___ All those people were really sick – I'm not like that so I got out of there

___ Apart from a few patients who were deep into their own stuff, most of the patients were really open-minded and we could talk about real things in an honest way

___ Before I started opening up to the others I felt really paralyzed about my problem, but once I got into the swing of talking honestly back and forth, I felt I could walk again

___ Before I went in the program I was afraid that my experiences would freak people out, but after listening to some of the others, my eyes opened and I stopped worrying

___ For the first time I didn't feel all alone in the world with my problem, because of the other patients

___ From talking with the others, it made me realize for the first time that my alcohol and drug thing was something I could overcome and that I could have a life

___ Hearing other patients talk about their experiences was definitely a highlight of the whole treatment program for me

___ I am very, very grateful to the other patients for being there

___ I don't believe in magic but there is something magical about just being with a group of people who understand

___ I felt a bond with most of the other patients and I felt that this helped me

___ I felt a bond with one or two of the other patients and I felt that this helped me

___ I felt about average with the other patients in terms of how I was doing

___ I felt I got more out of listening to the other patients than from staff

___ I felt that by sharing my story with other patients I could serve as a living warning not to go where I've been

___ I felt very different from the other patients in the treatment program and didn't connect

___ I found another patient who also thought it was all BS and we plotted to drink/use as soon as we got out

___ I made up my mind that if the others could stay clean and sober, I could do it too

___ I met someone there who has remained my best friend ever since and we keep each other clean and sober now

___ I picked up more tips and tools for how to stay clean and sober from listening to the other patients than I did from all the books we had to read

___ I still see some of the other patients at outside meetings

___ I'm grateful to the program mainly for putting me in contact with other people like myself

___ In some of the informal conversations I had with other patients I really got a chance to pour my heart out and that helped enormously

1 Body   2 Exposure   3 Activities   4 People   5 Feelings   6 Life Style   7 History   8 Culture   9 Treatment

1 Body   2 Exposure   3 Activities   4 People   5 Feelings   6 Life Style   7 History   8 Culture   9 Treatment

__ It took me quite a while before I could accept being like the others in some ways, and open up to them

__ It was a revelation to me to open up to other people about some of my bad stuff and not have the sky fall in

__ Most of the patients were really way different than me and it was hard to connect

__ My ears always perked up when people started talking about themselves

__ My feeling was that I did significantly better in "getting it" than most of the other patients

__ Nobody there had anything to teach me, I knew all this already

__ One of the things that keeps me sober somehow is the thought that if I run into somebody from the program they'll ask me how I'm doing

__ People looked up to me as a kind of leader or spokesperson among the patients

__ Seeing and talking with the other patients felt empowering like nothing else I have ever experienced

__ Some of the other patients told me that they got help from things I said, and that made me feel I was a worthwhile person

__ Some of the things that other patients said left a deep impression on me

__ Somehow I felt out of it and that I didn't measure up to the standard that the other patients set

__ Talking honestly to another person who had the same issue I did was like a miracle cure for me

__ They were a bunch of sickies in there and I was glad to get away from them

__ Until I got with other people and saw they were struggling with the same thing as myself, I had felt really hopeless

__ What a congenial group of people – I fit right in and we were like old friends right away

__ When a few of us would get together and talk informally during free time, it felt wonderful; I really felt connected and understood for the first time in a long time

__ When I heard stuff from the other patients it seemed much more real and credible to me than reading it in a book

__ When I realized from listening to the others that I was not alone, I just cried and cried for a while and then I felt a lot better

__ When I saw that with all my fancy career and SUVs and all, I had a lot in common with a teenage crack addict, it really gave me a new perspective

__ When I saw what some of the other patients had gone through it firmed up my resolve to turn myself around before that happened to me

__ When I see somebody now that I met in the program, I feel really proud that I'm still clean and sober and I keep my head up

__ When I was struggling with my problem all by myself I felt like I was walking with crutches, barely able to move; when I was able to open up to even one other person it was like throwing my crutches away and dancing

__ When the group would get into an exchange back and forth about some sobriety issue I felt much stronger and more determined to beat this thing than I ever did before

__ Whenever we patients started talking informally with each other, some staff would come and break it up

__ Without question the interaction with the others was the thing that propelled me and energized me to stay clean and sober after I got out

175. Thinking about the Company of Peers: Synergy

Treatment programs usually have you spend a major portion of your time in groups with other clients/patients. They do so for more than reasons of economy. Being together and interacting with others who have similar concerns can be a powerful healing experience. When two or more interact, the energy that flows between them can bring about changes in all of them that none of them could achieve in isolation. This energy-from-combination, or synergy, makes it possible for two or more to stay sober when they work together, even though each of them probably could not do it alone.

Synergy may seem miraculous to someone experiencing it for the first time, especially in a setting that touches some of the deepest emotions. But if you look around, you'll see the same miracle at work in thousands of ordinary settings, large and small. When people get together in a quilting bee, instead of stitching in isolation, they're tapping into the creative and bonding force of synergy. When football players huddle and clap their hands together and run a coordinated play, they're using synergy. Soldiers training as a squad, police officers calling in help, firefighters working as a team, surgeons and nurses doing a complex operation together, workers forming unions, merchants forming trade associations, oil producers forming cartels, parties holding conventions – wherever two or more get together to do a thing they couldn't do as well alone, good, bad or indifferent, they're tapping into the power of synergy.

The whole social division of labor, from one end of the world to the other, when it works, works because of the power of synergy. Why shouldn't you use synergy to help you stay clean and sober?

176. Seeing the Similarities

Your first reaction when you hear others talk in your groups may be to push them away mentally because their situations are in some ways different from yours – perhaps very different. You'll get more out of the group experience if you look for the similarities. If your drug was alcohol, you can certainly relate to someone whose drug was heroin, if you look for the similarities. If you are a company manager you can certainly relate to someone who has been in the gutter, if you look for the similarities.

By seeing the thing-you-have-in-common in all its diverse and multicolored forms, you'll be able to see your own individual situation in a more three-dimensional way. Have you had moments of sudden insight when you realized that you had more in common with the other people in the group than you thought at the outset? How did that make you feel?

In the next worksheet, put the first name (or initials, or a pseudonym) of other members of your group in Column 1. In Column 2, put an obvious way that the person is different from you. In Column 3, put some ways that the person is similar to you. Focus on the drug/alcohol issues.

Are you having trouble finding similarities with a particular person? Perhaps the fact that you both wound up in the same room together is just one big horrible mistake. That does happen sometimes. One thing you could do is to approach that person on the side and ask them if they see anything in you that is similar to something in them. Or ask a third person whether they see anything in common. Or you could just wait a bit, suspend judgment, and see what develops. Treatment can be remarkable in the way that perceptions and feelings change in even a short time.

Worksheet 50: Looking for Similarities

THINGS I HAVE IN COMMON WITH PEOPLE WHO ARE DIFFERENT FROM ME		
Name of Person	**How Different**	**How Similar**

1 Body   2 Exposure   3 Activities   4 People   5 Feelings   6 Life Style   7 History   8 Culture   9 Treatment

177. Change Runs Deeper When You Are Active

It's helpful to talk as well as listen. At times when you're changing inside, you sometimes won't know what you're really thinking and feeling until you hear it coming out of your mouth. Listening to lectures or speakers and watching videos is fine, but it's passive. Change inside you runs deeper and stronger when you become active. A well-run group where you can feel comfortable talking freely, from the heart, can be the highlight of your day.   Have you experienced such a group?

If you are a person who has difficulty speaking in the group, try making a list of the reasons why:

Reasons Why I Have a Hard Time Speaking in the Group:

_____

_____

_____

_____

If you are a person who has a tendency to talk too much, and who has a low tolerance for moments of group silence, try making a list of the reasons why:

Reasons Why I Tend to Talk Too Much and Dislike Silence:

_____

_____

_____

_____

_____

1 Body   2 Exposure   3 Activities   4 People   5 Feelings   6 Life Style   7 History   8 Culture   9 Treatment

178. Making "I" Statements

Talking with other people about common issues is more interesting, and fewer feelings are hurt, if participants remember to use "I" statements. This is a common rule of all kinds of self-help groups. For example, if someone expresses concern about going to a ball game and staying sober, you may respond: "I have gone to ball games and stayed sober by going with sober friends." Or: "I went to a ball game but the smell of beer everywhere was too much for me and I almost had a relapse." Both are "I" statements.

Rarely is it helpful to say: "You should not go, ball games cause relapses," or "Go ahead, ball games are no problem." Statements prefaced with "I" express respect for the other person's autonomy and intelligence. Can you see how "I" statements also reduce the likelihood of arguments?

Of course, if the person directly asks for advice, then statements in the form of "you should" or their equivalent are OK. Still, even if the person directly asks for advice, "I" statements are always appropriate, and are generally more appreciated and effective.

Have you observed that sometimes the people who are the shortest on experience are the quickest to dispense advice? It's been said that asking for advice at a self-help meeting is like trying to drink from a fire hose.

Under the "I" statement rule, you can still speak about things of which you have no personal experience, if you frame them like this: "I've heard ..." or "I've read ..." or "someone told me ...". If you don't have a basis for speaking either from personal experience or based on something you gained from others, the "I" statement rule suggests silence as the appropriate policy. Is that unfair?

In the next worksheet, translate the "you should" statements in the first column into "I" statements (second column).

Worksheet 51: Making "I" Statements

TRANSLATING "YOU SHOULD" STATEMENTS INTO "I" STATEMENTS	
"You Should" Statement	**"I" Statement**
You should never eat Dijon mustard, it will lead you to relapse	
You have to stay away from your old friends if you want to get sober	
You have to shut up and listen to the elders	
You should dump your relationship if they drink/use	
You have to go to x meetings in x days to get sober	
You have to work the program I worked or you will drink/use	
You have to read and follow this book or you will drink again	
You have to find somebody to lead you through the program or you will relapse	
The only way to stay sober is to _____	
Unless you do _____, you will drink again	

Body　Exposure　Activities　People　Feelings　Life Style　History　Culture　Treatment

1　2　3　4　5　6　7　8　9

179. A Support Group's Purpose Is To Support

The bottom line with group interaction in the treatment setting or afterward is whether it fortifies your sobriety. The group and its individual members work well when they support the inner struggle that you are waging to transform yourself into a sober person. To be effective, the group has to give each member respect and space. For you to benefit from the group, you need to be free to be who you are as a sober person.

Sometimes groups forget this; they get full of themselves, play God toward the individual, and demand that the members assume false personalities to fit in. These tendencies are unhealthy and will not strengthen your recovery. To endure, the change inside you needs to be real and freely chosen, and the sober you that is emerging needs to be authentic.

Have you experienced groups that became overbearing and oppressive? Yes No

Have you experienced groups that were supportive and respected your space and your effort? Yes No

Write a few observations here about the ways in which your support group reinforces your sobriety. If you feel that the group is doing something contrary to that goal, write about that:

_____

_____

_____

_____

Bottom line: at the end of the group session, do you feel that your sobriety is stronger, or weaker?

___ At the end of the group session, my sobriety feels stronger
___ At the end of the group session, my sobriety feels shakier

180. Give Your Treatment Program Your Feedback

A substance abuse treatment program is a health service provider, and most health service providers are keen to get patient feedback. If your treatment program does not have a feedback form for you to use, you can use the following worksheet. The ranking scale runs from –3 to +3, where the minus side means "tended to make me feel like I wanted to relapse" and the plus side means, "tended to strengthen my recovery." In the middle, zero means this program component was neutral, or you can't decide. Leave it blank if it doesn't apply; some items will apply only to an inpatient program.

Worksheet 52: Rate the Quality of Your Treatment Program

Program Component	← Relapse				Recovery →			Comment
	-3	-2	-1	0	+1	+2	+3	
Detox								
Intake interview/assessment								
Orientation								
Written material about program								
Breakfasts								
Lunches								
Dinners								
Snacks								
Smoking rule								
Candy/sugar rule								
Coffee rule								
Laundry								
Rooms								
Beds								
Other:								
Medical checkup								
Access to physician								
Physician's demeanor								
Nursing supervision								
Nurses' demeanor								
Access to my medical chart								
Prescriptions offered:								
Antabuse								
Naltrexone								
Buprenorphine								
Anti-depressants								
Methadone								
Urine tests								
Urine test reporting								
Individual counseling:								
Amount of time spent with me								
Availability								
Counselor's style								
Counselor's knowledge								
Counselor's responsiveness								
Counselor's respect for my beliefs/ culture /life style								
Receptiveness to my concerns								

Right margin tabs: 1 Body   2 Exposure   3 Activities   4 People   5 Feelings   6 Life Style   7 History   8 Culture   9 Treatment

Left margin (vertical): 1 Body   2 Exposure   3 Activities   4 People   5 Feelings   6 Life Style   7 History   8 Culture   9 Treatment

TREATMENT PROGRAM FEEDBACK FORM								
Program Component	← Relapse				Recovery →			Comment
	-3	-2	-1	0	+1	+2	+3	
Group education sessions:								
Movies/videos								
Educational speakers								
Staff lectures / discussions								
Handouts								
Other								
Twelve-Step Work								
Step 1 (Powerless)								
Step 2 (Higher Power)								
Step 3 (Surrender)								
Step 4 (Moral Inventory)								
Step 5 (Admit Wrongs)								
Step 6 (Character defects)								
Steps, generally:								
Process groups:								
Group leader's role								
Choice of topics								
Ground rules								
Other participants' roles								
In-house support group meetings								
Choice of groups offered								
Presentations by speakers								
Choice of topics								
Audience participation								
Written materials								
Family and Friends sessions								
Recreational activities								
Free time								
Library (reading materials)								
Preparation for re-entry								
Referral to follow-up care								
Choice of support groups offered								
Overall Rating of Program:								

Other comments about the program:

_____

_____

181. Write a Letter to Your Counselor

Chemical dependency counseling generally pays very little money. What keeps the counselors going is the belief that they are making a difference in your life and in society. If you would like to thank a particular counselor for what he or she has done for you in the treatment program, take a few minutes and write a letter. You could make the counselor's day and, incidentally, put them in a better frame of mind to be helpful to the next person. You know, positive reinforcement? The blank form letter below contains some suggested sentence starters; fill it in, or make your own.

Worksheet 53: Dear Counselor, Thank You

My name _____

Address _____

City _____

Date _____

To: _____, Counselor

Facility: _____

Street: _____

City, State Zip: _____

Dear _____

You have made a difference in my life because:

Thanks to you, I now understand that:

The way you treated me made me feel different about myself, namely:

You said something to me that I still remember:

I am grateful to you because:

Thank you for having been part of my recovery.

Sincerely yours,

Signed:

_____

Sidebar (right margin): 1 Body   2 Exposure   3 Activities   4 People   5 Feelings   6 Life Style   7 History   8 Culture   9 Treatment

182. Let Your Treatment Program Know How You Are Doing

A treatment facility can't know whether its program is working unless you, the client, check in with the program on a regular basis after discharge and let them know how you are doing. Below is a set of suggested short forms you could clip out and mail to your treatment program. You can ignore these if your treatment program already has its own follow-up system. These forms are for three months, six months and one year after your discharge. Ideally you should check in with the program annually for at least five years; you can easily make your own forms for that purpose.

Please photocopy and cut out the forms. You might date all three of them now and post them on your refrigerator or someplace where you can look at them and be reminded to send them in.

Worksheet 54: Let Your Treatment Program Know How You Are Doing

Three Months

Dear Treatment Program:

I was a client in your facility from _____ to _____

___ I have been clean and sober continuously since discharge
___ I relapsed
    ___ I relapsed for a while but am clean and sober now
    ___ I relapsed and am still drinking/using

Comments:
_____

Signed:
_____

Six Months

Dear Treatment Program:

I was a client in your facility from _____ to _____

___ I have been clean and sober continuously since discharge
___ I relapsed
    ___ I relapsed for a while but am clean and sober now
    ___ I relapsed and am still drinking/using

Comments:
_____

Signed:
_____

One Year

Dear Treatment Program:

I was a client in your facility from _____ to
_____

___ I have been clean and sober continuously since discharge
___ I relapsed
    ___ I relapsed for a while but am clean and sober now
    ___ I relapsed and am still drinking/using

Comments:
_____
_____

Signed:_____
___

183. People Say: About Going To Support Groups

___ I have never attended any recovery support group meetings
___ I can't bear the idea of going into a room with people who are alcoholics or addicts
___ I would like to attend meetings but I don't do it for no reason I can put my finger on
___ I'm deathly afraid I'll meet somebody I know, so I don't go
___ I like the groups because I meet all kinds of people from the town I would never know otherwise
___ I don't go to meetings but I participate in support groups over the Internet
___ I started going to these meetings because I was told I had to in order to stay sober
___ I got referred to my support group by a counselor at a treatment program
___ I have to go to the meetings and get a slip signed
___ My counselor gave me a choice of 12-step and non-12-step support groups to attend
___ I have attended meetings of only one organization
___ I have attended meetings of several organizations
___ Counting everything, I have attended approximately _____ (*number*) meetings
___ I stopped going to meetings but still see friends I met there
___ I no longer have any contact with people I met at meetings
___ Practically all of my social life now is with people I met at meetings
___ I didn't connect with any of the people at meetings
___ I tried to connect with people at meetings but they put me down
___ I connected with one or a few people at meetings and this helped me stay sober
___ I connected with one or a few people at meetings and we relapsed together
___ I connected with a lot of the people at meetings and this helped me stay sober
___ I connected with people but this made no difference to staying sober
___ I feel I have a lot in common with the people in my meetings
___ I learn something from other people at just about every meeting
___ A lot of the people I see at meetings are weirdoes
___ A lot of the people I see at meetings are nice and I like them

1 Body   2 Exposure   3 Activities   4 People   5 Feelings   6 Life Style   7 History   8 Culture   9 Treatment

1 Body 2 Exposure 3 Activities 4 People 5 Feelings 6 Life Style 7 History 8 Culture 9 Treatment

__ I go because the meetings help me stay sober
__ I go because I meet people and see them afterwards

184. Thinking About Going to Recovery Support Groups

Some people manage to recover without attending groups. Something goes "click" in their minds, more or less, and they stop drinking/using, period. Based on your own experience, do you think such people are better off, somehow, than people who get clean and sober using support groups? Why or why not?

__ People who recover on their own are better off
__ People who use support groups are better off
__ Not sure

Why:
_____
_____

Some people are deathly afraid to enter a support group meeting. They say that they would be mortified if they met someone who knows them. Can you think of some things to say to such a person to reassure them that it's OK? What is the worst thing that could happen if they did meet someone who knows them? Do you think that the fear of meeting someone else is the real root fear in every instance?

Explain:
_____
_____
_____
_____

Some people talk as if going to a support group meeting were a punishment. They'll use phrases such as "Alcohol brought me here" or a sarcastic expression such as "My best thinking got me here." Wouldn't it be more accurate to say, "My desire to recover from alcohol got me here"? Or, "My recovery got me here"? Isn't it literally true that going to a support group – as opposed to, say, going to a bar and drinking – reflects a person's best thinking? Do you agree that sarcasm about "thinking" is misplaced here?

In your community, does a recovering person have a choice about what types of support groups to go to? If a person doesn't feel comfortable with the 12-step approach, is an alternative available? Do you think that having a choice of support groups is a good thing? Why or why not?

__ A choice of abstinence support groups is a good thing

__ A choice of abstinence support groups is not a good thing
Explain:

_____

_____

Have you participated in a recovery support network over the Internet? If so, what kind (social network, chat room, email list, forum, other)? Do you find recovery support via the Internet helpful for your sobriety? How would you compare it to the kind of support you can get from face-to-face meetings?

__ Have not tried Internet
__ Have used Internet

Advantages/disadvantages of Internet support compared to face-to-face group support, in your experience:

_____

_____

_____

If a person has an issue with alcohol and also with another drug such as marijuana and/or heroin, do you think it's better that they go to two or three separate groups, one for each drug, or do you think that an inclusive support group (one that supports recovery from alcohol and other drugs together) would be preferable? What are your reasons?

__ Better to deal with all chemical dependency issues in the same group
__ Better to deal with each addictive substance in its own separate group

Why:

_____

_____

_____

 Some people attend support group meetings only because their alternative is jail. Do you think that they get something positive out of meeting attendance? Do you think that it is a good thing for the meeting to have a large proportion of the participants attending against their will? What have been your experiences with this situation? If you believe this is a problem, what do you think could be done about it?

__ No experience with this
__ I am familiar with this and I don't see a problem
__ I am familiar with this and it causes problems

1 Body   2 Exposure   3 Activities   4 People   5 Feelings   6 Life Style   7 History   8 Culture   9 Treatment

1 Body   2 Exposure   3 Activities   4 People   5 Feelings   6 Life Style   7 History   8 Culture   9 Treatment

What I think should be done:

_____

_____

For some people, their recovery support group meeting provides social contacts; for some it is the only social life they know. How do you feel about that? Do you want recovery groups to make up your entire social life? Or do you want to find a balance?

___ OK if recovery groups are my whole social life
___ I want a social life beyond recovery groups
___ I'm not interested in the social aspects of recovery groups

My reasoning:

_____

_____

_____

Some people look at their recovery group participation as a lifelong commitment. How do you feel about that?

___ Lifelong commitment OK if that's what it takes to stay clean and sober
___ I'd rather go for a while and then stay clean and sober on my own
___ I'm not sure about this at all, I'm going to play it by ear

My reasoning:

_____

_____

185. People Say: My Meetings and My Sobriety

___ I feel free to speak my mind in the meeting
___ I feel I could speak but only if I said the approved phrases
___ I want to speak but feel too intimidated or insecure
___ In the meetings I go to you are expected to sit and listen to other people speak
___ The meetings I go to are so big that only a few people can speak
___ The meetings I go to are small enough for everyone to have a say
___ In the meetings I go to you are expected to give and get feedback from other people
___ In my meetings, feedback is not allowed
___ I feel OK about the meeting's rituals
___ I feel some of the meeting's rituals are offensive to my beliefs
___ I feel the meeting's rituals go on so long there's little time left for anything else
___ I feel some of the meeting's rituals are unsanitary
___ I feel people in the meeting accepted me the way I am without judging me

__ Some of the people in the meeting are judgmental

__ The atmosphere in the meeting was preachy

__ The meeting felt like being in Sunday School

__ I am one of the people who helps lead the meeting

__ I have leadership responsibilities in the organization that holds the meetings

__ I help the meeting by setting up, making coffee, passing the basket, cleaning up, etc.

__ I just go to get my slip signed

__ I always make a point to be clean and sober the day of the meeting

__ I drink/use drugs before I go to the meeting (or during breaks)

__ I stay after the meeting and socialize

__ I get out as soon as I can

__ I find the meeting interesting and I pay attention to what is said

__ It's interesting when people tell their experiences but when they start the Higher Power talk my mind wanders off

__ I feel uplifted when people talk about their spiritual enlightenments

__ All the religious talk turns me off and I want to be out of there

__ The people have a great sense of humor and I enjoy myself in the meeting

__ I am mostly bored during the meetings and my mind tends to be elsewhere

__ After each meeting I feel stronger in my sobriety

__ I never or rarely feel any cravings during the meeting

__ I often feel a craving during the meeting

__ I drink coffee at the meetings

__ I eat cookies or other sweets at the meetings

__ I smoke at the meetings

__ After each meeting I feel like going out to drink/use but I resist

__ After each meeting I feel like going out to drink/use and I usually do

__ How I feel afterward depends on what I heard at the meeting

__ How I feel afterward depends on what I said at the meeting

__ If I don't go, I feel my sobriety gets shakier

__ I don't feel the meeting has any effect on my sobriety

__ I look on the meeting as an important source of support for my sobriety

__ I relapsed right after attending a meeting because of something that happened in the meeting

__ I planned to relapse before going to a meeting and went ahead and did it despite going to the meeting

__ I had planned to relapse before going to a meeting but something that happened in the meeting stopped me and I did not relapse

__ I relapsed while I was going to meetings regularly, but not right after a meeting

__ I stopped attending meetings because I had decided to relapse

__ After I stopped attending meetings I lost my sobriety consciousness and relapsed

__ I keep (kept) on attending meetings after I relapsed

__ I keep (kept) on relapsing while attending meetings

__ I had relapsed a lot but stopped relapsing after I started going to meetings

1 Body   2 Exposure   3 Activities   4 People   5 Feelings   6 Life Style   7 History   8 Culture   9 Treatment

186. Twenty-One Questions to Ask About a Support Group

1 Body   2 Exposure   3 Activities   4 People   5 Feelings   6 Life Style   7 History   8 Culture   9 Treatment

Support groups are as varied as individuals. Even within the same organization, meetings may differ from place to place and day to day. If you don't like your current meeting, try another one. If you don't feel comfortable in any of the meetings in your locality, start your own. Here are some questions you might ask as you evaluate your support group experience.

1) Does the group recognize that people are individuals and that everyone has to work out their recovery their own way? What assistance and encouragement does the group offer me to help me work out my recovery in a way that fits who I am?

2) Does the group's philosophy encourage me to look within myself for the resources to make my recovery work? Does it explain how it is possible for me to become clean and sober, and to remain that way long term, by changing my behavior and my outlook?

3) Does the group recognize that I am inherently a worthy person despite my past use of alcohol/drugs, and despite all the awful things I might have done? Does it help me to identify and to develop further the worthwhile, healthy, competent parts of my character?

4) Does the group's philosophy encourage me to take responsibility for my own recovery?

5) Are the basic principles of the group simple enough for an average person to understand and to practice without a mentor?

6) If the group requires the newcomer to get a mentor in order to get the full benefit of its program, what measures does it take to ensure that its mentors are trained and qualified to handle the responsibility?

7) Does the group keep to a single standard for success and failure, so that if I fail the fault is mine but if I succeed the credit is also mine? Or is there a double standard?

8) Does the group recognize that I am not paralyzed and that I can over time and with effort develop my powers to stay clean and sober, just as a muscle can grow stronger through exercise?

9) Does the group help me rebuild my self-esteem? Does it support me in building up the ego strength that a person needs to survive? Does it recognize that an ego is part of a healthy personality?

10) Does the group help me achieve balance in my life by recognizing that I can be on the receiving as well as the giving end of wrongs, harms, and injustices? Does it go beyond the harm I may have caused, and empower me to amend also the real injustices I and other members of my community may have suffered?

11) Does the group's meeting format make me feel like a passive spectator at a show or like an active participant in a loop of support?

12) Does the group's meeting format allow me to talk back and forth comfortably with the other participants, like in conversation with friends? Can I get and give feedback?

13) Is the group's literature gender-neutral? If the group's original texts stem from a culture where women were considered less than full equals, have the texts been modernized in subsequent editions? As a woman, do I feel that my particular experience and perspective are given equal respect in the group's literature?

14) Does the group respect my religious beliefs or disbeliefs? Am I under pressure to modify my theological views in order to participate fully in the group's recovery process? If addiction is like diabetes or asthma, why should a person's beliefs about a supernatural power make a difference?

15) Is the main focus of the group meetings on the current happenings in the participants' lives, so as to assist them in living clean and sober?

16) Does the group limit the recital of people's drunk and drugged histories at meetings to the minimum necessary to remember that drinking/using was harmful?

17) Does the group continually update and revise its teachings in the light of scientific discovery about addiction? Does it disseminate knowledge about new anti-addiction medications that are becoming available? Is it open to scientific research about its own processes, and does it support research in the medical field?

18) Does the group extend an equal welcome to persons addicted to alcohol and to other drugs? Does it offer all-round support to persons with multiple substance issues? Does it recognize the commonality of all forms of chemical dependency, and does it strive to unite all kinds of chemically dependent people into a shared pool of knowledge and into a single recovery community?

19) Does the group provide education to its members on the hazards of nicotine addiction and does it provide its members with encouragement and support to quit smoking?

20) Does the group frame its claims of effectiveness in a modest, realistic manner consistent with modern medical practice?

21) Does the group accept its failures and acknowledge that its approach is not for everyone? Does it define itself as one among multiple and equally valid pathways to a common destination?

1 Body   2 Exposure   3 Activities   4 People   5 Feelings   6 Life Style   7 History   8 Culture   9 Treatment

Sidebar: 1 Body 2 Exposure 3 Activities 4 People 5 Feelings 6 Life Style 7 History 8 Culture 9 Treatment

187. My Plan for My Treatment and Support Group Participation

___ I plan to complete the treatment program in which I am currently enrolled
___ I plan to enter treatment at some time in the future
___ I plan to look around for a treatment program that has high professional
    standards and offers a variety of therapeutic options

In more detail, my plan for my treatment is:

_____

_____

_____

___ I plan to continue with my current support group
___ I plan to get continuing support for my recovery in face-to-face groups
___ I plan to get continuing support for my recovery in online Internet groups
___ I plan to investigate all the available options for support groups
___ If I cannot find a support group that I feel comfortable in, I plan to start one

My plan for my support group participation, in more detail, is:

_____

_____

_____

Three-Month Review

_____

_____

_____

Date:_____

One-Year Review

_____

_____

_____

Date: _____

Preventing Relapse

At any fork in the road, one branch leads toward a stronger sobriety, and the other leads ultimately toward relapse. Most of the exercises in this workbook have tried to shed light on the many varieties and flavors of this basic choice.

If you have the luxury of always doing an exhaustive Sobriety T-chart analysis (see Chapter One) before every decision in your life, and if you have uncommonly sharp foresight, you may never need to concern yourself with relapse prevention. Similarly, you may never need a smoke detector or a fire extinguisher.

However, in real life people sometimes make decisions first and do the analysis afterward, or not at all. Situations also come up where people seem to be going in a circle and cannot see a fork in the road that would lead to new ground. At times like these, it's useful to be able to recognize a relapse-bound path or a near-relapse situation, when your path takes you perilously close to the edge. You may then be able to make timely corrections and avoid the fall, or at least minimize the impact and limit the damage.

If a relapse does happen, it can be a valuable educational experience for all involved. One utility of a support group is to serve as a living laboratory where people try different action plans and share the results with one another. A relapse that happens in isolation is a terrible waste. This chapter includes exercises that the person who has relapsed could work by way of getting a deeper understanding and sharing the lessons of the experience.

In this book, relapse prevention is not considered a distinct domain or work area. All of the domains are about relapse prevention. To put it more positively, all of the domains are about empowerment of your sober self. Relapse is what happens when your work in any of the nine domains falls short. Therefore this chapter is mainly in the nature of a quality control checkup on your earlier work. The skills you develop in this chapter are critical reflection on your previous work, and timely correction of mistakes.

Here you'll first review the motivation that started you on the road to freedom from alcohol and other drugs. Then you'll have a closer look at the relapse phenomenon, and give yourself some checkups for early relapse warning signs. It's been known for a long time that relapses don't really strike out of the blue. They don't begin with the first intake of the drug. Leading up to that first intake there is a long process of preparation that takes place more or less consciously. The signs of that pre-intake relapse process can often be identified and flagged, and the downward slide can be aborted.

An unusual feature of this chapter is the worksheet on page 273, *My Relapse Plan*. The idea here is that if someone is intending to relapse, it might be helpful to plan the relapse all the way through. Possibly, you may change your mind.

Several checklists in this chapter help you identify where in the nine domains you probably need to do more work, or better work, in order to put more distance between yourself and the relapse cliff. If you have had a relapse, the worksheet on page 283 helps you flag the domain where the problem lies. A short recovery checkup on page 270 and a more detailed one on page 287 similarly contain pointers to the work areas where additional effort may be required to keep relapse at bay. Some people begin their work in this book with those checklists as a way of deciding which domains are the most immediately urgent for building their Personal Recovery Program.

188. How and Why I Stopped

Sometimes a near-relapse situation arises because the person never understood or has forgotten why they stopped drinking/using to begin with, or because the situation has changed so that those reasons no longer obtain.

___ One day it just came to me out of the blue that I had to stop drinking/using and I did

___ One day something dramatic happened and I stopped

___ I had been sick and tired of drinking/using and thinking about stopping for
_____ *(time)*

___ There was a series of events that led up to my stopping

___ I came to the decision to stop all by myself

___ Other people played a role in my decision to stop

___ Members of my family asked me to stop

___ A doctor or other professional told me to stop

___ I thought if I did not stop, certain bad things would happen to me

___ I thought if I did stop, certain good things would happen

The main ideas in my mind originally when I stopped drinking/using were:

_____

_____

_____

_____

_____

Do the reasons why I originally quit no longer hold? (For example, has the person who urged me to get clean and sober left my life? Has my medical diagnosis changed?)

     __ The original reasons are gone
     __ The original reasons are still there
     __ Some of the original reasons are still there, others have gone

Now that I have been clean and sober for some time, is my understanding of the reasons for staying clean and sober broader and deeper than it was originally?

     __ Yes, I see more now
     __ No, my understanding is less deep than it used to be
     __ It is the same

If yes, what reasons to be clean and sober do I see now that I did not see originally?

_____

_____

_____

If no, what part of my original reasons for staying clean and sober have I tended to forget about?

_____

_____

_____

Note that there are daily exercises that can be used to keep alive the memory of one's original reasons to get clean and sober; see My Daily Do, Page 70.

189. People Say: My Desire to Stay Clean and Sober

Some people get into relapse trouble early on because their desire to be clean and sober is nonexistent, or has faded, or flickers, or is thin and abstract. Some people pass through a period of craziness where they feel the desire to be clean and sober only when they are drinking/using, but when they are clean/sober, all they can think about is their next drink/hit. It may take a while for the point to sink in that purposeful actions, not merely wishes, make a recovery. As with any difficult learning project, misconceptions, false starts and mistakes are common at the start; and some of them result in relapse. Try this checklist:

__ I don't feel any desire within me to stay clean and sober; I'm only doing it
     because I have to
__ I feel a desire to stay clean and sober but it is so small that sometimes I can't
     find it

___ I feel a sharp desire to stay clean and sober sometimes but I can't hold on to it

___ When I feel the desire to stay clean and sober I try to lock on to that feeling and hold it

___ I feel a strong desire to stay clean and sober most of the time

___ The desire to stay clean and sober is my normal feeling, anything else is exceptional

___ I do feel a desire to stay clean and sober but it's only "in my head" and not "in my gut"

___ My desire to stay clean and sober is both in my gut and in my head; when I smell alcohol or drugs I gag or feel nauseous and I get away as fast as I can

___ I only feel the desire to stay clean and sober when I've started drinking/using; when I'm sober I mainly feel a desire to drink/use

___ I don't feel anything positive about drinking/using any more; if I were to go back there it would be because I wanted to destroy myself

___ I'm so glad I'm not drinking/using any more; it had become crazy-making

___ I read recovery books while I'm drunk/high, so drinking/using is part of my recovery

___ I feel sad and relieved when I read books about active alcoholics/addicts – sad for them, relieved that I'm sober now

___ Once I actually stopped drinking and using, I understood on a gut level that this was the only way for me to live

___ As long as I attend recovery groups it's OK for me to continue drinking/using

___ My brain was a mess of rationalizations and self-deception until I gave myself a kick in the pants and actually stopped

___ I want to stay clean and sober, provided it doesn't mean I have to stop drinking and using

___ Staying clean and sober has become the most important priority in my life

___ I might feel a stronger desire to be clean and sober if I felt I had more reason to be alive

___ I might feel more reason to be alive if I were to stop drinking/using

___ When I feel the desire to drink/use I act on it immediately, but when I feel the desire to stay clean and sober I ignore it until it goes away

___ When I feel the desire to stay clean and sober, I act on it immediately, but when I feel the desire to drink/use, I procrastinate and don't act on it

190. Thinking About the Desire to Be Clean and Sober

Obviously, if a person has no desire to be clean and sober, they will relapse at the next opportunity.   Some people in prisons, hospitals or similar settings where alcohol/drugs are difficult to get on short notice – or where penalties for use are prohibitive – may be abstinent in their behavior, but mentally they remain drinkers/users. Their drinking/drugging is merely on hold. They are not counting up the days of their sobriety; they are counting down the days until they can drink/use again.

Do you think that a period of enforced abstinence can nevertheless work to bring about recovery, if it awakens a person's own desire to become clean and sober? As the French say, sometimes the appetite comes with the eating. Have you seen instances where enforced abstinence has worked? Have you seen examples where it did not work? What do you think accounts for the outcomes you saw?

_____

_____

_____

Sigmund Freud divided the human personality into three parts: id, ego and superego. The id is the seat of instincts, desires and pleasures; it says "I want." The ego is the seat of rational, self-interested calculation; it weighs the alternatives and concludes "I will." The superego is the voice of society's mores and taboos; it says "you should" or "you must."

Assuming that you see some usefulness in this scheme, where do you feel your desire to get clean and sober comes from? Where do you feel your desire to drink/use comes from? Do you see some threads of your sober striving that come from the id? (See the section on _Recapturing Pleasure_ in the Fifth Domain (Feelings), at Page 117.) From the ego? Conversely, when you look at your desire to drink/use, do you see some parts of it that come from the superego? (Check the Eighth Domain, _My Culture_.) From the ego? Do you see an advantage, in terms of relapse prevention, to having your sobriety anchored in all three areas?

_____

_____

_____

_____

_____

_____

The desire to get clean and sober often forms in the mind long before the person takes action on it. Was this true in your case? How long did you feel a desire to be clean and sober before you first actually stopped drinking/using?

_____

Can you see how a desire to relapse can also form in the mind long before the person takes action to relapse? Yes   No.

Have you had arguments in your mind between your desire to be clean and sober, and your desire to drink/use? Yes No

If so, describe some of these arguments: what were the voices, and what did they say? Did you take any action that revealed your inner struggle, such as going into a store to buy, and leaving without buying? Write about these experiences here:

_____

_____

_____

_____

Do you agree that one cannot force a person to want to be clean and sober?   Yes
No

What kinds of things, in your experience, increased your motivation to be clean and
sober? What kinds of things impaired that motivation?

_____

_____

Do you feel more motivated or less motivated to do something if you are told
that you have to do it? Do you like to have choices?   Yes No

Why or why not?

_____

_____

191. When Someone Else Has Relapsed

Sometimes people get into relapse danger because someone they looked up to
as a model has relapsed; this occurs, for example, when a sponsor in a 12-step
group relapses. In any support group, a member's relapse can tug the other
members downward, just as their support will tend to pull the falling member
upward. Think of mountaineers roped together on a slope. Which of these
reactions applies to you?

__ That person's relapse created a pull on me in the relapse direction
__ I distrusted this person and their relapse has made my sobriety, if anything,
      stronger
__ I don't feel affected one way or the other
__ I was not surprised this person relapsed; I saw it coming
__ This person relapses all the time, it was nothing new
__ I could have done something to maybe prevent this person from relapsing
__ Someone else could have done something to maybe prevent this person from
      relapsing
__ The group could have done something to prevent this relapse
__ Nothing could have been done to keep this person from relapsing
__ This person's relapse has upset and shocked me
__ I want this person to come back to the group and try again
__ I'd just as soon this person didn't come back into the group
__ I have learned something useful for my own recovery from this person's relapse

If you have had the experience of dealing with the relapse of someone in your
group, you may have had occasion to reflect on the deep issues that arise from

the social nature of human beings. No one is an island, but connectedness can be painful. If the relapse is serious and involves loss of life, you may be reminded that staying clean and sober is not an abstract issue; it has to do with survival.

If you have experienced someone else's relapse, write about how this has made you feel and what you learned from the experience:

_____

_____

_____

_____

_____

Can you ever help a person who relapsed by following them into relapse?   Yes No

If you relapse out of "sympathy" with such a person, what effect will that have on them?

_____

_____

In view of the probability that someone in your support group will experience a relapse at some time, do you think you are better off working on your recovery in isolation?   Yes No

Can you see advantages to being part of a group experience that sometimes includes someone's relapse? Yes No

If you are able to be of help to someone who is in danger of relapsing, or who has relapsed, how does this make you feel about yourself?

_____

Can helping someone else also help you? Explain:

_____

_____

_____

What if you are a member of a group in which the great majority of people relapse? Should you just accept this as the nature of the beast, and struggle on to become one of the handful of survivors? Should the group's standards of admission be raised? Should the group's approach be re-examined to see in what way it might be made more effective for more people? Should you give up on that group? Should you give up on groups in general?
Discuss:

_____

_____

_____

_____

192. Expectations about Relapse

As with anything else, your expectations will influence your outcomes. If you believe that relapse is inevitable, it probably will be. Here is a short checklist to help you spot arguments that, in some people's minds, create an expectation that they will relapse or that they ought to relapse.

__ I believe that everyone who gets into recovery inevitably relapses
__ I believe that some people will relapse, some people won't, and it's beyond their control
__ Relapse just happens, like sh*t, and there is no point in trying to figure anything out about it
__ Statistics show that relapse is common, so it will probably happen to me
__ Addiction is a relapsing disease and I have it, therefore I will relapse
__ The disease progresses no matter what you do, so relapse is inevitable
__ I have no control over my addiction so I am bound to relapse eventually
__ Relapse is a punishment for being a defective person, and I am one
__ I would have to work a perfect recovery program to avoid relapse, and I can't
__ When it comes to alcohol and drugs I am basically paralyzed, so relapse is inevitable
__ Unless I work X program I am doomed to relapse, but X makes no sense to me, so I will end up relapsing
__ Unless I do my recovery the way Z did his recovery, I will inevitably relapse, but I can never be like Z, so I am bound to relapse
__ Relapsing is what alcoholics/addicts do, and I'm one

___ _____

If you have checked one of the items in this list, use the space below (or a separate sheet) to write a counter-argument. This could be a good topic for group discussion.

_____

_____

_____

In engineering, "redundancy" means having a back-up system. Redundancy is an important safety feature. Can you see how having more than one recovery approach available can be a good thing for relapse prevention? Yes No

193. Termites That Prepare the Mind for Relapse

To paraphrase another Yogi Berra expression: "Ninety per cent of relapse is half in the mind." Here is a collection of notions that sometimes take up residence in the mind of a person in recovery and gnaw away at the foundations. Each of them has a plausible introduction, but a shaky conclusion. If one of these troublemakers is at work in your head, put a check mark next to it and write a commentary about it below.

__ I am disappointed in sobriety. (I was promised a rose garden)

__ I'm a bad person. (I should do the world a favor and drink myself to death)

__ I'm just an alcoholic. (So I should relapse, since that's what just-alcoholics do)

__ I'm doing so well in my sobriety. (So I should have a drink to celebrate)

__ I'm out of town, who'll ever know? (I will, but I am not an important person in my life)

__ I'm losing my mind. (Maybe drinking/using will restore me to sanity)

__ My addiction is to heroin, not alcohol, so I can safely have a drink now and then. (Once I drink I'll forget all about the trouble heroin got me into)

__ My sobriety is ironclad. (I don't have to work my program any more)

__ By drinking, I'll really get even. (At my funeral they'll be sorry they were mean to me – if anybody shows up)

__ Certain people want me to relapse. (And I'm only too glad to oblige them)

__ Drinking/drugging is the only real pleasure I ever knew. (I'll forget about all the pain and misery it brought me)

__ I am cured of my addiction. (I can now drink or use like non-addicts)

__ I can show these idiots how to stay sober. (My own program is perfect, I don't need to work on it any more)

__ I can stop anytime I want. (I just don't want to, right now)

__ I can't handle my shame and guilt. (So I'll add to my shame and guilt by relapsing)

__ I can't handle the emotional pain. (So I'll make it worse)

__ I guess I just haven't hit bottom yet. (Let me pull something even worse, that'll help)

__ I have a progressive fatal disease. (It's going to get me eventually, even if I stay sober, so why fight it?)

__ I have relapse dreams, so why not go there for real. (I have to act out everything that happens in my dreams)

__ If people see me not drinking they'll guess I'm on the wagon because I'm an alcoholic. (So I better drink and leave no doubt in their minds)

__ I'll never be able to undo all the harm I've done to other people. (So I might as well drink myself to death)

__ I'm insane. (You can't expect a crazy person to get sober)

__ I'm just a defective person. (I'll never get it together for recovery, why try?)

__ I'm making no progress, it's hopeless. (I might as well give up)

__ I'm more enlightened than the average person in recovery. (I can have the occasional drink or drug without risk)

__ I'm not an alcoholic. (So I can have just one or two drinks, like social drinkers)

__ I'm not really myself unless I'm high. (My sober self doesn't live up to my drunk self's high standards)

__ I'm only staying sober to impress X. (I myself am not important enough to stay sober for)

__ I'm powerless against addiction. (I might as well stop trying to fight it)

__ I'm sick of hanging around with all these drunks and addicts. (I'm not one, I can drink or use just a little bit and stop when I want)

__ I've made up my mind I'll never drink again; case closed. (So why bother working any kind of recovery program?)

__ If I stay sober I'll lose all my friends. (Such wonderful friends, they only spend time with me when I'm drunk/high)

__ If it's a choice between going to this meeting or drinking, I'll drink. (I'll forget about trying other meetings or trying to create the kind of meeting that will help me)

__ It's all hopeless. (Might as well check out)

__ My body is falling apart. (Alcohol/drugs will really improve my health, yeah)

__ My character defects are so great I can't ever recover. (Drinking/using will really improve my character)

__ My disease is alcoholism, so I can safely use marijuana. (Once I use marijuana, I'll forget what my disease was)

__ My life is unmanageable. (Drinking/using will really help me get on top of it, yeah)

__ Nobody cares whether I relapse or not. (I'm nobody)

__ Nobody will know whether I relapsed. (I'm nobody)

__ The person who wants me to stay sober is an asshole. (So I'll prove that I'm an even bigger one by relapsing)

__ The world is against me. (Might as well head for the exit, it's hopeless)

__ There's nothing the matter with me. (So why do I need a recovery program?)

__ Trying to change myself or my life is pointless, so f*ck it. (I'd rather screw myself over with drugs and alcohol)

__ _____

Are there items on the list that you recognize as current occupants gnawing away in your mind? If so, write a commentary on a separate sheet that examines each one and puts it to rest.

194. Relapse Smoke Alarms

The purpose of smoke alarms is to alert you to a fire that you can't see yet. Many decisions in life start in the unconscious part of the mind and only rise into awareness later. For example, the decision to change jobs may start out as a problem with getting up in the morning, a feeling of depression, a series of accidents or near-accidents on the job, irritability with co-workers, etc. Only later does the person become consciously aware that this job was not a good fit, and make a conscious plan to change it.

In a similar way, some people run into problems with their recovery without at first being consciously aware of it. Their unconscious mind labors on some recovery issue that absorbs part of their energy and affects their mood and maybe even their muscular coordination. On the surface they remain unaware that anything particular is wrong.

Here is a checklist of signals that may indicate a recovery problem smoldering beneath the surface of your consciousness. Knowing how to read the warning signs from your own unconscious can be a useful relapse prevention skill.

___ I feel like I have a secret but I don't know what it is
___ I get quiet around my sober friends for no particular reason I can express
___ I'm looking forward to something special but I can't articulate what it is
___ I feel mentally like I'm pregnant but I'm not
___ I'm so preoccupied that I stumble over my words
___ I'm so busy processing something that I take out the wrong key, or go to the wrong door, or make other goofs for no obvious reason
___ I'm preoccupied to the point where I trip over my feet
___ I get nervous or twitch a lot even though there's no obvious source of current stress
___ I get hung up on compulsive activity like mindlessly playing Solitaire for hours on end
___ I go to meetings but I pass instead of checking in, or I check in very superficially
___ I think of reasons not to go to my usual meetings at all, or just don't go, without a good reason I can think of
___ I'm late to recovery meetings or appointments without a real excuse
___ When I get to some obvious trigger situation, I don't quickly avoid it or block it
___ When I see liquor or drug stuff, I let my eyes linger on it and don't immediately shut down my thinking about it
___ I ignore parts of my usual recovery program for no good reason, or I ignore all of it
___ I get gloomy or elated in an unusual way for no visible reason
___ I have weird drinking/using dreams night after night
___ I feel that my life is going to change soon but I can't say how or why
___ I feel as if I were going on a trip soon, but I have no real-life travel plans
___ I have the sense that I'm going to die or get sick soon, for no obvious reason
___ I get physical symptoms of stress (e.g. indigestion, insomnia, breathing problems, rashes, etc.) without any manifest reason
___ I get irritable, harsh, unfair, or aggressive for no reason I can explain
___ I suddenly feel like a doormat and let people walk all over me, when I don't have to

___ I feel like I'm going to get revenge on people soon, but can't say exactly how or for what

___ I cut people out of my life and isolate myself without being able to say truthfully why

___ I look for and accept opportunities to get into risky situations for my sobriety

___ I let my mind dwell on drinking or using without thinking it through to the harmful consequences

___ I make plans to look up old drinking/drugging buddies, when I don't really have to, without making firm plans for how to stay sober once I get together with them

___ I go back into places where I used to drink/use when I don't have to, and without making a firm plan for how to stay clean and sober there

___ I somehow end up with liquor or drugs in my house or car and I don't energetically get rid of them

___ I suddenly remember some stash of liquor or drugs I had squirreled away a long time ago, and when I find it I don't throw it out

___ I suddenly feel relieved as if a load was off my mind, but I can't say why or what

___ I feel as if some doom is impending, but I can't say why or what

___ _____

___ _____

___ _____

195. A Quick Relapse Check-Up

The trouble with a checklist such as the one in the previous section is that the symptoms can be due to other causes. For example, you could unconsciously feel a sense of doom because of the stock market or the Mideast or global warming; many clean and sober people do. Smoke detectors may go off from frying chicken. There may be no cause for concern if you find that some of these items apply to you.

Still – if you have checked several of the items on the list, wouldn't it be wise to give yourself a quick relapse check-up? Action may be especially urgent if your checked items include increased exposure to alcohol/drugs. Assuming that you have done some work in the nine domains of this workbook, you could do a review here, for example:

- Have I made progress in addressing my "Body" issues, or am I letting some problem in that area fester and grow? (First Domain)

- Have I really done the best I can to minimize my exposure and to adopt a Daily Do exercise? Or am I being careless or reckless about getting into trigger situations, and am I neglecting my everyday reminders? (Second Domain)

- Have I made progress in learning to do my life's activities clean and sober and in starting up new activities that interest me? Or am I barely functional and doing very little different from when I was drinking/using? (Third Domain)

- Have I worked out who are the friends and who are the opponents of my recovery, and am I making progress in improving my people relationships? Or am I spending too much time with people who are a drag on my recovery, and not enough with people who care for me as a sober person? (Fourth Domain)

- Have I succeeded in building more clean and sober pleasure into my life? Have I identified and learned to deal with my trigger feelings, if any, and do I feel better about my emotional life? Or am I treating recovery as a punishment and retreating into numbness? (Fifth Domain)

- Have I pinpointed my major life style issues and have I made progress in repairing any damage that addiction did to my life style? Or have I resigned myself to the way things were and given up trying to solve my real-life problems? (Sixth Domain)

- Have I reviewed my history and come to an understanding of what part of my life was me and what part was my addiction? Do I have a clearer sense of who I am, where I came from and where I am going? (Seventh Domain)

- Have I identified the sources of support and the problem areas for my recovery in my culture, and have I begun to figure out my role in it? Or am I just another depressed, isolated couch potato soaking up beer commercials? (Eighth Domain)

- Have I made the necessary decisions about treatment and support groups, and do I know how to go about getting what I need from these resources? (Ninth Domain?)

- Above all, have I understood that my recovery is my decision and my responsibility?

As you do this workbook review, listen to your feelings and to your body. Consult with a savvy friend if you have one. Do you find some stressful blank spots, emotionally painful areas, clenched-jaw issues, foot-tapping lines, gut-wrenching sections, or other stuck points? If so, might your unconscious mind be preoccupied with, overwhelmed by, and unable to resolve some of these problem areas? Is your unconscious emotional processing engine overheating? Is that what the "smoke alarm" is trying to tell you?

If you consistently get a number of "hits" on the *Smoke Alarm Checklist* (Page 269), one appropriate response might be to go back and work on one or more of the problem areas you identified in your relapse check-up, above.

> ▶ Action may be particularly urgent (red alert!) if you are getting into new situations where you have drugs/alcohol within reach.

If you bring the resources of your conscious mind to bear on these issues – along with your other resources, such as professional help and group support, if you have them and want them – you may be able to make progress on the problems, get your unconscious unstuck, and move on toward a stronger, freer recovery. You'll also feel better.

If you ignore your unconscious preoccupations, they may go away – or they may erupt to the surface of your consciousness weeks, months or even years later as a "made" decision to abandon recovery and return to drinking/using. Frying chicken left unattended can catch fire and burn the house down. Some people relapse because a crisis catches them unprepared and overwhelms them. But in many instances, they steered into the crisis situation from far away with their eyes wide open. They will claim that circumstances overwhelmed them, but they persistently ignored the warning signs and deliberately put themselves at risk. How does this approach to relapse differ from the person who frankly decides to relapse? Discuss your thinking about this issue:

_____

_____

_____

196. Recognizing Relapse Styles

Relapses come in different forms. The "Type A" relapse is a blunt, sudden return to heavy drinking/using – a bender. The person jumps back into the addiction with both feet. The person usually plans this relapse ahead of time. Sometimes they will hole up somewhere, put everything else aside, and concentrate on drinking/drugging as much as possible as fast as possible until money or consciousness end, whichever comes first. This style of relapse resembles suicide. There's more about it in Section 10, below.

By contrast, the "Type B" relapse comes on tiptoes. The person begins with a single drink or dose, "just one," followed by a pregnant pause that may last hours, days, or longer. It may seem that this was merely a slip, an isolated accident. But it soon turns out that the initial drink/dose was merely the thin end of the wedge, and more is to follow. By a set of slippery rationalizations, the one drink/use leads (after some time) to another, and then after a shorter time to a third, and after a still shorter time to more and more, until the person has pulled out all the stops and returned to their former level of drinking/using, or worse. This style of relapse resembles a seduction. It may take weeks, months, or years for it to reach full development. It leads to the same place as the Type A, but it comes on differently and takes longer to get there. There's more about this type in Section 12, Page 278.

Have you seen or experienced either of these types of relapse?   Yes No

Have you experienced a different type, or a hybrid variety?   Yes No

What can you learn about relapse from knowing about the different approaches that people take to get there?

_____

_____

197. My Relapse Plan

People who consciously plan their relapses get points for honesty, but usually not for preparedness. They rarely think beyond laying in an adequate supply. The next worksheet presents an outline of typical issues that arise further down the relapse road. If you're planning a relapse, you can use this worksheet to plan it all the way through – and perhaps change your mind in the process.

Worksheet 55: My Relapse Plan

MY RELAPSE PLAN	
Substance I plan to use first	
Source where I plan to get the substance	
What I will say if I am seen getting the substance	
Place where I will hide the substance until ready to use	
Amount of money I plan to devote to the first drink/hit	
Source of the first money	
Place where I plan to take the first drink/hit	
Date I plan to do the first drink/hit	
Time of day I plan to do the first drink/hit	
Why I haven't done this relapse earlier	
Why I can't wait and do this relapse later	
Who if anyone will be with me when I do the first one	
Story I am going to tell others to explain what I am doing	
How I will keep the first one secret from people who care	
Story I am telling myself to convince myself this is not a relapse	__ I'm cured of my addiction now, I can handle drinking/using __ I never was an addict, I can drink/use normally __ I deserve a little reward, I can have just one __ This is just a little slip __ This is just an experiment to see if I can handle it now __ I just need one more blow-out before I commit to recovery __
Other substances I plan to use after I get started	

MY RELAPSE PLAN	
Total budget for this relapse	__ Drugs/alcohol $_____ __ Transportation $_____ __ Shelter $_____ __ Food $_____ __ Medical care $_____ __ Other $_____ Total $_____
Source of the money for the whole relapse budget	
Will the rent or mortgage be paid during my relapse?	__ Yes __ Not sure __ No
Will the utility bills be paid during my relapse?	__ Yes __ Not sure __ No
Will I be able to meet my other obligations during my relapse?	__ Yes __ Not sure __ No
Will I miss any appointments, birthdays, anniversaries; sales, concerts, get-togethers or other events because of this relapse?	__ Yes __ Not sure __ No
Will I have a job or business when the relapse is over?	__ Yes __ Not sure __ No
Will I have a roof over my head when the relapse is over?	__ Yes __ Not sure __ No
Will this relapse cause the end of a relationship I'm in?	__ Yes __ Not sure __ No
How will my family members react to this relapse?	
Am I – could I be – pregnant?	
Having spent time in recovery, will I be able to really enjoy my drinking/using without feeling stupid and guilty?	__ Yes __ Not sure __ No
How will I get transportation during this relapse?	
If I drive a car during this relapse, can I afford a drunk driving rap?	__ No
Number I will call if I need medical care as result of relapse	
Person who will put up bail for me in case I need it	
How will I get food during this relapse, if I want any?	
Will my relapse substances interact with any medications I'm taking?	__ Yes __ Not sure __ No
Person who will come looking for me in case something happens to me during relapse	
Am I carrying identification?	__ Yes __ No
Will I have clean clothes and underwear during and at the end of this relapse?	__ Yes __ Not sure __ No

MY RELAPSE PLAN	
Will I shower, shave and take care of my personal hygiene during this relapse?	__ Yes __ Not sure __ No
Do I plan to end my life with this relapse?	__ Yes __ Not sure __ No
In case of a medical emergency, have I left legally binding instructions whether to resuscitate me?	__ Yes __ Not sure __ No
Will I be having sex with strangers, or will strangers be having sex with me, during this relapse?	__ Yes __ Not sure __ No
In case sex happens, do I have condoms and will I have control to make sure they are used?	__ Yes __ Not sure __ No
Have I signed organ donor papers so my usable body parts can help someone else, just in case?	__ Yes __ Not sure __ No
Are there children to consider?	__ Yes __ No __ Not sure
If there is a dog, cat, birds, fish or plants to consider, will they be taken care of during this relapse?	__ Yes __ Not sure __ No
Are any of my family members liable to die during my relapse?	
Are any of my friends liable to die during my relapse?	
In case I black out and kill somebody during this relapse, am I prepared to put up with the guilt?	__ No
How will I keep my belongings from being ripped off during this relapse?	
Will newspapers pile up outside my door during this relapse?	__ Yes __ Not sure __ No
Will I miss any important mail during this relapse?	__ Yes __ Not sure __ No
Have I made a will and is it located where it can be found, in case?	__ Yes __ Not sure __ No
Will my health insurance cover another round of detox and treatment?	__ Yes __ Not sure __ No
How will I handle it if the phone rings during my relapse?	
How will I feel physically when I am done with this relapse?	
How will I detox after this relapse?	
How much fun will that detox be?	
Will I be able to hide the fact that I relapsed?	__ No __ Not sure __ Yes
How will I rebuild the trust of the people close to me, if any?	

MY RELAPSE PLAN	
Will my next recovery be easier or harder than this one?	__ Easier __ Harder __ I may not have another recovery left in me __ Not sure
What will people in my recovery meetings say when they hear about my relapse?	
How will I explain my relapse to people?	
How will I feel about starting my recovery out from Day 1 again?	
What will my counselor(s) say when they hear about my relapse?	
Will I feel better or worse about myself for having done this relapse?	
What message will I have sent with this relapse?	
Will my friends respect me more after this relapse?	
Will people feel sorry for me that I relapsed?	
Will people love me more because of my relapse?	
Will this relapse make people be sorry for the way they treated me?	
If this relapse is a cry for help, will it be answered?	
What problem of mine will this relapse solve?	
How will the world be different as a consequence of this relapse?	
The point of this relapse is:	

198. Hitting the Panic Button

At the moment when a person who has been in recovery for some time takes the first drink/hit, two conflicting reactions tend to occur within the brain. There is a rush of intoxication that brings back the old euphoric feelings of addiction. Simultaneously there is a sensation of panic, like the moment before a collision, because ending recovery is a psychological, physical, and social disaster.

Have you ever had a drinking/using dream and woken up in a cold sweat, terrified that you have blown your sobriety? Then you've experienced a taste of relapse panic.

Which of these two opposite reactions – euphoria or panic – predominates in a particular instance depends on the individual and on the situation. Many people ignore the panic or misinterpret it as a reason to drink/use more. But for some people, the moment of panic serves as a last-chance alarm that brings their inner sobriety powers to red alert and energizes them, in one last desperate effort, to fling away the bottle or the rig and flee the scene to safety. Even people who have studiously planned to go on a bender sometimes recoil in rational terror and save themselves when the substance first hits their bloodstream.

Instant reaction is the key to survival in relapse panic. You may have only a second or two before the effects of the drink or drug overpower your body's response-to-danger chemistry. This is not a time for reflection or argument; it's a time for reflex response by the major muscles. Like a pilot hitting the eject button, you need to put significant physical distance between yourself and the drink/drug NOW, or it's too late.

As with any powerful emotional experience, this kind of incident calls for a supportive debriefing. Whatever your support systems may be, now is the time to use them. You've had a slip, but you've avoided a major catastrophe. You've escaped a possible death trap with only minor injuries. If you have a counselor, call. If you have a support group, insist on sharing and getting feedback. If you keep a journal, write in it. This could be a powerfully enlightening and energizing experience for your recovery, and an educational lesson for everyone fortunate enough to have shared it with you.

199. Slippery Logic That Lubricates the Seduction-Style Relapse

A person who quick-ejects from a bender-style relapse may still fall prey to the Type B variety – the gradual seduction that may take weeks, months or years.

A hallmark of the slow-seduction type of relapse is persistent mental preoccupation with the next drink/drug. Having "broken the ice" with the first one, the person spends hours, days, weeks, months or (rarely) years thinking and thinking and thinking about the next one. In some people, this becomes an obsession that crowds out all other mental activity.

Much of the reasoning that people do in the pregnant pause between their first one and their next one seems twisted and laughable to the sober mind. The checklist that follows gives a fair sample. But anyone who has been there will tell you that this lame parade of rationalizations seemed brilliant at the time.

If you have experience with this kind of relapse, put a checkmark next to all the arguments that you have used on yourself; be sure to enter and share any new ones of your own addicted brain's invention.

Even if you've never experienced this kind of relapse, it may be worth doing the exercise for prophylactic reasons. If you can prepare your mind to recognize and break down this kind of reasoning ahead of time, you may have a better chance of derailing a Type B relapse if you ever fall into one. Seduction doesn't always have to succeed; if you can see the con, you may be able to break it.

__ Since I handled the first one without any problem, I can obviously handle another one

__ Since I stopped after the first one, I can have any number and stop whenever I want

__ Since I was able to stop after the first one, I obviously never was addicted, so I can have another one

__ Since I was able to stop after the first one, I obviously am cured of my addiction now, so I can have another one

__ Since I was able to stop after the first one, I am obviously recovered now, so I can have another one

__ I'm not really relapsing, I'm practicing moderation management, so I can have another

__ I'm not really relapsing, I'm practicing controlled drinking/using, so I can have another

__ I'm not really relapsing, I'm drinking/using normally again, so I can have another

__ I'm not really relapsing, I'm doing drink counting, and I can have another

__ I'm not really relapsing, I'm experimenting with my tolerance, and so I can have another

__ It's not a relapse because I have nothing to relapse from, so I can have another

__ This isn't the drug I'm addicted to, so I can have another of these

__ I'm not really relapsing, I just had a slip, and it would still be just a slip if I have another

__That first one was just for a special occasion; fortunately, there's another occasion coming up that's just as special

__ That first one was just because I had a really difficult moment; and I feel another difficult moment coming on

__ Why "must" I not drink/use? I will stop making myself miserable with "musts" and follow my preferences and have another

__ It's true that every time I've tried to limit my drinking/using in the past ten years it hasn't worked, but the manly thing is to keep trying, so I should have another

__ As long as I drink/use for the purpose of enjoyment and not for the purpose of evading my psychological problems, it's OK to have more, so I can have another

__ As long as I drink slowly instead of gulping, it's OK to have more, so I can have another

__ It's OK to have another one as long as I don't get drunk, and I didn't, so I can have another

__ As long as I only drink/use to be sociable, not to try to solve my problems, it's OK to have more, so I can have another

__ That first one was just to celebrate my recovery and it's worth celebrating again, so I can have another

__ That first one was to give me a different perspective on my recovery, and that was interesting and worth doing again soon

__ That first one was just a break to give me the strength to go on with my recovery; I'm feeling like I need another break soon

__ I still have some left after the first one; if I keep it around I might get triggered to drink/use later, so I better do it now

__ If I were to avoid having another it would seem as if I thought I had a problem, so I should have another to prove that I don't

__ If I were to agonize over having another one it would tend to suggest that I have a problem, so I'll have another one without thinking about it

__ Since I blew my recovery anyway, I might as well go all the way and have another one or two or twelve

__ Having had this one makes me feel so guilty and ashamed that I can't handle it and I need to have another one to make me feel better

__ _____

__ _____

__ _____

__ _____

200. Turning Nonsense Around

All of the slippery arguments in the previous checklist end up with the express or implied conclusion that "I can have another." Can you take each of these arguments and come to the opposite conclusion? For example:

- Slippery argument: "Since I handled the first one without any problem, I can obviously handle another one."

- Same argument turned around: "I handled the first one without a problem, but I think I'll stop right there and not push my luck. I'm not going to play Russian roulette."

- Slippery argument: "I'm not really relapsing, I'm drinking/using normally again, so I can have another"

- Same argument turned around: "Maybe I'm not really relapsing and maybe I'm drinking/using normally again, but if that's the case I'll do what any normal person would do and never touch the sh*t again, considering the grief it's caused me."

Using these examples, for each argument on the slippery logic checklist that has run through your mind, write a counter-argument that starts from the same premise but comes to the conclusion that it's better to stop. (Use a separate sheet).

201. When Drinking/Using Is No Fun Anymore

It's been said that the experience of recovery can pretty much spoil the fun of drinking/drugging. If you have fallen back into drinking/using, you'll find that your clean and sober self hasn't disappeared. It may even speak more insistently. Many people continue to feel the urge to get free of drugs/alcohol even while they're under the influence. Does this describe you?

    __ I totally pretend to function like a clean and sober person while I'm high
    __ If I admit to myself that I'm under the influence, I feel miserable
    __ With a bottle in front of me, I read sobriety literature
    __ I go to sobriety meetings (or recovery chat rooms) while I'm under the
        influence
    __ I call up sober friends while inebriated and pretend to be sober
    __ I give people advice on how to stay clean and sober, even though I'm not

The common denominator here is a tortured consciousness. Long gone are the days when you could drink/use without worries. When you relapse after experiencing a period of recovery, you will probably feel less comfortable and more troubled than you did before you stopped drinking/using in the first place. The whole alcohol/drug scene now reveals itself to your enlightened eyes as infinitely cynical and depressing. The memory of recovery remains alive in you and now exercises its own seduction. Embrace it if you get the chance.

202. Don't Beat Yourself Up

One of the most common feelings after a relapse is shame, humiliation, and worthlessness. If negative feelings of this type motivate you to stop drinking/using, that's fine. But for many people, these powerful depressing feelings only reinforce the urge to drink/use. "I drink because I'm ashamed, and I'm ashamed because I drink." (Try the *Working with Strong Trigger Feelings and Cravings Worksheet* on Page 136 if this applies to you.) Beating yourself to an emotional pulp may not be the best way to energize yourself to move forward.

Recovery from relapse is easier if you focus mentally on your strengths, even though your strengths may seem much less obvious. When you have a ton of relapse and a grain of sobriety, concentrate on the grain. Compare these two approaches:

Worksheet 56: Focusing on Weakness or Strength

FOCUSING ON WEAKNESS	FOCUSING ON STRENGTH
My relapse proves I'm helpless	Before my relapse I had 12 days clean, so I'm not totally helpless
I'm no good	Being sober for 12 days showed I'm not a total wimp
I'll never get sober	I thought I could never get sober but I did it for 12 days which is more than I ever thought I could do
I did such horrible things during my relapse	I've been sober all day and I'm starting to take care of business again
I deserve to be really punished for my relapse	I deserve another chance and I'm going to do better this time around
I can't figure out why I'm such a loser	I have a pretty good idea what actions I need to take to avoid a repeat of this incident
I'm the biggest piece of sh*t in the world, I'll never accomplish anything	I'm not any worse than a lot of other people who have gotten sober; if they can do it, so can I

It doesn't take a rocket scientist to see that the person who focuses on their strengths is more likely to break out of the relapse cycle than the person who sees only their shortcomings and defects. Recovery from relapse begins in the mind. Somewhere in the chaotic and polluted war zone of the relapsed brain, the hope must arise that recovery is possible.

The message of hope is, "Yes, I can!" The vital belief in one's own competency, despite the burden of disempowering emotions, supplies the energy to take essential survival actions, such as flushing the addictive substance down the toilet and making sober contact with supportive people.

203. Debriefing and Re-Entry after Relapse

One way or another, many people manage to terminate their relapses before the relapse terminates them. The things that give traction to people's survival instincts and motivate them to get out of the relapse cycle are as varied and unpredictable as the impulses that bring people out of addiction and into recovery in the first place. One utility of a large workbook such as this one is to present a wealth of diverse issues, so as to increase the probability that one of them will be the trigger that activates a person's recovery impulse and leads them back to solid ground. Recovery from relapse is, fortunately, a very common experience.

When you are clean and sober again, it may be useful to figure out what happened to bring about the relapse and to take preventive measures against a repeat. Because remembering a relapse can be emotionally stressful, it may be especially helpful to debrief with supportive friends. Even if you are stable now, it is a service to others to share your relapse experience so that others can have the opportunity to learn by hearing rather than by doing.

If you have a support group and are ready to give your debriefing, is your group ready to receive it? Few people will readily explore their relapses with a group that is judgmental, opinionated, and likely to overwhelm the person with unsolicited advice. If you relapsed you probably already feel bad enough without having other people dump on you. Sometimes people leave their support group permanently after a relapse because of the group's judgmental attitude. Do you think this kind of attitude advances the group?

It may be helpful to think of your recovery as a project that has never been done before. This is strictly true. Other people have made their recoveries, but they aren't you. There are no ready-made blueprints for the recovery of YOU. You can and should learn from other people's experiences, but the bottom line is that you have to design and build and maintain your recovery yourself. In any such project, mistakes are inevitable.

In the real world, no computer program, no blueprint, no recipe, no business plan, no serious project of any kind goes from first draft through completion without errors and omissions. Making mistakes and learning from them is the nature of progress. Time spent in blaming and shaming is time wasted. Once you have identified what went wrong, move your thinking forward to the path ahead. Will similar situations such as the one that tripped you up arise again? If so, what will you do differently next time? Visualize yourself navigating the next trouble spot and emerging successfully with your recovery intact.

The next section of this work area contains a debriefing outline that allows you to get a grip on what went wrong last time and focus ahead so that you can strengthen your recovery program in this problem area.

204. My Post-Relapse Debriefing Outline

You will note that the Relapse Debriefing outline (below) approximately follows the system that a physician might use in assessing a patient, beginning with a history and ending with a plan of action. In analyzing your relapse you are, in effect, becoming your own therapist and counselor.

You are in a position to know yourself better than anyone else, if you work at it; you are always there when you need yourself; and your fees are reasonable. The more skillful and confident you become at being your own therapist, the better are your chances to survive any challenge to your recovery.

Worksheet 57: Post-Relapse Debriefing

REPORT ON MY RECENT RELAPSE – AN OUTLINE	
Date I put the first drink/dose of this relapse into my body	
Circumstances of first input	
I. Pre-Input	
My continuous clean and sober time prior to putting first drink/dose into my body this time:	
Date that I made the conscious decision to drink/use this time:	
"Termites" at work in my mind prior to making decision to drink/use: (See Page 267)	
Warning signs of possible relapse before the day I made the decision to drink/use: (Refer to "Smoke Alarms" checklist, Page 269)	
Action I took to respond to warning signs of possible relapse:	
Pre-relapse status of my concerns about my physical and mental health: (first Domain)	

REPORT ON MY RECENT RELAPSE – AN OUTLINE	
Pre-relapse status of my efforts to minimize my exposure to alcohol/ drugs, to create safe space and time, and to do Daily Do exercises: (Second Domain)	
Pre-relapse status of my progress in learning to do activities sober and to acquire sober new activities that interest me: (Third Domain)	
Pre-relapse status of my work to maximize my recovery support from people and to minimize contact with people who oppose my recovery: (Fourth Domain)	
Pre-relapse status of my efforts to bring more pleasure into my recovery, to recognize and handle my trigger feelings, and to develop a more satisfying emotional life: (Fifth Domain)	
Pre-relapse status of my work to repair the impact of drinking/using on my life style and improve my real-world situation: (Sixth Domain)	
Pre-relapse status of my efforts to get oriented in my culture in a clean and sober manner: (Seventh Domain)	
Pre-relapse status of my work to understand my personal history, to separate what was me from what was my addiction: (Eighth Domain)	
Pre-relapse status of my involvement with treatment and with support groups: (Ninth Domain)	

Report on My Recent Relapse – An Outline	
Pre-relapse status of any other concerns of relevance:	
Summary of major unresolved problem areas in my recovery, pre-relapse:	
II. Post-Input Relapse Course	
Interval between first drink/use and last drink/use of this relapse:	
Type of relapse onset (sudden, gradual, or other):	
Substances used, sequence, amounts:	
Immediate consequences of this relapse:	
Ideas/feelings that motivated me to get out of the relapse:	
External influences that motivated me to get out of the relapse:	
III. Plan to Prevent Recurrence	
Specific changes I'm going to make so that I have a more successful outcome next time:	

205. Down Is Not the Way to Up

People who rejected every life ring offered to them and are sinking back into their old pattern of intoxication still need not and should not give up on recovery. Relapse can be a complex, twisty process, just as recovery can be, and opportunities to step off its downward course and return to a clean and sober life can arise at any moment. Seize them if you can.

It's important to know that worse is not better. Your chances of recovery do not improve as you sink lower and lower in life. Although some people do bounce back from the gutter, they are the rare exception. Studies show that your chances of recovery go down as you do. The more you lose – job, family, shelter, car, health – the more liable you are also to lose the battle for recovery and for life itself. Don't delude yourself that by sinking deeper and deeper into relapse, you're really coming closer to your turnaround point, so that your relapse is really a stealth recovery tool. That is lunacy.

206. Summary: My Relapse Prevention Checklist

The best relapse prevention is to work on getting to know yourself and building and updating your Personal Recovery Program. Unless you happen to be one of the lucky individuals who perfectly match the parameters of one of the off-the-rack recovery programs, it does little good to adopt one as is. At the very least, you have to rework it and adapt it from start to finish until it becomes truly yours. Otherwise, it may sit inside you like an alien transplant and in time you will reject it.

Many decades of experience have gone into the finding that effective treatment is individualized (National Institute on Drug Abuse, see *Introduction*, Page **Error! Bookmark not defined.**). Institutionalized programs may in rare cases come close to the ideal of individualized treatment, but the treatment you give yourself can match your needs perfectly.

Here is a checklist that may be useful in tuning up your personal recovery program and in modifying it as your feelings and your situation develop. You are not static; your recovery program needs to develop as you do. Perhaps, like a snake, you can shed your old one from time to time and grow a new one, very similar to the old one, but bigger, fresher, more supple, and more comfortable.

Worksheet 58: Recovery Tune-Up and Relapse Prevention Checklist

MY RECOVERY TUNE-UP AND RELAPSE PREVENTION CHECKLIST	
___	I remember why I originally wanted to get clean and sober
___	I now see additional reasons to stay clean and sober, beyond what I saw to begin with
___	I understand and use the method of analyzing my choices in terms of the Sobriety Priority, choosing S over A (Chapter One)
___	I know what my issues are concerning my body and my mental health, and I am working on them (First Domain)
___	I minimize my exposure to alcohol/drugs to the degree necessary for my recovery (Second Domain)
___	I know what my main trigger situations are and I have worked out a method to either avoid them or handle them clean and sober (Second Domain)
___	I have safe places and safe times where I can go to recharge my recovery fuel cells (Second Domain)
___	I start my day with a carefully thought-out personal affirmation and reminder ritual (Second Domain)
___	I have learned to handle all my necessary activities in a clean and sober manner, and have learned to avoid for the time being those that I cannot yet manage (Third Domain)
___	I have started clean and sober new activities that fill my time and engage my interest (Third Domain)
___	I know who the people are who support my recovery and I am developing closer relationships with them (Fourth Domain)
___	I am learning how to open up my new way of living to others and how to feel comfortable in my new identity as a person who does not drink or use (Fourth Domain)
___	I am doing my honest best to work on improving my ongoing relationships in a way that is positive for my recovery (Fourth Domain)
___	I am getting better at dealing with people who oppose my recovery and in learning to manage them or avoid them (Fourth Domain)
___	I am paying attention to my feelings and learning to recognize and accept them (Fifth Domain)
___	I am recapturing the pleasures that alcohol/drugs took over (Fifth Domain)
___	I am doing something clean and sober every day to make me feel good (Fifth Domain)
___	I know at least three ways of handling strong trigger feelings when they come up (Fifth Domain)
___	I feel good about being clean and sober now (Fifth Domain)
___	I recognize what my old emotional issues are and I have a plan for handling them (Fifth Domain)
___	I know the impact of my past drinking/drugging on my work situation and I am working on it (Sixth Domain)
___	I understand the impact of my past drinking/drugging on my housing situation and I am doing what can be done (Sixth Domain)
___	I recognize the impact of my past drinking/drugging on my living situation, and I am making the appropriate moves (Sixth Domain)
___	I see the impact of my past drinking/drugging on my social life, and I am putting effort into it (Sixth Domain)
___	I can see the effects of my past drinking/drugging on my housekeeping and personal hygiene, and I am taking the appropriate steps (Sixth Domain)
___	I understand the relationship between my past drinking/drugging and my sex life, and I am doing what I consider best for my recovery (Sixth Domain)

	MY RECOVERY TUNE-UP AND RELAPSE PREVENTION CHECKLIST
___	I recognize the impact of my past drinking/drugging on my financial situation, and I am doing the best I can (Sixth Domain)
___	I know the relationship between my drinking/drugging and my health insurance, and I am acting accordingly (Sixth Domain)
___	I am doing what needs to be done regarding my legal situation (Sixth Domain)
___	I am attending to any other life style issues that I feel would strengthen my recovery (Sixth Domain)
___	I understand that my sobriety is the foundation of all my life style improvements (Sixth Domain)
___	I understand that becoming addicted can happen to anyone who drinks or uses and that I am not a bad person because it happened to me (Seventh Domain)
___	I have a clearer picture of who I was before I got sidetracked by substance use, and I accept the original clean and sober me as valid and worthwhile (Seventh Domain)
___	I have calculated and summed up the cost of my past substance use in terms of time and money, and made better plans for those resources in the future (Seventh Domain)
___	I have separated out the parts of my past life that were due to my addiction, and have a clearer sense of my strengths and weaknesses as a clean and sober person (Seventh Domain)
___	I have emotionally said good-bye to the person I was when I was drinking/using, and have finished grieving, and I have a clearer sense of purpose in my life as I move forward as a clean and sober person (Seventh Domain)
___	I am learning to recognize and to distinguish the messages in the culture around me that promote addiction and those that are supportive of my recovery (Eighth Domain)
___	I feel more oriented about the social, political and economic interests that have an influence on the setting in which my recovery is taking place (Eighth Domain)
___	I am making progress at becoming a member of my communities in a way that affirms my recovery (Eighth Domain)
___	I have explored the treatment resources available to me and I have made the maximum possible use of them for my recovery under the circumstances (Ninth Domain)
___	I am an actively participating member of a community of people who are working on their own recoveries from substance addictions and who support me and look to me to support them (Ninth Domain)
___	I have a better sense for what is going on inside of me and I monitor myself frequently for possible relapse early warning signs
___	I recognize the mental bugs that could undermine my recovery program and I know how to handle them when they show up
___	If despite my best efforts I should relapse, I have prepared myself to eject immediately and to defeat the seductive self-talk that would lead me deeper into the pit
___	I understand that staying clean and sober is my responsibility and that no one else will or can do it for me
___	I will not drink or use, no matter what

My Recovery Plan for Today

Some situations call for sobriety planning on an hour-by-hour basis. Use this worksheet when you feel that you would benefit by a more fine-grained structure in your life, or when you feel a crisis situation coming on, or in unusual situations like trips out of town, weddings, funerals, vacations, business conventions, etc. Be sure to build into it your Daily Do or other recovery exercises (see Page 70). Here is an example:

Worksheet 59: My Recovery Plan for Today (Example)

TIME / ACTIVITY / PERSON / EMOTION	RISK LEVEL FOR ME	MY PLAN
7:10	–	Do my Daily Do
7:55 Return to work after two weeks in rehab. I'm going to run into Dave B., my former dealer, in the break room. All kinds of triggers for me.	Red alert	Don't go near the break room, bring thermos from home instead, avoid the SOB
Lunch. What if drug zombies L. and V. invite me to go eat at the tavern with them?	Warp 7 danger	Early in the day, ask T. and F. to go to lunch in the cafeteria with me, then I can tell L. and G. I'm already busy if they ask me.
2 pm annual Performance Evaluation by Terry, my manager. I feel very insecure and anxious.	No immediate danger but could be Big Trouble when I get home. I might be very depressed, or I might want to "celebrate."	Definitely plan to have coffee with S. (sober friend) right after work and then go to a meeting this evening and unload it on the group.

On Page 291 there is a blank Sober Day Plan to photocopy.

When the day is over and you are safely in bed and out of danger, take a moment and think (or write some notes) about the following issues:

- Did I anticipate the major trouble spots?
- Were my feelings what I thought they would be?
- Did my evasive maneuvers work?
- Did I do OK in the situations where I had to confront the issue head on?
- Was it helpful to talk about the issues with my friend?
- Was it helpful to discuss the issues in my support group?
- What have I learned from today?
- What could I do better next time?

Worksheet 60: My Recovery Plan for Today

My Sober Day Plan for: _____ (date)

TIME / ACTIVITY / PERSON / FEELING	RISK LEVEL FOR ME	MY PLAN

Chapter Thirteen

My Recovery Plan for This Week

The Sober Week Worksheet works on the same idea as the Sober Day Plan. Use it when you have the hour-by-hour details pretty much in hand, but need to get a more strategic overview of what is coming up for you. The Sober Week Plan is also handy if you participate in a check-in at a weekly recovery meeting. Here is a filled-in example. A blank weekly worksheet for photocopying is on the next page. When the week is over, you can do a "Week in Review." You could pretend you're doing the Sunday evening news broadcast.

Worksheet 61: My Sober Week (Example)

DAY	ACTIVITY/PERSON/EMOTION	RISK LEVEL	MY PLAN
Mo	Day off	Serious!	Take car in to be fixed, dentist appointment at 11, etc. (STAY BUSY!!)
Tu	Back to work	OK	
We	Eve: bowling	Alert	Stay away from Frank the boozehound, hang with Larry instead
Th	Routine	OK	Go to meeting, prepare mind for tomorrow:
Fr	Mother's visit	Red alert!	Take her to Appleby's and finally tell her I don't drink anymore and don't want to be around it.
Sa	Ditto	ditto	Take her to museum, park, anyplace but Louie's.
Su	Mother gone, collapse	High alert	Definitely go to meeting and de-brief.

Worksheet 62: My Recovery Plan for This Week

My Sober Week Plan for Week Beginning: _____

DAY	ACTIVITY /PERSON/ FEELING	RISK LEVEL	MY PLAN
Mo			
Tu			
We			
Th			
Fr			
Sa			
Su			

207. My Week in Review (Example)

Last week I faced the following challenges to my sobriety:

Dealing with free time
Handling re-entry into the work environment
Surviving a family visit

These things were challenges to my sobriety because:

When I have nothing else to do my first impulse is to get loaded
My work environment is filled with drug associations and people
My mother can really stress me out

I solved these challenges by doing the following:

I stayed busy on Monday doing things to take care of myself
At work I made a point to hang with people who do not do drugs and to stay
away from the dealers and the druggies I used to run with
I talked about what is going on with me at my meeting and got feedback
I asserted myself with Mom and took her to non-drinking places where I
wouldn't have to deal with her getting drunk and get into gut-wrenching
arguments; I actually enjoyed some parts of her visit, unbelievable as it
seems

I learned the following about my recovery plan from my experiences this week:

If I plan my day to stay busy, I can avoid the idle-hands problem
It makes a difference who I hang with at work
Talking at the meeting and getting feedback is really helpful to me
If I put my foot down with my Mom I can survive at least a short visit

Next week I will face the following challenges to my sobriety:

It should be a regular type week ... I'll keep on keeping on ... my main
problem may be the beginnings of boredom setting in at work again ...
should I think about going back to school? Taking a night class?
Starting a relationship? ... This is something I can talk about in my
meeting.

208. My Week in Review

Last week I faced the following challenges to my sobriety:

_____

_____

_____

These things were challenges to my sobriety because:

_____

_____

_____

I solved these challenges by doing the following:

_____

_____

_____

I learned the following about my recovery plan from my experiences this week:

_____

_____

_____

Next week I will face the following challenges to my sobriety:

_____

_____

_____

Chapter Fourteen

My Recovery Plan for My Life

In this chapter you can begin to map out a longer view of your recovery road. Remember, as always, that this is not about people in general; it's about who you are as an individual. All the work you have been doing in the nine domains has prepared you to understand better who exactly you are and what you need to do to lead your life in a clean and sober way.

It may be especially advisable to use a pencil in this chapter. Serious engineers, architects, programmers, business people – any people who make plans for real life – know that revisions and modifications are the rule, not the exception.

209. Overview of This Chapter

In writing out your life plan, you could start by reviewing the "My Plan for …" sections of the nine domains and copying out or summarizing the most important points. The chapter begins with a worksheet for that purpose.

When you have the pieces all laid out, one possible next move is to look for connections between them – overlapping fact patterns that show up in all or several domains. The second section of the chapter discusses connections.

If there is more than one issue, it makes sense to prioritize them. That is the purpose of the section that follows.

With that done, the general concept for addressing each concern has to be translated into the gory details. There is a worksheet for that purpose.

Finally, you can summarize your life plan in your own words in a form that is suitable for sharing with others.

Worksheet 63: Summing Up

SUMMING UP MY WORK FROM THE PREVIOUS CHAPTERS	
Domain	**My Main Issues**
(1) **My Body** (see Page 56)	
(2) **My Exposure** (see Page 71)	
(3) **My Activities** (see Page 90)	
(4) **My People** (see Page 112)	
(5) **My Feelings** (see Page 146)	
(6) **My Life Style** (see Page 162)	
(7) **My History** (see Page 206)	

SUMMING UP MY WORK FROM THE PREVIOUS CHAPTERS	
Domain	My Main Issues
(8) My Culture (see Page 229)	
(9) My Treatment and Support Groups (see Page 258)	
Other concerns I want to build into my life plan:	

210. Making Connections

Do you see connections between some different domains in your *Summing Up Worksheet*? For example, do you notice that your summaries of your Exposure, your Feelings, your Activities and your People Domains all point at the same set of facts in your life? Are there big overlaps?

For example, if your boss demands that you take prospective clients to nightclubs and get them drunk as a sales technique, this same set of facts will show up from different angles in your Exposure, Feelings, Activities and People work areas.

Or if you find yourself repeatedly tempted to do drugs when feeling worthless after a series of unsuccessful job interviews following your rehabilitation from a major injury, this same set of facts will show up in your Body Domain, your Feelings Domain and in your Life Style Domain, at a minimum.

Use this space to identify any fact patterns in your life that overlap two or more domains in your earlier work in this book:

_____

_____

_____

_____

_____

_____

_____

_____

_____

_____

_____

_____

_____

211. Lining Up Issues in Order

If you have identified only one set of facts that shows up as a concern for you in several different work areas, your starting point is obvious. But if you have identified several sets of facts that are of concern to you, it may be helpful for you to decide which of them is the most important to solve first.

For example, Sandy lives in a crack-infested run-down apartment building (heavy exposure, repeated triggers) and works in a bar (not a safe space and no social support for recovery) and has a partner who abuses prescription drugs (a close-range opponent of Sandy's recovery, heavy emotional triggers). Sandy realizes that this is a pattern in Sandy's life (unresolved emotional issue). Sandy by this point attends recovery support group meetings regularly and does a "Daily Do" every morning. What does Sandy do next?

Maybe the place to start is by moving to a better neighborhood. But if Sandy's partner is spending their moving money on drugs, then maybe the place to start is to end that relationship.

Or maybe Sandy's partner would be willing and able to get into treatment? Or maybe Sandy can get active in a Residents' Association to drive out the dealers and force the landlord to fix up the place? Or should Sandy start by getting counseling to deal with Sandy's psychological pattern?

Or should Sandy avoid real-life changes and concentrate on learning blissful acceptance of things as they are?

You may want to make several Sobriety T-Charts (Chapter One) to get clarity if you have a multi-issue situation, such as this one. Talking it out and getting feedback from your support group can be especially helpful here. Other people could help you "think outside of the box" and see solutions that didn't occur to you.

It's difficult enough to prioritize two or three issues. If your list has more than three issues, it might be helpful first to trim it down to the Big Three. A long list can loom so large that you could feel overwhelmed and get nothing done. It might also be helpful to write the issues down on small pieces of paper and shuffle them around until you find an order that makes the most sense.

Sometimes it's necessary to break each issue down into its details before the best order of priorities emerges. Try skipping ahead to the "Gory Details" section and then come back here and finish prioritizing.

When prioritizing issues, it's often necessary to get more information about one of the options. For example:

- Is there a treatment program that would accept Sandy's partner?
- Would Sandy's partner agree to go, if a program were available?
- Is there an apartment in a less drug-infested neighborhood that Sandy can afford?
- Would a move put Sandy closer to a good recovery meeting?
- Is a Residents' Association already in place or would Sandy have to start it up?
- Are there other jobs for someone with Sandy's qualifications?
- How much would a counselor charge?

Use this space to begin a list of the questions you need answered in order to finish prioritizing <u>your</u> problems.

_____

_____

_____

_____

_____

_____

_____

How can you tell whether you have prioritized your issues in the best way? The optimum order for attacking your problems is the one with good *transitions*.

You have the best order when your solution to the first one puts you in a good position to solve the next one, and so down the line.

Skilled pool players make this sort of analysis all the time – at the end of each shot, the cue ball should be in a good position for the next shot.

When the issues aren't lined up well, the opposite happens: after you solve the first one, the next one is more difficult than it was to begin with.

When you have the information you need in order to understand what your choices are, and have thought about all the different possible ways to tackle the issues, and have discussed it with as many other people as you can get to listen and give you feedback, then write your list into the next worksheet in the order in which you plan to proceed:

Worksheet 64: My Issues, Prioritized

MY RECOVERY ISSUES IN THE ORDER IN WHICH I PLAN TO WORK ON THEM	
I plan to start with my first issue, which is:	
The solution to this issue will put me into a good position to tackle my second issue, which is:	
The solution to this issue will put me into a good position to tackle my third issue, which is:	

In this case, Sandy decided to open a separate bank account and go to school part time. Sandy's partner couldn't pay the rent and when Sandy was absolutely firm about not financing the partner's drug trips, the partner moved out. Sandy got a clean and sober roommate, studied extra hard, and got over the heartbreak. In a few months Sandy had a certificate and got a better job, and with that money moved to a cleaner neighborhood and found a counselor to help work on some old issues to break Sandy's problem relationship pattern.

Sandy understood that staying clean and sober is the necessary foundation for solving any life problem. When people are clean and sober, they can develop the clarity of mind to see that the life they have slid into is a pit out of which they must climb, or drown. When people are clean and sober, they can make intelligent plans for the future, and even more important, they can make the difficult and sometimes emotionally painful moves that have to be made to carry them out. With sobriety, a person can get to work on old issues and make inner advances to go with the external improvements.

Knowing that remaining clean and sober was the foundation of everything, Sandy took care to move forward mentally, socially and culturally in recovery throughout this period of life changes.

In addition to Sandy's "Daily Do" affirmation, and regular participation in a meeting that discussed its members' current life issues, Sandy turned off the TV and bought a computer, got on the Internet, read for hours about recovery issues, and joined a sober chat and email list.

Above all, Sandy used the Sobriety Priority as a tool for making decisions in life, and in every tight spot – such as when the drug-using partner moved out – Sandy remembered: Sobriety Is My Priority, I Don't Drink Or Use No Matter What.

212. **The Gory Details**

A recovery plan that only consists of good intentions is as effective as no recovery plan at all. As with anything else, "the devil is in the details." Use this section to take the general concepts from your previous worksheet (*Worksheet 64: My Issues, Prioritized*) and translate them into practical, working details. The key questions to answer are Who, What, When, Where, Why and How Much.

For example, when Sandy from the previous example decided to go to school part time, this general plan had to be broken down into numerous details before Sandy could make it work. What school? What courses? What times? Where were the classes? What about transportation? What certificate would the classes lead to? Could Sandy afford the tuition?

Use the next worksheet to break down your Issue No. 1 into its gory details. Make sure that you build your sobriety maintenance practices into your plan at the detail level. Make additional copies of the worksheet for additional issues you have identified.

After you have detailed all your issues, do your segues still work? Sometimes breaking down general concepts into their practical details reveals flaws in the order of priorities, and it's necessary to go back and revise the order of attack. It is common in all kinds of real world situations to cycle through this kind of process (from prioritization to working out the details) several times before it all clicks.

It's also helpful to make a backup plan, just in case you run into Murphy's Law. It's rare for everything to go according to plan. When you run into the inevitable snags and breakdowns, remember: IDDOUNMW – I Don't Drink Or Use No Matter What.

Worksheet 65: Detailed Plan Execution

BREAKING MY RECOVERY PLAN DOWN INTO DETAILS: ISSUE NO. _____	
General statement of the objective (copied from Worksheet 64: My Issues, Prioritized)	
Who do I need to get involved in order to do this plan?	
What do I need to do in order to get ready and then to carry through to the finish?	
Where do I need to be? How will I get there?	
When is this going to happen, and how much time will it take? What conflicts will it raise?	
How does this project relate to my recovery? Will it interfere with my relapse prevention program?	
Where will I get the resources required to complete this plan?	
How will completion of this plan put me into a good position and give me momentum to tackle my next issue?	

213. Conclusion: Sharing My Plan with Others

You have probably done many hours of work getting to this point. It could be very helpful to other people if you were now to share your conclusions. What others would probably find most valuable is a summary in your own words. You could copy it and make it available. If you are working with a group, you could collect your and other people's condensed programs in a binder and make that available to newcomers. Writing a summary could also help you clarify and firm up your plan in your own mind.

In doing your summary, you may want to use the domain structure of this book as rough scaffolding, or you could ignore all that and go directly to the heart of your concerns. It's your program – write it your way.

One final suggestion: You might include in your summary a paragraph on how you have changed in the process of constructing this recovery program of yours. The carpenter not only builds the house; more importantly, the house builds the carpenter. The most important product of your sweat on this workbook is not the book; it is the clean and sober YOU.

Worksheet 66: My Personal Recovery Plan (Summary)

Date: _____

_____

_____

_____

_____

_____

_____

_____

_____

_____

_____

_____

_____

_____

_____

_____

_____

_____

_____

_____

_____

_____

_____

_____

_____

_____

_____

_____

_____

_____

_____

(Continue on an extra sheet)

Also by the workbook author:

Empowering Your Sober Self:
The LifeRing Approach to Addiction Recovery

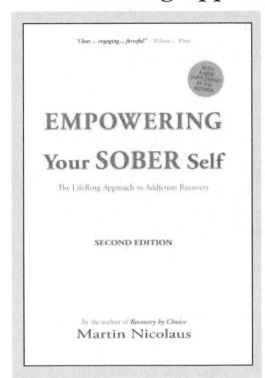

Second Edition

The one book to read for an all-around introduction to LifeRing

Written for the person who wants to get free of alcohol/drugs, for their friends and relations, and for the professionals who treat them

By Martin Nicolaus

Foreword by William L. White

"Offers a sane and secular approach to seeking sobriety and a sophisticated, insightful, and well documented view of the philosophy and practice that are at the heart of this LifeRing approach. This book offers a perspective on recovery that can motivate change in clinicians and researchers as well as among individuals struggling to find their sober selves." — *Carlos DiClemente Ph.D., Professor and Chair, Department of Psychology, University of Maryland.*

Second Edition published 2014 by LifeRing Press
Order online: https://lifering.org
Questions: publisher@lifering.org
Toll-free: 1-800-811-4142
Order directly from LifeRing Press for fastest delivery

How Was Your Week?

Bringing People Together in Recovery the LifeRing Way – A Handbook

Second Edition (2015)

By Martin Nicolaus

"How Was Your Week?" is the question that opens most LifeRing meetings. This book describes the surface process of the LifeRing meeting format and the deeper healing, empowering forces at work within it. The book is principally a handbook for the people who lead and support LifeRing meetings ("convenors") but will also be of value to other readers who want a thoughtful, reasoned exposition of the LifeRing approach.

"A masterful job. ... Many recovery mutual aid groups have floundered or collapsed because they failed to clearly define their mission and methods. _How Was Your Week?_ defines the mission and methods of LifeRing Secular Recovery with remarkable clarity and enthusiasm. This book is a significant achievement that will be an invaluable aid ..." – Bill White, Author, _Slaying the Dragon: The History of Addiction Treatment and Recovery in America_.

"Through his books and articles, LifeRing author Martin Nicolaus provides the recovery community with what it most needs – a vast variety of individual paths toward sobriety and improved living. For those who have failed to find a comfortable place in the twelve-step community, Nicolaus' books lead the way to another chance. – Lonny Shavelson, Author of _Hooked: Five Addicts Challenge Our Misguided Drug Rehab System_.

How Was Your Week?

Order online: https://lifering.org
Questions: publisher@lifering.org
Toll-free: 1-800-811-4142
Order directly from LifeRing Press for fastest delivery

Looking for a support group in tune with this workbook, or for a workbook study group?

LifeRing on the Web:

www.lifering.org

The front door to the LifeRing recovery world. LifeRing news, meeting schedule, chat room, social network, email lists, blogs, FAQs, readings, and much more.

Chat rooms open 24/7 – drop in anytime.

LifeRing Live:

LifeRing Service Center
Toll free: 1-800-811-4142
Email: service@lifering.org